Media Pluralism and Online News

Media Pluralism and Online News

The Consequences of Automated Curation for Society

EDITED BY

Tim Dwyer and Derek Wilding

Bristol, UK / Chicago, USA

First published in the UK in 2023 by
Intellect, The Mill, Parnall Road, Fishponds, Bristol, BS16 3JG, UK

First published in the USA in 2023 by
Intellect, The University of Chicago Press, 1427 E. 60th Street,
Chicago, IL 60637, USA

Copyright © 2023 Intellect Ltd

All rights reserved. No part of this publication may be reproduced, stored in a retrieval system, or transmitted, in any form or by any means, electronic, mechanical, photocopying, recording, or otherwise, without written permission.

A catalogue record for this book is available from the British Library.

Copy editor: MPS Limited
Cover designer: Tanya Montefusco
Cover image: The image was developed using OpenAI's text to image generator, DALL.E 2.
Production manager: Laura Christopher
Typesetter: MPS Limited

Hardback print ISBN 978-1-78938-848-0
Paperback print ISBN 978-1-78938-857-2
ePDF ISBN 978-1-78938-849-7
ePUB ISBN 978-1-78938-850-3

To find out about all our publications, please visit our website. There you can subscribe to our e-newsletter, browse or download our current catalogue and buy any titles that are in print.

www.intellectbooks.com

This is a peer-reviewed publication.

Contents

List of Figures and Table	vii
Acknowledgements	ix
1. Introduction *Tim Dwyer and Derek Wilding*	1
2. The Contemporary Policy Context: Plurality, Diversity and Automated Curation *Derek Wilding and Tim Dwyer*	28
3. New Directions in Media Pluralism and Diversity Interventions *Derek Wilding and Tim Dwyer*	67
4. Problem Definitions in European Policy Debates on Media Pluralism and Online Platforms *Kari Karppinen*	97
5. Automation, News and Social Media Pluralism *Jonathon Hutchinson, Tim Dwyer and Derek Wilding*	118
6. Researching Online News Media Diversities in China and South Korea *Tim Dwyer and Jonathon Hutchinson*	143
7. Investigative Journalism and Media Pluralism: Voices from the Global South *Saba Bebawi*	179
8. Conclusion *Tim Dwyer and Derek Wilding*	197
Notes on Contributors	221
Index	223

Figures and Table

Figures

3.1	Ofcom media plurality measurement framework.	69
3.2	Ofcom table on weekly readership of UK national newspaper groups.	71
3.3	Ofcom share of reference for retail providers used 'Nowadays' for news.	73
3.4	Ofcom consumption survey.	75
3.5	ACMA's 'key Measures of Diversity and Localism'.	80
3.6	ACMA's 'Indicators of Diversity and Localism'.	82
3.7	PA distribution by groups of publishers.	90
3.8	Topic distribution by groups of publishers.	90
5.1	The Philip DeFranco show's YouTube page.	131
5.2	*Russell Brand* YouTube page.	133
5.3	The YouTube page of the friendlyjordies.	135
6.1	Intercoder reliability by purpose.	154
6.2	Intercoder reliability by topic.	155
6.3	*Sixth Tone*: relationship between images and clickbait titles.	157
6.4	*Shine*: relationship between high image count and public affairs content.	158

Table

6.1 Sample of WeChat Official Accounts Publishers. 153

Acknowledgements

This book emerges from an Australian Research Council (ARC) project 'Media Pluralism and Online News' (DP 180100034) which began in 2018 and formally concluded in 2023. We would like to thank the ARC as well as the staff of the research portfolios at the University of Sydney and the University of Technology Sydney, who provided a very useful stream of advice in relation to the project. We would like to thank our co-investigators on the project, Saba Bebawi, Jonathon Hutchinson and Kari Karppinen. We are grateful to our colleagues in our places of work, the Department of Media and Communications at the University of Sydney, the Centre for Media Transition at the University of Technology Sydney, and the Department of Social Research, Media and Communication Studies at the University of Helsinki who provided the intellectual contexts to pursue the important goals that underpin the project.

The project was well underway before COVID-19 hit, so fortunately, we were able to undertake field interviews in Brussels, Florence, London, Seoul, Tokyo, Shanghai and Beijing before the pandemic restricted our travels. We were also able to present our research at several conferences including the European Communication Research and Education Association's 2018 annual conference held in Lugano, Switzerland at the Universita della Svizzera Italiana.

Jonathon Hutchinson presented a paper with Heather Ford at the Ludwig Maximillians University of Munich conference 'Automation, News and Algorithms' in May 2018 which was a useful event to inform our thinking regarding developments in the computational aspects of news.

We hosted a meeting at the University of Sydney in 2019 with the South Korean (RoK) Committee on the Impact of Media Concentration whose members are appointed by Ministry of Culture, Sports and Tourism. We were able to compare research with Chair Young Uk Kim and his fellow committee members, which proved to be a very fruitful exchange of ideas on media pluralism policies and media concentration.

Our colleagues at the Sydney Informatics Hub, in particular, Joel Nothman and Chao Sun brought the best of data science to the project, enabling data analysis at scale and demonstrating their talents in guiding the production of the project's excellent computational tools.

Many interlocutors were very helpful for us in researching pluralism in their national contexts. We like to thank Lesley Hitchens, Steve Barnett, Des Freedman, Justin Schlosberg, Martin Moore, Angela Phillips, Frances Cairncross, Ingrid Lambrecht, Han Woo Park, Heejin Lee, Leslie Tkach-Kawasaki, Junku Lee, Takeshi Fujitani, Albert Lu, Qihui Gao, Jin Guo, Jianguo Deng, Wei Lu and Yun Wu.

Without the hard work and insight of our RAs, it would have been a much more difficult project. Our sincere thanks to Tim Koskie and Weiwei Xu, along with interns Vidya Kathirgamalingam, Joshua Green and Olivia Nunes Malek, along with Rosa Alice, administration and communications officer at the Centre for Media Transition.

Our meetings with media regulators Ofcom (UK) (Tom Wicken, Jonathan Mackay, Lewis McQuarrie) and the ACMA (Australia) (James Cameron, Creina Chapman and colleagues) were very productive. Other important meetings for us were at DG Connect in Brussels with Suzanne Vanderzande and David Friggieri; and at the CMPF in Florence, including Elda Brogi, Iva Nenadic, Marko Milosavljevic and Luc Steinberg.

Chapter 6 draws on and adapts previously published research on our Chinese and Korean fieldwork that had appeared in the *Journal of Contemporary Eastern Asia* and *Journal of Global Media Studies*. The data collection, modelling and dashboard development were implemented by the Sydney Informatics Hub, a Core Research Facility of the University of Sydney. We would like to specifically acknowledge the work of Dr Chao Sun in constructing the WeChat dataset. We would like to thank the following people who provided us with insights into the Korean news ecology: Yongwoon Shim, Senior Research Fellow, SK Telecom; Daewon Kim, Director Government Relations & Policy Affairs, Kakao; Sung Jin Yang, Editor of Digital Content, The Korea Herald; Jin-Hyung Kim, Managing Director International Affairs and Business, Yonhap News Agency; and Se Uk Oh, News Trust Project, Korean Press Foundation. We would also like to thank Kyungmi Choi at TBS-FM in Seoul.

We would like to thank the team at Intellect including Julia Brockly, Tim Mitchell and Laura Christopher for their excellent guidance.

Finally, we are very grateful for excellent comments from our two reviewers, one anonymous and the other from our colleague, Emeritas Professor Graham Murdock – who managed to succinctly move from Adam Smith to algorithms in his generous suggestions – and we have reproduced his argument in Chapter 1.

1

Introduction

Tim Dwyer and Derek Wilding

This book represents our research and critical reflections from a four-year Australian Research Council-funded 'Discovery Project' entitled 'Media Pluralism and Online News'.

The broader purpose of the project was to track the dynamic developments in the way news is produced, distributed and consumed online and to account for this in public policy designed to promote media pluralism (Media Pluralism Project 2019). The researchers were also seeking to transition the understanding of media pluralism by studying contemporary European policy approaches and a series of innovative news practices, including through making use of a big data approach to collecting media content. To that end, the project reviewed the best international policy practices, and we conducted interviews with policymakers, regulators and academic experts in Europe and Asia, and we used computational data collection for empirical analysis of news articles on a variety of platforms.

One of the principal aims of the 'Media Pluralism and Online News' project was to discover methods of computationally evaluating media pluralism that are relevant for assessments of multi-platform news ecosystems. We investigated how the concept of 'public affairs' allows us to separate out and identify the categories of news content that contribute to media pluralism (Media Pluralism Project Dashboard 2020). Our view is that this term is useful in showing the news content that should be valued; that is, content which is constitutive of a news public good, and, for which, the business model is in a state of crisis.

In this context, an understanding of major trends in dominant media-tech, including *platformisation*, data surveillance flows, and broader system-wide innovation in connectivity and distribution informs the research; these developments all portend radical implications for news consumption. Algorithmic visibility of news has emerged as a core concept for those researching questions of media pluralism. News content distribution is embedded in platform power and regulatory debates in relation to how access is shaped by automated machine-learning processes. Research indicates that the way audiences become exposed to news content will increasingly be a matter of these automated, platform-based mechanisms (Wilding et al. 2018; Helberger 2018; Helberger et al. 2018; Helberger 2021).

As Wilding et al. (2018) note, in the context of a discussion regarding the importance of obtaining a diverse news diet for quality and informed citizenship, 'Algorithmic filtering methods, however, run the risk of constraining diversity, which may cause information blindness for consumers' (p. 58). They anticipate that a reverse situation is also possible: that algorithmic or automated news content may lead to more diverse content when that objective is 'programmed in' to a platform's algorithms. To develop this point a step further, we see that in either scenario, whether or not there is likely to be more or less diversity in content, which is always an important consideration arising in online news contexts, platforms *are* curating such provision in novel computational ways. This departs from the predominately human curation of news content that operated in the pre-digital world. Such filtering processes are, of course, the source of ongoing debates regarding their intrinsic merit or otherwise.

Bodo's discussion of algorithmic agency and platforms in *News, Algorithms and Automation* provides an account that places the consequences for news distribution into stark relief. His research distinguishes the use of algorithmic personalization by digital news organizations from that used by platform intermediaries. In the latter context, he argues:

> Platforms upset the logics of news production, delivery and consumption in more than one way: they compete for advertising revenues with news organizations; through their control of access to audiences, they play an increasingly important role in news delivery; and through their own personalization efforts, they are able to set their own agendas, at the expense of news media.
> (Bodo 2019: 1056)

This power to curate the news, then, and to indirectly 'set their own agendas', lies at the core of their societal influence. Virality, popularity, misinformation and disinformation together with the personalized delivery to audiences is a demonstrable shift accompanying the rise of tech-media platform intermediaries. For Bodo, these developments are linked to 'economic, technological and sociocultural conditions of the production, distribution, and consumption of news' and the 'algorithmic control of information flows and the customization of the information environment around each of us constitute the latest development in that process' (Bodo 2019: 1070). The platform logic of personalization is characterized by abundant personal usage data (and datafication more broadly), vast amounts of user and publisher content, an aggressively ad-based business model, 'almost limitless technological and financial resources' and a more diffuse approach to editorial or curatorial oversight (Bodo 2019: 1070). Quite rightly, too, Bodo's view is that the role of these algorithmically personalized controls is ultimately a matter for how societies wish to interpret their impact on the prevailing forms of governance.

Helberger's research points to the increasingly important role that personalized recommender systems now play in news distribution, arguing that recommender systems can be theorized in terms of four main varieties of algorithmic recommendation. First, she argues that liberal recommenders inform within limits of what people want/expect. Second, participatory recommenders map the diversity of ideas and opinions in society, responding to differences in information needs, styles and preferences. Third, deliberative recommenders nudge people to encounter different perspectives, serendipity, as well as activating people to comment, share and the like. Finally, constructivist recommenders can nudge people to encounter and acknowledge minority opinions but also support seeking out the like-minded (Helberger 2021).

While these varieties of priorities for algorithmic recommender systems are particularly relevant for the responsibilities of public service media (PSM) sites and platforms, they can be applied more broadly in relation to certain categories of commercialized personalized media delivery. Public service media have a recent history of blending machine-determined automation alongside human-driven curation to effectively operate in expanding automatic media content environments. For example, YLE, the Finnish public service media broadcaster, has long given its journalists the ability to target their content via an insights dashboard that presents them with audience performance data (Hutchinson and Sørensen 2021). The next step for public media operators is to enable a form of exposure mechanism, similar to the Helberger (2021) model, to determine where the targeted content will appear in these kinds of news content delivery mechanisms. Given the historical trajectory of PSM, it seems logical to develop the application of this kind of pathway not only for traditional public service media but more broadly to help safeguard democracy.

Just as all media content is not targeted for all audiences on social media, algorithmic media can target diverse audiences for news content. This algorithmic thinking can be described as a form of 'hidden innovation', exemplifying research and development that begins in public media, and which is then adopted by the broader commercial media sector (Cunningham 2013). The idea of aligning content production with audience analytics is nothing new of course – but how it is applied to satisfy aspects of exposure mechanics within automated media has emerged as the frontier of news and algorithmic studies. Helberger's recommender model (discussed in more detail below) is well suited to media produced by organizations with a legislated social cohesion purpose; in other words, public service media (2021). Indeed the concept of targeted exposure, based on algorithmic alignment, is also related to the content exposure management techniques employed by certain social media influencers. Bishop (2019) notes that this targeted approach towards specific exposure visibility is typically a strategy of content producers seeking maximum visibility within algorithmically determined environments – something news distribution is yet to fully address. However, we would make the observation that the application of this model to more traditional commercial media contexts where editorial and business priorities can innately conflict, renders some of the more interventionist varieties of recommender models a less plausible proposition.

The need to take new platform distribution processes into account in assessments of media pluralism has been recognized by EU Member states in EU Council deliberations. In the Council's discussions regarding findability and discoverability of pluralistic content, it has foreshadowed that future media policy needs to consider how algorithmic manipulation affects users' exposure to informational content and news sources as well as their overall consumption. Significantly, though, the Council has gone a step further by recommending that Member States' media policies should consider 'must show' rules and criteria for discoverability and findability to favour media pluralism and cultural diversity. The Council specifically invites the European Commission to:

> continue and further develop research to identify potential risks to media pluralism and further understand the changed position of editorial media outlets in relation to social media, search engines, video-sharing platforms and other media platforms; concepts of information science should explicitly be taken into account.
> (Council of the EU 2020, paragraph 25)

Although the EU is the leading development of this approach, there are indications that it could feature in policy or regulatory arrangements in other jurisdictions. In Australia, as explained further below, the recent legislation that prompted the dominant digital platforms Google and Meta to make payments to news organizations includes a requirement that the platform develop a proposal to 'recognise original [...] news content when it makes available and distributes that content', along with an obligation to inform news organisatons of certain algorithmic changes that might have a significant effect on their referral traffic. However, as Lee and Molitorisz (2021) point out, these aspects are not in operation as the legislative scheme itself is designed to come into effect only if the two platforms make insufficient progress in their own commercial agreements with news providers; these agreements need not contain provisions dealing with algorithmic governance.

INTRODUCTION

The main reason behind the call for greater transparency is that there is now a body of evidence that has shown us how social media news sharing on platforms, driven by algorithms, shapes how news stories are selected, distributed, discussed, and valued (Martin and Dwyer 2019; Flew et al. 2021). The overall impacts of digital intermediaries (social media, search, online news and aggregation platforms) on news indicate important trends in the way audiences now get access to journalistically produced news content. Transformations wrought by the rise of algorithms and artificial intelligence in online intermediaries, including in social media feeds and search and online news sites themselves mean that our exposure to news and information products is shaped by our own usage (Pasquale 2015: 79; 2017). It is not an overstatement to recognize that these digital modes of distributing and discovering news are baked into a new logic of the media–industrial complex. In other words, news as a public good has been recast by private interests in platform capitalism (Srnicek 2017). In turn, this gives heightened meaning to the resurgence of interest in news as a public good – evident for example, in the work of the Australian Competition and Consumer Commission (ACCC 2019) and the OECD (2021) – and emphasizes the importance for research on journalism and critical algorithmic studies to engage with rapidly evolving policy.

Algorithmic curation of news articles in tech-media spaces now relies on the routines and logics of automated plaformization, shaping how news content becomes visible for audiences. The influence of platformization on journalism, including the use of new metrics and performance priorities, has emerged as a key part of the online news ecosystem, shifting the foundations of how audiences will discover sources of news and information. These processes are the terrain of this volume.

What is at stake for online news audiences?

The subtitle for our book, *The Consequences of Automated Curation for Society*, focuses on what we understand to be the high stakes arising from the unprecedented rise of tech-media platforms and news distribution shaped by algorithmic manipulation.

In 2020, the University of Canberra's *Digital News Report* found that around 52 per cent of Australians get news via social media, and the number is growing (Park et al. 2020: 50). Facebook also boasts of its investments in news via deals with publishers and new products such as Facebook News. The Reuters Institute for the Study of Journalism in a five-nation survey found that the primary source of news ranged from 31 per cent of people in Germany using social media as their main source of news to 45 per cent in the United States to 66 per cent in Brazil (Newman et al. 2019 in Flew et al. 2021).

The consequences of being beholden to the algorithmic provision of news by platforms was made shockingly clear the day Facebook decided to shut down the visibility of news and information sites on the platform for 17 million Australians in early 2021. The move was widely anticipated in the context of the Australian Government's decision to legislate for a mandatory bargaining code for news, in response to recommendations by the competition regulator, the ACCC (2019) in its Digital Platforms Inquiry (DPI) report, two years previously.

In a move that attracted a great deal of international attention and indeed scrutiny, the Australian government enacted a law in early 2021 that puts in place a mandatory code to help support the sustainability of the Australian news media sector. The key rationale for the new law is to address bargaining power imbalances between digital platforms and Australian news businesses. One of the main recommendations of the ACCC's (2019) DPI was to establish a 'bargaining' code (which was initially to be voluntary, until the government decided that to have any impact it needed to be mandatory). The code provides for a system of 'final offer' arbitration between news media businesses registered with the Australian Communications and Media Authority (ACMA) and designated 'responsible digital platform corporations'. The term 'designated' has emerged as a very 'over-determined' one; to be designated requires a failure on the part of certain platforms to enter into sufficient commercial arrangements with news content businesses.

However, platform corporations have not been put onto the designated list and Meta and Google have already entered into contracted commercial arrangements with news media businesses that former ACCC Chair Rod Sims has estimated exceed AUD 200 million annually (Butler 2021). This pre-emptive move was widely interpreted as an attempt to avoid being caught in a regulatory net that would not be on the most favourable terms for the platforms (Dwyer 2021).

The Mandatory News Media Bargaining Code has a requirement to provide registered news businesses with advance notification of planned changes to an algorithm that will significantly affect 'covered' news, to provide information about the collection and availability of user data; and to develop a proposal to recognize original news (Senate 2021). This is intended to capture algorithm changes which involve an active decision to modify how content will be distributed on a designated digital platform service. The Code provisions are not intended to apply in situations where the algorithmic changes are mostly automated or a result of machine learning. The policy intent is that changes are likely to be considered significant if they are likely to result in an approximately 20 per cent or greater change in referral traffic to registered news businesses as a whole (Senate 2021: 1.126). The key point here is that the enforcement processes, including very significant fines, will not be available because of the lack of designation under the legislation. Against this background, the decision of Meta (then known as Facebook) to shut down news in the days before the legislation was passed to give effect to this scheme was widely interpreted as a form of blackmail and an attempt to prevent the government from proceeding with the new law.

In Australia, the ABC's online headline was: 'Facebook just restricted access to news in Australia: Here's what that means for you' (ABC Online 2021). The impact was well reported around the world. A sample of international news headlines caught the key aspects of story:

> 'Australia's Scott Morrison slams Facebook's move to block news as "arrogant."' (*South China Morning Post*)
> 'Facebook ban on news in Australia provokes fierce backlash.' (*Financial Times*)
> 'Australia Reacts to a Facebook Without News.' (*The New York Times*)
> 'Facebook's Australia news ban: what is the social media giant up to and how will you be affected?' (*The Guardian*)

When Australian users (including those living abroad) attempted to share a news story on Facebook they received the following pop-up message: 'This post can't be shared: In response to Australia's proposed new Media Bargaining law, Facebook will restrict publishers and people in Australia from sharing or viewing Australian and international news content.'

Richard Glover, a popular Australian radio presenter on the public service broadcaster, writing in the *Washington Post* posed the question:

> People and governments everywhere have wondered whether the world has allowed American tech giants to become too powerful and too central to the way our societies work. What would happen if they suddenly chose to use that enormous power to win an argument with a democratically elected government?
>
> (Glover 2021: n.pag.)

Glover was not alone in thinking through the stark consequences of these events in terms of Facebook as a news source: 'The problem is that many Australians have developed the habit of using Facebook as their access point to news and information.' Facebook pages run by Government departments responsible for fire and emergency services, hospitals, charities, domestic violence support groups all went dark.

Publishers' Facebook pages were replaced with an information page with contact details only. Net data analytics group *Chartbeat* noted that from 5.30 a.m. on the morning of 18 February 2021 (the morning after), the traffic sent to Australian and international publishers fell off a cliff, going down to a trickle except for a few anomalous publisher sites that were still able to link to their news on the social media platform (Benton 2021a).

This was not the first time that that Meta had threatened to metaphorically 'shoot the hostages' to achieve its own political or comercial ends (Benton 2021b). Another occasion when Meta used its market clout was in 2017 when it undertook live experiments to the newsfeed by introducing a new 'Explore Feed' product in Slovakia, Sri Lanka, Serbia, Bolivia, Guatemala and Cambodia, moving news stories to the new feed. It meant that users needed to click on the new product to access their favourite news sites, and it resulted in the biggest drop in organic reach seen to that point in time (Struharik 2017).

A further example is when Facebook shut down completely in August 2018 for 45 minutes, providing a glimpse into the world without Facebook news (Whittaker et al. 2018). The result confirmed that without a newsfeed, users go straight to publishers' mobile apps and news sites. *Chartbeat* data indicates that built in mobile aggregators emerged as important referrers, driving 'significant traffic to publishers' (Schwartz 2018: n.pag.). These aggregators include *Apple News*, *Google Chrome Suggestions*, news aggregator *Flipboard* and the *Google News* app which is pre-installed on Android devices. Publisher owned apps also gain when the Facebook news feed is not available and these went up by as much as 40 per cent in 2017 during the 'Explore Feed' incident (Struharik 2017). But perhaps the most heartening message for news publishers in the 2018 dark mode event was that news users seek out alternatives and can change their practices in a matter of seconds.

Similarly, platforms have changed content curation algorithms without warning, reducing traffic to news websites, as occurred with Facebook in 2017 and 2018 (Flew et al. 2021). There have also been very well-documented cases of audience manipulation by Facebook (Martin and Dwyer 2019). In early 2018, Facebook with no warning decided to flick the algorithmic switch to prioritize posts made by friends and family over public content. In this action, Facebook was actively *de*prioritizing professionally made news journalism, and in effect allowing a lesser quality information to dominate news feeds. The other less well-publicised instance of algorithmic change was when in March 2018, Facebook tweaked the algorithm to favour local news. They first rolled out the changes in the US market, claiming that this was to ensure that readers were being exposed to content that was more meaningful in their community contexts.

Such instances are all clear evidence of the power of the platform to control the delivery of news content. The actions of the platforms to curate content and to shape what becomes more, less or even *in*visible demonstrate their power. However, some research is beginning to emerge indicating that the impact of these kinds of algorithmic changes on the businesses models of different categories of news institutions (digital native, print, PSM, social news and television) in terms of referral traffic, can be quite variable. For example, Bailo et al. note that referral traffic to public service media organizations in Australia has proven to be quite resilient to the 2018 prioritization of 'family and friends' changes in Facebook's algorithms, whereas social news was detrimentally impacted (Bailo et al. 2021).

Online news and platform power

For Helberger, the ability of platforms to make algorithmic changes of this kind is an example of their communicative power and indeed the main problem with solving questions of diminishing structural diversity in the media. She makes the point that platforms are not concerned with the provision of diverse forms of news and information; instead, they seek to control exposure to available information. Platforms, she argues, 'stage encounters with media content, affect the "findability" of content, order and prioritise existing content, manage and direct user attention as a scarce resource, and influence the choices consumers make' (2018: 162). Therefore, platforms' roles in curating opinion power should not be underestimated. In their recent work colleagues at the University of Amsterdam note that their research, 'aims not only at better understanding shifts of opinion power, but also at developing ways and informing policy debates and regulatory thinking on how to deal with concentrated power in the media' (Seipp et al. 2023: 2).

Schlesinger locates power in relation to a 'regulatory field', adapting Bourdieu's formulation, and suggests that the 'upsurge of British activism' by relevant agencies is related to the way 'they exercise power over cultural production, circulation and consumption' (Schlesinger 2020). He maps a litany of what are, at their core, content concerns on platforms and which herald significant consequences for society: 'fake news, exposure to harmful or illegal content, anti-competitive behaviour, misleading political advertising, the uses of consumer data, expressions of violence and terrorism, online indecency and interference by foreign governments in the domestic electoral process' (Schlesinger 2020).

Underlying many of these issues, the development of algorithmic patterns in online news distribution and consumption through platformization dynamics has inevitably given rise to a call for a renovated set of questions and re-framings for policymakers in nation states (Wilding et al. 2018; Flew and Wilding 2020: 6). In effect, these changed dynamics require new orthodoxies for expanding conceptions of voice pluralism based largely on media ownership; they require rethinking and adapting the long-standing policy objectives for media plurality. Fenton et al. (2020) argue that in the context of increasing media concentration, there is a need for counter narratives and mechanisms 'to promote meaningful plurality'

(2020: 104). Therefore, these authors argue that the performance of news algorithms should be scrutinized so that they do not 'unduly favour particular types of news providers and voices over others' (2020: 105). We agree that this is the reality of online news distribution over intermediary platforms where the algorithms have a direct role in the selection of news articles surfacing on platforms, at both aggregate and individual levels. However, in this context, we would distinguish 'meaningful plurality' from the conceptualisation of 'sufficient plurality' – critiqued by Gibbons (2015: 22–27) among others – used in UK law. The latter is concerned with the hard political decision limits or thresholds in law and regulation which impact on the number and 'sufficiency' of voices, while the former focuses on expanding formulations that apply in new media ecologies. As Valcke et al. (2016: 2) have observed, 'the concentration of where the audience goes – in terms of aggregators and sites – is every bit as damaging to pluralism as limitations on spectrum and concentration of ownership'.

The preparedness to completely turn off the availability of news in these ecologies represents a phase-shift in platform power. Writing in *The Conversation* in relation to the social value of news distributed by platforms, Dwyer noted that executives from Google and Meta told an Australian Senate committee that they were prepared to take drastic action if Australia's news media bargaining code, which, as noted above, would force the internet giants to pay news publishers for linking to their sites, came into force (Dwyer 2021).

People realize news is important – that it shapes their interactions with the world and provides meaning and helps them navigate their lives. So the threat to withdraw services from the Australian media landscape was all about wanting to convey a sense of power to Australian lawmakers. At the same time, the rhetorical flourish from the platform behemoths was also about how news meant little to them in financial terms, a claim that was at odds with research indicating that 52 per cent of Australians were currently getting their news via social media platforms (although, news access on social media varies with age and platform usage) (Park et al. 2020, 2021).

Australia's Treasurer, Josh Frydenberg described Meta's action to turn off news in people's Facebook news feeds as 'heavy handed' and 'confirming the immense market power of these digital giants' (Snape 2021). Predictably, Meta argued that poorly drafted legislation was to blame. When Meta's Simon Milner appeared to give evidence at a public hearing of the Senate Economic Legislation Committee, inquiring into the Treasury Laws Amendment (News Media and Digital Platforms Mandatory Bargaining Code) Bill, he was questioned about the intentions of Meta in sending Facebook news to black in Australia for a week. The senior spin doctor was questioned in relation to the social responsibility of 'turning off' a swathe of government and community health information sites that were caught up in the

INTRODUCTION

Facebook dragnet (Taylor 2021). In part, Milner's justification for the social media platform's action was that the definition of news in the new law, as argued in the corporation's written submission, was 'so broad and vague that they will inevitably result in differences in interpretation and result in large, overreaching ambit claims from news publishers' (Facebook 2021: 27). The argument was made that 'core news' and 'covered news' – the legislative categories of news that help establish who has access to regulated bargaining, mediation and arbitration over remuneration for news content – could include any content that 'reports, investigates or explains events of public significance at a local level'. The submission also questions the use of the phrase 'of interest to Australians' in the new law. This lack of specificity in the definition of news, Meta argued in its submission, would result in 'overreaching ambit claims for news publishers' (Facebook 2021: 27).

As we explain in Chapter 2, this issue of the definition of 'news' was one that researchers in the *Media Pluralism Project* were frequently reminded of during the many hours spent in classifying news stories scraped from online brands. Was a particular story *news* – even though it could also be classified as 'sport', or 'health information', or 'celebrity'? We noted that the varieties of news would often depend on where one's gaze was directed: online news sites, blogs, entertainment news sites all push out different contents that could be interpreted as examples of a range of media forms, genres and topics.

Meta's decision to block access to Facebook news for Australians had quite an adverse impact on health (including vaccination and COVID-19) information, weather and other unexpected community pages hosted on the social media platform. The 'collateral damage' sites affected by the decision included the mental health information line, 1800 Respect, the WA Department of Fire and Emergency Services, the Hobart Women's Shelter and the Bureau of Meteorology, among many others (Smyth et al. 2021; Snape 2021).

Joel Nothman, the lead data scientist on our project, suggested that there would have been some weeks of data analytics work in creating the blacklist of sites that Meta prevented from surfacing in Australians' newsfeeds. It is possible to surmise, then, that the humans in that curation process made some bizarre and yet also quite telling decisions about what constitutes a source of 'news' from Meta's perspective.

Despite these concerns over news content definitions, the Treasury Laws Amendment (News Media and Digital Platforms Mandatory Bargaining Code) Act 2021 was passed by parliament on 25 February 2021 and commenced on 2 March 2021. The efficacy of the model it institutes and its claimed long-term benefits – the long-term sustainability of public interest journalism – remain in doubt (Winseck 2021; Centre for Media, Data and Society 2021: 241).

Nonetheless, this desire of platforms to demonstrate their power to the Australian lawmakers goes to the heart of the problem of what was at stake. This was, and is, an issue about monopoly power – a well-documented phenomenon in the history of capitalism.

Google and Meta have dominated web search and social media, respectively, in ways that echo the great US monopolies of the past: rail in the nineteenth century, then oil and later telecommunications in the twentieth century. All these industries became fundamental forms of capitalist infrastructure for economic and social development. Dwyer (2021) has argued that all these monopolies required legislation to break them up in the public interest.

Monopoly power in the tradition of these earlier forms of corporate power seeks to control its own destiny to the detriment of the public interest. As the twenty-first century mega corporations who now dominate the face of the internet, digital platforms have at times acted like this around the world, even if the extent of their market power varies across the services they provide and in different countries. Canadian media scholar, Dwayne Winseck, has provided a clear analysis of the ways in which the platforms operate, noting that in the struggle over the passage of new legislation seeking to address a power imbalance between traditional media and the platforms, this imbalance

> allows the biggest global platforms to impose take-it-or-leave-it conditions on users in terms of data and privacy protection and on creators in terms of who gets paid how much and who gets to see [...] when it comes to the data generated around a YouTube video, for example. Such things must change.
>
> (Winseck 2021: n.pag.)

Des Freedman has argued that monopoly power needs to be challenged, and to that end asks, 'what is the nature of this influence and what does "media power" actually mean?' (Fenton et al. 2020: 7). 'Does it refer to the ability of major platforms and outlets to shape agendas and disseminate content in line with their own interests'? He notes that: 'Their power is vested in economic and political control of communications landscapes – a dominance that is scarcely comparable to the far more limited opportunities for individuals to deploy their own symbolic resources' (8). Productive in the Foucauldian sense, media power for Freedman is also amorphous and machine-like. Platform power via social media algorithms manifests as a form of deeply embedded executive media power. As Srnicek has argued, the network effects of corporations such as Meta and Google mean that 'more users beget more users which leads to platforms having a natural tendency towards monopolisation (and) a dynamic of ever-increasing access to more activities and therefore to more data' (Srnicek 2017: 45).

INTRODUCTION

This proposition of laying bare the coded priorities of platforms is not new. Relatedly, there have been calls for a regulated audit of Facebook's news algorithm; the purpose is described by Winseck:

> Opening the black box is also needed to address a crucial question that has forever defined the relationship between those who own and control communication networks/distribution, on the one side, and set-top boxes, TV services and program rights holders, on the other: who controls the data about individual users/audiences and on what terms do the other parties get a peek at that data–data that is essential for them to know their audience and craft their wares?
>
> (Winseck 2021: n.pag.)

In the context of the Mandatory Bargaining Code stand-off with the Australian government, Google threatened to cut users off from their search engine, and Meta said it would remove links to news articles in users' Facebook feeds – whether from Australian or international sources. Google withdrew its threat, while Meta made good on its before retreating when it secured amendments to the proposed legislation. And although Google did not follow through with their threats, Google had already run small-scale experiments to test removing Australian news from search. So clearly this was a demonstration that the threat to withdraw from Australia was serious, or at least, serious brinkmanship.

In a speech given a few weeks after the 6 January 2021 attacks on the US Capitol, Apple CEO Tim Cook pointed out how personal information collected through tracking by Facebook and other social media can push people towards more misinformation and hate speech as a by-product of the efforts to show them more personalized ads.

'What are the consequences of not just tolerating but rewarding content that undermines public trust in life-saving vaccinations?' Cook asked. 'What are the consequences of seeing thousands of users join extremist groups and then perpetuating an algorithm that recommends more?' (Liedtke 2021: n.pag.).

COVID-19 created a perfect storm for the circulation of disinformation and misinformation. Social media platforms such as Facebook, Twitter, Instagram, YouTube or Tiktok are often the distributors of these dangerously ill-informed views. Dis/misinformation is a fundamental problem of social media platforms considering their role in dynamically re-shaping a post-public sphere. Anti-vaxer content emanating from celebrity influencers is shored up by billions in advertising connected to this content.

A report by the UK House of Commons Sub-committee on Online Harms and Disinformation, *Misinformation in the COVID-19 Infodemic*, was published in July 2020. It was noted that the COVID-19 pandemic was a test case for how platform corporations were approaching the problem of misinformation. The report argued:

> Platform policies have also been too slow to adapt, while automated content moderation at the expense of human review and user reporting has had limited effectiveness. The business models of tech companies themselves disincentivise action against misinformation while affording opportunities to bad actors to monetise misleading content
>
> (House of Commons 2020: 3)

The report makes the point that warning labels and tools introduced by the platforms have been inconsistently applied, especially in relation to high-profile accounts. An example of platform power can be seen when Meta stopped censoring posts about the Wuhan lab outbreak theory of the pandemic in May 2021. Previously seen as a fairly fringe theory that had been dismissed by WHO experts, Meta changed tack as the popularity of these conspiracy theories grew (Lima 2021). The company made this policy change following moves at the White House to push formal investigations into the origins of COVID-19 and claims to have consulted with health organizations including the WHO (Dwoskin 2021). The question of where the COVID-19 virus originated was always a major topic but arguably the new ban was an indication of Meta and other western social media giants' ability to control the narrative.

Many suggest that the owners of these giant social media platforms have essentially constructed the new public square and are clearly in the business of deciding what is and is not of interest to their audience–consumers. The attention economy and the emotional-information needs of people were made for each other. Unfortunately for society, as Vaidhyanathan has argued, the 'disinformation machine' has 'the added feature of often being irresistible to the clicking fingers of Facebook users and thus the distributive power of Facebook algorithms' (Vaidhyanathan 2018: 185).

In other words, the much-vaunted debates of how the functions and roles of news media publishers merge with those of platforms are now a reality. Both traditional online news media sites and newer, born digital sites can now be seen as variants of news publishers who have provider relationships with digital platforms. Algorithmic mediation occurs at both news publisher and the platform redistribution locations, and this is proving to be very significant.

Another illustration of this power to curate the news, and in so doing to fundamentally shape key societal narratives that are highly consequential for audiences, is the moderation and censorship practices of social media platforms such as Facebook, YouTube and Twitter. Platform curation becomes automated when the popularity aspects of algorithmic virality comes into play. Recent recruitment advertisements by Facebook for the two positions of 'Content Curation Manager, News' and 'Content Program Manager, News' provide some further insights regarding the news curation practices on the social media platform. A 'Content Curation Manager, News' position advertisement specifies an 'experienced journalist' who is skilled in 'identifying credible news content, making editorial decisions, and responding to breaking news' and who can 'identify cultural trends across a diverse spectrum of topics'. The person should also be able to 'collaborate with our product teams to improve user experience and internal tools' (Facebook 2021b). For the 'Content Program Manager, News' position, Facebook was looking to hire a person with a 'strong editorial and analytical background' and a 'deep knowledge of digital news media' (Facebook 2021b). The proximity to a traditional news editors' skill set is telling for these positions, supporting the case that Facebook's newsfeed is very carefully curated involving human and machine-learning elements. Despite claims to the contrary, news and information provision is core business on the platforms.

A large-scale survey 'Australia Talks' by Australia's public service media organization, the ABC, found that 94 per cent of participants found misinformation on platforms to be a significant problem. Researchers at Canberra University found that the general concern about false and misleading information online was high at 64 per cent, when the global average was 56 per cent (Park et al. 2021). The 'Australia Talks' survey also found that 79 per cent of Australian did not know which sources of information to trust (ABC 2021). Relatedly, the First Draft group have noted the following aspects from transparency reports due under the new Australian Code of Practice on Disinformation and Misinformation, which was launched in February 2021:

- Facebook reported it removed more than 110,000 pieces of COVID-related misinformation generated by Australian accounts between March and December 2020.
- Twitter reported Australia-specific approximate data for July–December 2020, with 37,000 Australian accounts actioned for violations of the Twitter Rules.
- TikTok noted the platform removed 651 videos mentioning COVID-19 or coronavirus between October 2020 and March 2021 for violating the company's misinformation policy.
- In March 2021, Google blocked or removed over 11,000 coronavirus-related ads from Australia-based advertisers for policy violations (First Draft 2021).

These and other reports from the platforms show that they have taken some action to address the problems associated with misinformation and other harmful content. However, given the maximization of audiences is critical to the platforms' business model, there is an inherent disincentive to take meaningful action which seriously affects distribution. Furthermore, the sheer volume of disinformation and misinformation on social media platforms and search engines calls for new strategies of prevention in relation to the regulation of social media platforms. The preliminary reports of the ACCC's DPI and the UK's Furman Report ('Unlocking Digital Competition') both suggested that one way to intervene in this issue is to have a process of auditing the algorithms which generate socially corrosive content. This is an issue we will consider further in the discussion in the next section and in Chapter 2.

Automated news media curation and resources for citizenship

The backdrop to the current phase of the commercialised internet is long and well documented, as media scholar Graham Murdock has noted. He observes:

> Adam Smith's *The Wealth of Nations*, his manifesto for a capitalism organised around minimally regulated markets published in 1776, emerged within a few short weeks of the American Declaration of Independence founding a republic based on the popular vote. From that point on news media have been assigned a central role as the primary sources of the information, analysis, explanation and debate over issues of common concern citizens require for political participation and social inclusion.
> (Murdock 2022: n.pag.)

In their influential essay 'Information poverty and political inequality: Citizenship in the age of privatised communications', Murdock and Golding (1989) argue that citizenship can be defined as not simply about the political process. 'It is about the conditions that allow people to become full members of the society at every level.' This understanding must therefore entail the necessary communications and information resources to 'exercise […] full and effective citizenship in the contemporary era'. They make the point that this is not a new insight and that liberal democrats 'have long recognised that access to adequate information and to diversity of debate and representations is a basic precondition for the effective functioning of a democratic polity and for the full exercise of citizenship rights' (1989: 183). Murdock and Golding were focused on the impact of the broader processes of privatization, deregulation and neoliberal marketization, and how this had fundamentally reorganized citizens' access to news and information. We would argue that these same ideological trends continue to drive automated curation in platformized media ecologies.

INTRODUCTION

From the outset, the commercial organization of news production was in tension with the role of news as resource for citizenship. These tendencies underpin automated news content provision in contemporary media-tech platforms (Srnicek 2017). News media publishing conglomerates such as News Corporation or the Daily Mail Group operate to further concentrate their communicative power in collaboration with media-tech platforms. As a clearly recognized characteristic of commercial media, private ownership therefore carries the risk that news media will be deployed in the service of partisan interests.

At the same time, factors such as high fixed costs associated with traditional media and the network effects associated with higher circulation have meant that concentration of ownership has often been a feature of media markets. The economic power of platforms continues the traditional media industrial practice that enables advertising finance to prioritize reader attention and engagement that in turn prioritizes sensation and entertainment over public interest news. In the past, in an effort to counter these dynamics, regulation has been developed and public subsidy and ownership introduced. Recent developments in Europe and Australia to legally require platforms to compensate or share revenue with media publishers is the latest manifestation of measures taken to correct failing news media markets.

The role of algorithms in structuring the provision of news and information is now critically consequential for the citizenship of all internet users. Indeed it's possible to identify three major shifts that have accelerated from the start of the twenty-first century:

1. The increasing centrality of digital platforms, particularly Facebook and Google in the West, and their Chinese platform equivalents, as being primary points of access to news for many citizens.
2. The consequential migration of control over news selection and presentation from the human decisions of journalist and editors, informed by professional criteria of newsworthiness, to 'automated curation' organized around algorithmic filtering systems directed to personalizing delivery.
3. The challenges this shift presents for policies designed to ensure media pluralism and how these challenges might be met (Murdock 2022).

A recent discussion paper prepared by the Digital Regulation Cooperation Forum (DRCF), consisting of UK regulators the Competition and Market Authority (CMA), Ofcom, ICO (Information Commissioner's Office) and the Financial Conduct Authority (FCA) is titled 'Auditing Algorithms: the existing landscape, the role of regulators and future outlook' (DRCF 2022a). It was accompanied by a partner paper titled, 'The benefits and harms of algorithms: a shared perspective from the four digital regulators' (DRCF 2022b). Together the papers represent the first steps by these British regulators to intervene in a landscape of digital algorithms characterized by personalization by predominantly private corporations. Relevantly for the potential harms arising for news content distributed over digital platforms, major harms identified include:

3.3.1 Access: Limiting people's exposure to alternative viewpoints
The use of algorithms to target content online, particularly on social media platforms, could result in internet users being repeatedly exposed to the same type of information. As has been well documented, many of today's platforms deploy sophisticated recommendation algorithms, which adapt as they learn more about the type of content users tend to engage with. In many cases, this results in users being presented with more of the same innocuous content, such as a favourite TV show or a friend's social media posts. However, in other cases this type of targeting can result in people being repeatedly shown content that is misleading or damaging, such as antivax conspiracy theories, or even violent content.

(17)

In China, measures have been put in place that require large platformized corporations (Bytedance, Tencent Holdings Ltd) to provide detailed information of their algorithms to the Cyberspace Administration of China. This requirement shows a clear recognition by Beijing of the need to regulate the ways in which these corporations' algorithms direct content on their platforms. The companies are required to explain how the algorithms work, and this goes on the public record. Under these new regulations, companies must also submit non-public information which includes a self-appraisal on the security of the algorithms, the kinds of data they collect, including if this is sensitive biometric or identity information, and what data sources are used to train algorithms (Zhang 2022).

Access to the full range of mediatized media and communications therefore is dependent on the platform politics and affordances of the internet giants such as Alphabet (Google), Meta (Facebook) and Apple in the West and their equivalents such as Baidu, WeChat, Weibo, Douyin (TikTok), and mobile corporations like Xiaomi and Huawei in China.

As a result, it is necessary to situate the specific problems of algorithmic curation within the wider context of concentrated communicative power and the distortion of democratic debate. Algorithmic curation is often second order curation – that is, selected from material that has already been curated by dominant media organisations. It follows from this that any policy intervention to address the specific issues raised by algorithmic curation must be part of a wider discussion of the possibilities for recasting public communication in the service of democracy.

INTRODUCTION

In this context, throughout this book, we want to emphasize the role of algorithms and automation in the organization of news delivery practices. We are concerned with the way in which automation (including AI and machine-learning processes) curates how news media content is shaped and distributed in platformized contexts, and how this impacts media pluralism for citizens and consumers. Increasingly, the consumption of news is shaped by algorithmically driven processes that select, filter and surface this content to our news feeds and search engines.

In the final stages of preparing the book for publication we were surprised by Ofcom's release of a 'discussion document' which had a very similar title as the book: *Media Pluralty and Online News* (Ofcom 2022). At various points throughout this book we consider this document and other work of Ofcom. While some of Ofcom's concerns intersect with our own, we are more ambitious in our appeals for understandings of how automated curation affects society, while also somewhat constrained in our attempts to craft an approach to measuring and regulating for media pluralism in a market such as Australia where policy in this area has long trailed that of the United Kingdom.

There are profound consequences arising from these processes of automated curation for individual citizens, and for societies in aggregate. Operating in the background of our digital lives, news publishers, social media platforms and search engines are central actors in these developments, and their decisions ultimately determine what news publics can access. When news content is automatically curated using algorithms whose priorities include topicality and popularity this raises red flags for regulatory authorities. Agenda setting by large privately owned corporations brings questions of power, influence, transparency and legitimacy to the fore. Are governments and their regulatory agencies in a position to intervene in the public interest? It's clear that the health of our public infospheres is implicated in these media technologies; and policymakers need to be alive to their modus operandi in order to ameliorate their worst impacts through public policy interventions.

Overview of the chapters

Chapter 2 reviews several of the foundational concepts used in the book to assess diversity, plurality and developments in automated curation of online news. We analyze the Australian policy and regulatory framework for media pluralism comparing it with the United Kingdom, exploring evolutions in policy and scholarly thinking since the core regulatory settings were developed 30 years ago. In this chapter, we review the interplay between competition law and media regulation, and the place of a public interest test for media mergers.

In Chapter 3 'New directions in media pluralism and diversity interventions', we analyze the state of the Australian media policies and regulation for achieving media plurality (*qua* diversity as the dominant discursive framing), recognizing the consequences of this ineffective and unsustainable regulation that is no longer fit-for purpose. Again, drawing comparatively on developments in the United Kingdom and the EU, we explore possible ways forward for industries which are undergoing rapid structural transformations. We argue that although there is clear evidence of innovation, additional measures will need to be taken if the objective of a diverse, pluralized media capable of responding to non-merger concentration as well as media mergers, is to ever be achieved.

Emerging from a long hibernation in the space, the ACMA released a policy paper in December 2020. We note that the ACMA's proposed 'news measurement framework' is a serious attempt to provide a framework to assess media pluralism in the age of algorithmic news delivery. Perhaps most innovatively, its framework explores the dual policy challenges of diversity and localism. Broadly consistent with the original policy framework developed by Ofcom (2015) in the United Kingdom in its Measurement Framework for Media Plurality, it builds on insights from the Media Pluralism Monitor developed by the Centre for Media Pluralism and Freedom (CMPF) (see, e.g., CMPF 2022) for the EU, as well as the Diversity Index formerly used by the Federal Communications Commission in the United States.

In Chapter 4, Kari Karppinen examines the shifting rationales of European media pluralism policies. Karppinen argues that as a fundamental media policy aim, the notion of media pluralism has usually been invoked in European media policy debates around issues such as media ownership concentration, subsidies, and the role of public service media. These debates have been marked by conflicting rationalities of market oriented and more cultural or democratic policy paradigms, and their conflicting conceptions of what media pluralism entails. In recent years, debates on media pluralism have increasingly shifted to emphasize questions around the power of digital platforms, algorithms, disinformation, and related digital risks. These debates now add a new layer of ambiguity to the debates on media pluralism, including new problem definitions, policy interests and potential solutions.

This chapter discusses how these new issues have changed the policy rationales and objectives in current European policy debates. It then reviews recent European media policy documents produced by the Council of Europe, the EU institutions as well as monitoring reports, such the Media Pluralism Monitor (recently redesigned to take into account the impact of digital developments), to discuss continuities and breaks in how media pluralism is defined and justified as a policy objective and the problems and solutions with which it is typically associated.

INTRODUCTION

In Chapter 5, 'Automation, news and social media pluralism', Jonathon Hutchinson, Tim Dwyer and Derek Wilding seek to locate less orthodox forms of news and information within culture and technology debates regarding new and emerging platform intermediaries. They make the argument that the rapidly changing context of social media platforms brings with it important implications for voice plurality and wider assessments of news diversity. This ecosystem's evolution has resulted in not only a shift in how news is produced but also how it is produced for new platform-specific affordances such as visibility, shareability and what they refer to as algorithmic suitability. They further argue that exposure to media diversity on social media platforms will depend on the combination of interactions between producer, the consumer and the platform. It is suggested that public service media can play an important role in media diversity across increasingly automated systems of our platformed societies.

Chapter 6 provides insights generated by our project fieldwork into new ways of researching media news diversity within the mass scale popularity of the Asian media forms that are increasingly relied upon on a daily basis in China and South Korea. We argue that not only do these east Asian nation-states provide heuristic insights into the meanings of news media diversity but they also indicate that the historical and socio-cultural underpinnings of these locales and their unique processes of platformization have deeply impacted the ways that news and information are now distributed and consumed.

In Chapter 7, Saba Bebawi examines investigative journalism and media pluralism, framing her analysis in terms of 'Voices from the global south'. Bebawi argues that in many parts of the global south, the media have been mainly state-controlled and the practice of investigative reporting, which aims to 'dig deeper' and uncover facts on various issues of concern, has been regarded as foreign and problematic. News reporting in these regions, therefore, has historically been controlled and opinion pieces have been monitored. Nevertheless, we are currently witnessing the rise of investigative journalism in many countries of the Global South due to an increase of awareness for the need for such a form of journalism, facilitated with funding as a result, in addition to online opportunities for publishing.

For Bebawi, investigative journalism has been a key component of media pluralism in terms of the production of truth telling discourses in national and international polities. The availability of these voices in the Global South has emerged as critical for a political reportage that accounts for identity and structural inequality. This chapter, therefore, aims to map and uncover the extent to which investigative journalism – as a form of knowledge building journalism that is slowly emerging – is developing in these regions.

In the concluding chapter, we revisit some of the key themes that emerge in the book and signpost the way ahead for media pluralism policy and online news in light of some clear and present risk scenarios. Automated processes of online news curation rely on the shifting priorities of algorithmic mechanisms that lack transparency for their audiences. In using the term 'automated curation' in the book, we wished to emphasize the machinic and non-human agencies that accompany platform distribution of online news.

We have shown that it is critical that policy makers adjust their focus on the role of social media and platform distribution in order to take into account the potential for new ways of encountering media diversity and plurality in media markets. Innovation in methods of measuring pluralism is achievable, but rejuvenating media pluralism policies will need to be undertaken in a manner that takes into account the possible impact of algorithmic news recommenders. This kind of policy reform will need to look closely at how algorithms increase users' engagement at the expense of personalised content suggestions that are useful for democratic living and social participation. The gap between providing sustainable regulations and policies for the longer term, and the reforms put forward in a recent Australian Senate inquiry into media diversity – which we consider further in the following chapter – indicate this will continue to be a highly politicised terrain.

REFERENCES

ABC Online (2021), 'Facebook just restricted access to news in Australia: Here's what that means for you', 18 February, https://www.abc.net.au/news/2021-02-18/facebook-news-ban-what-just-happened-post-zuckerberg/13166710. Accessed 19 February 2021.

ACCC (2019), *Digital Platforms Inquiry*, Final Report, 26 July, https://www.accc.gov.au/publications/digital-platforms-inquiry-final-report. Accessed 21 February 2021.

ACMA (2020), *News in Australia: Diversity and Localism – News Measurement Framework*, ACMA, Melbourne, December. Commonwealth of Australia (Australian Communications and Media Authority) 2020, https://www.acma.gov.au/sites/default/files/2020-12/News%20in%20Australia_Diversity%20and%20localism_News%20measurement%20framework_1.pdf. Accessed 21 February 2021.

Australian Broadcasting Corporation (2021), 'Australia Talks shows most Australians are concerned about misinformation and fake news', https://www.youtube.com/watch?v=tKEqUEjLVkg. Accessed 27 May 2021.

Bailo, Francesco Meese, James and Hurcombe, Edward (2021), 'The institutional impacts of algorithmic distribution: Facebook and the Australian News Media', *Social Media & Society*, 7:2, April–June, pp. 1–13, https://doi.org/10.1177/20563051211024963.

Benton, Joshua (2021a), 'In Australia, Facebook's ban on sharing news stories has sent publishers' traffic tumbling', *Nieman Lab*, 18 February, https://www.niemanlab.org/2021/02/in-australia-facebooks-ban-on-sharing-news-stories-has-sent-publishers-traffic-tumbling/. Accessed 23 February 2023.

Benton, Joshua (2021b), 'Facebook got everything it wanted out of Australia by being willing to do what the other guy wouldn't', *Nieman Lab*, 23 February, https://www.niemanlab.org/2021/02/facebook-got-everything-it-wanted-out-of-australia-by-being-willing-to-do-what-the-other-guy-wouldnt/. Accessed 23 February 2023.

Bishop, Sophie (2019), 'Managing visibility on YouTube through algorithmic gossip', *New Media & Society*, 21:11, pp. 2589–606.

Bodó, Balázs (2019), 'Selling news to audiences – A qualitative inquiry into the emerging logics of algorithmic news personalization in European Quality News Media', *Digital Journalism*, Special Issue: Algorithms, Automation, and News, 7:8, pp. 1054–75, https://doi.org/10.1080/21670811.2019.1624185.

Butler, Ben (2021), '"Look at that penalty": After taking on Google and Facebook, Rod Sims departs ACCC with a warning', *The Guardian Australia*, 19 December, https://www.theguardian.com/australia-news/2021/dec/19/look-at-that-penalty-after-taking-on-google-and-facebook-rod-sims-departs-accc-with-a-warning. Accessed 23 February 2023.

Center for Media, Data and Society (2021), *Media Influence Matrix*, Media Reform Coalition, November, UK: CMDS/CEU Democracy Institute, November, https:///cmds.ceu.edu/sites/cmcs.ceu.hu/files/attachment/basicpage/1923/mimukfinalreport_0.pdf. Accessed 19 July 2023.

Centre for Media Pluralism and Media Freedom (2022), *Monitoring Media Pluralism in the Digital Era: Application of the Media Pluralism Monitor in the European Union, Albania, Montenegro, the Republic of North Macedonia, Serbia and Turkey in the Year 2021*, Fiesole FI: European University Institute, 30 June, https://cadmus.eui.eu/handle/1814/74712. Accessed 19 July 2023.

Council of the European Union (2020), Council conclusions on safeguarding a free and pluralistic media system (7 December 2020, 2020/C 422/08), para. 21, https://eur-lex.europa.eu/legal-content/EN/TXT/PDF/?uri=uriserv:OJ.C_.2020.422.01.0008.01.ENG. Accessed 19 July 2023.

Cunningham, S. (2013), *Hidden Innovation: Policy, Industry and the Creative Sector*, Brisbane: University of Queensland Press.

DRCF (2022a), Digital Regulators Cooperation Forum, 'Auditing Algorithms: The existing landscape, the role of regulators and future outlook', 23 September, https://www.gov.uk/government/publications/findings-from-the-drcf-algorithmic-processing-workstream-spring-2022/auditing-algorithms-the-existing-landscape-role-of-regulators-and-future-outlook. Accessed 19 July 2023.

DRCF (2022b), Digital Regulators Cooperation Forum, 'The benefits and harms of algorithms: a shared perspective from the four digital regulators', 28 April, https://assets.publishing.service.gov.uk/government/uploads/system/uploads/attachment_data/file/1071221/DRCF_-_Algorithmic_Harms_and_Benefits_Paper.pdf. Accessed 19 July 2023.

Dwyer, Tim (2021), 'Is news worth a lot or a little? Google and Facebook want to have it both ways', *The Conversation*, https://theconversation.com/is-news-worth-a-lot-or-a-little-google-and-facebook-want-to-have-it-both-ways-153787. Accessed 19 June 2023.

Dwoskin, Elizabeth (2021), 'Facebook's reversal on banning claims that covid-19 is man-made could unleash more anti-Asian sentiment', Washington Post.com, 27 May, https://www.washingtonpost.com/technology/2021/05/27/facebook-covid-man-made/. Accessed 19 July 2023.

Facebook (2021a), Submission to the Senate Economics Legislation Committee on the Treasury Laws Amendment (News Media and Digital Platforms Bargaining Code) Bill 2020, 18 January, Submission 50, https://www.aph.gov.au/Parliamentary_Business/Committees/Senate/Economics/TLABNewsMedia/Submissions. Accessed 19 July 2023.

Facebook (2021b), Careers site, job ads for 'Content Curation Manager, News', and 'Content Program Manager, News', https://www.facebook.com/careers/v2/jobs/162208452465190/. Accessed 19 July 2023.

Fenton, Natalie, Freedman, Des, Schlosberg, Justin and Dencik, Lina (2020), *The Media Manifesto*, Cambridge, Medford: Polity.

Finn, Ed (2018), *What Algorithms Want: Imagination in the Age of Computing*, Cambridge: The MIT Press.

First Draft (2021), Newsletter, Centre for Media Transition, *UTS*, https://www.uts.edu.au/sites/default/files/2022-01/CMT%20E-Newsletter%20-%2028%20May%202021.pdf. Accessed 19 July 2023.

Flew, Terry, Gillett, Rosalie, Martin, Fiona and Sunman, Lucy (2021), 'Return of the regulatory state: A stakeholder analysis of Australia's Digital Platforms Inquiry and online news policy', *The Information Society*, 37:2, pp. 128–45, https://doi.org/10.1080/01972243.2020.1870597.

Flew, Terry and Wilding, Derek (2020), 'The turn to regulation in digital communication: The ACCC's digital platforms inquiry and Australian media policy', *Media, Culture & Society*, 43:1, pp. 48–65, Online First, https://doi.org/10.1177/0163443720926044.

Gibbons, Thomas (2015), 'What is "Sufficient" plurality?', in S. Barnett and J. Townend (eds), *Media Power and Plurality: From Hyperlocal to High-Level Policy*, London. Palgrave Macmillan, n.pag.

Glover, Richard (2021), 'Australia is standing up to Facebook and Big Tech. It shouldn't fight alone. 25 February', *Washington Post*, https://www.washingtonpost.com/opinions/2021/02/19/australia-facebook-google-news/. Accessed 19 July 2023.

Helberger, Natali (2018), 'Challenging media diversity – Social media platforms and a new conception of media diversity', in M. Moore and D. Tambini (eds), *Digital Dominance: The Power of Google, Amazon, Facebook and Apple*, New York: Oxford University Press, pp. 153–75.

Helberger, Natalie (2021), 'On the democratic role of news recommenders', in N. Thurman, S. C. Lewis and J. Kunert (eds), *Algorithms, Automation and News: New Directions in the Study of Computation and News*, London: Routledge, pp. 14–33.

Helberger, Natali, Karppinen, Kari and D'Acunto, Lucia (2018), 'Exposure diversity as a design principle for recommender systems', *Information, Communication & Society*, 21:2, pp. 191–207, https://doi.org/10.1080/1369118X.2016.1271900.

INTRODUCTION

House of Commons (2020), *Misinformation in the COVID-19 Infodemic*, London: Digital, Culture, Media and Sport Committee (Sub-Committee on Online Harms and Disinformation), Second Report of Session 2019-21, 21 July 2020, p. 3, https://committees.parliament.uk/publications/1954/documents/19089/default/.

Hutchinson, Jonathon and Sørensen, Jannick (2021), 'Can automated strategies work for PSM in a network society? Engaging digital intermediation for informed citizenry', in M. Túñez-López, F. Campos-Freire and M. Rodríguez-Castro (eds), *The Values of Public Service Media in the Internet Society*, New York: Palgrave Macmillan, pp. 59–75.

Lee, Karen and Molitorisz, Sacha (2021), 'The Australian News Media bargaining code: Lessons for the UK, EU and beyond', *Journal of Media Law*, August, pp. 1–18, https://doi.org/10.1080/17577632.2021.1963585.

Liedtke, Michael (2021), 'Apple's iPhone privacy clampdown arrives after a 7 month delay', *Sydney Morning Herald*, 27 April, https://www.smh.com.au/technology/apples-iphone-privacy-clampdown-arrives-after-7-month-delay-20210427-p57mlt.html?utm_content=ALSO_IN_THE_NEWS&list_name=2031_smh_busnews_am&promote_channel=edmail&utm_campaign=business-am&utm_medium=email&utm_source=newsletter&utm_term=2021-04-27&mbnr=MTIwMjE3OTE&instance=2021-04-27-07-35-AEST&jobid=29303648. Accessed 19 June 2023.

Lima, Cristiano (2021), 'Facebook no longer treating "man-made" Covid as a crackpot idea', *Politico*, 26 May, https://www.politico.com/news/2021/05/26/facebook-ban-covid-man-made-491053. Accessed 19 July 2023.

Martin, Fiona and Dwyer, Tim (2019), *Sharing News Online. Commendary Cultures and Social Media News Ecologies*, Cham: Palgrave Macmillan.

Media Pluralism Project (2019), 'The role of a pluralistic media in Australia's democracy', Project Website Blog, https://mediapluralism.org.au/2019/05/the-role-of-a-pluralistic-media-in-australias-democracy/. Accessed 19 June 2023.

Media Pluralism Project Dashboard (2020), Computational tool available at https://mediapluralism.sydney.edu.au. Accessed 19 July 2023.

Murdock, Graham (2022), personal communication, 26 August.

Murdock, Graham and Golding, Peter (1989), 'Information poverty and political inequality: Citizenship in the age of privatised communications', *International Journal of Communications*, 39:3, pp. 180–94.

Newman, Nic, Fletcher, Richard, Kalogeropolous, Antonis, Levy, David and Nielsen, Rasmus Kleis (2018), *Reuters Institute Digital News Report 2018*, Oxford: Reuters Institute for the Study of Journalism, http://media.digitalnewsreport.org/wp-content/uploads/2018/06/digital-news-report-2018.pdf?x89475. Accessed 19 July 2023.

OECD (2021), *Competition Issues Concerning News Media and Digital Platforms: Background Note by the Secretariat. OECD Directorate for Financial and Enterprise Affairs*, Competition Committee, 3 December, Paris, https://www.oecd.org/daf/competition/competition-issues-in-news-media-and-digital-platforms.htm. Accessed 19 June 2023.

Ofcom (2015), 'Measurement framework for media plurality: Ofcom's advice to the secretary of state for culture, media and sport', *Statement, Ofcom*, 5 November, https://www.ofcom.org.uk/consultations-and-statements/category-1/media-plurality-framework. Accessed 30 January 2023.

Ofcom (2022), 'Media plurality and online news', Discussion Document, *Ofcom*, 16 November, London: Ofcom, https://www.ofcom.org.uk/research-and-data/multi-sector-research/media-plurality. Accessed 30 January 2023.

Parliament of Australia (2021), Treasury Laws Amendment (News Media and Digital Platforms Mandatory Bargaining Code) Act 2021, https://www.legislation.gov.au/Details/C2021A00021. Accessed 19 June 2023.

Park, Sora, Fisher, Caroline, Lee, Jee Young, McGuinness, Kieran, Sang, Yoon Mo, O'Neil, Mathieu, Jensen, Michael, McCallum, Kerry and Fuller, Glen (2020), *Digital News Report: Australia, 2020*, Canberra: News and Media Research Centre, University of Canberra, https://apo.org.au/node/305057. Accessed 19 June 2023.

Park, Sora, Fisher, Caroline, McGuinness, Keiran, Lee, Jee Young and Macallum, Kerry (2021), *Digital News Report: Australia, 2021*, Canberra: News and Media Research Centre, University of Canberra, https://www.canberra.edu.au/research/faculty-research-centres/nmrc. Accessed 19 June 2023.

Pasquale, Frank (2015), *The Black Box Society: The Secret Algorithms that Control Money and Information*, London: Harvard University Press.

Pasquale, Frank (2017), *The Automated Public Sphere. Legal Studies Research Paper*, No. 2017-31. Baltimore: University of Maryland, Francis King Carey School of Law, http://ssrn.com/abstract=3067552. Accessed 27 June 2023.

Schlesinger, Phillip (2020), 'After the post-public sphere', *Media, Culture and Society*, 42:7&8, pp. 1545–63, https://doi.org/10.1177/0163443720948003.

Schwartz, Josh (2018), 'What happens when Facebook goes down? People read the news', 22 October, Nieman Lab, https://www.niemanlab.org/2018/10/what-happens-when-facebook-goes-down-people-read-the-news/. Accessed 19 July 2023.

Seipp, Theresa, Helberger, Natali, de Vreese, Claes and Ausloos, Jef (2023), 'Dealing with opinion power in the platform world: Why we really have to rethink media concentration law', *Digital Journalism*, https://doi.org/10.1080/21670811.2022.2161924.

Senate (2021), Treasury Laws Amendment (News Media and Digital Platforms Mandatory Bargaining Code) Bill 2021: Revised Explanatory Memorandum, https://parlinfo.aph.gov.au/parlInfo/download/legislation/ems/r6652_ems_c352c005-974d-47e4-8999-35a566907f89/upload_pdf/JC001309_Revised%20EM.pdf;fileType=application%2Fpdf.

Smyth, Jamie, Murphy, Hanna and Barker, Alex (2020), 'Facebook ban on news in Australia provokes fierce backlash', *Financial Times*, 18 February, https://www.ft.com/content/cac1ff54-b976-4ae4-b810-46c29ab26096.

Snape, Jack (2021), 'Facebook reinstating health and safety pages but government says damage to reputation has been done', *ABC Online*, 18 February, https://www.abc.net.au/news/2021-02-18/facebook-credibility-brought-into-question-health-emergency-news/13166318.

Srnicek, Nick (2017), *Platform Capitalism*, Cambridge, Malden: Polity Press.

Struharik, Filip (2017), 'Biggest drop in Facebook organic reach we have seen', Medium.com, 21 October, https://medium.com/@filip_struharik/biggest-drop-in-organic-reach-weve-ever-seen-b2239323413.

Taylor, Josh (2021), 'Facebook's botched Australia news ban hits health departments, charities and its own pages', *The Guardian*, 18 February, https://www.theguardian.com/technology/2021/feb/18/facebook-blocks-health-departments-charities-and-its-own-pages-in-botched-australia-news-ban.

Vaidhyanathan, Siva (2018), *Anti-Social Media: How Facebook Disconnects Us and Undermines Democracy*, New York: Oxford University Press.

Valcke, Peggy, Picard, Robert and Sukosd, Miklos (eds) (2016), *Media Pluralism and Diversity: Concepts, Risks and Global Trends*, New York: Palgrave Macmillan.

Whittaker, Meredith, Crawford, Kate, Dobbe, Roel, Genevieve Fried, Kaziunas, Elizabeth, Mathur, Varoon, Sarah Myers West, Richardson, Rashida, Schultz, Jason and Schwartz, Oscar (2018), *AI Now Report 2018*, New York: AI Now Institute, https://ainowinstitute.org/AI_Now_2018_Report.pdf.

Wilding, Derek, Fray, Peter, Molitorisz, Sacha and McKewon, Elaine (2018), *The Impact of Digital Platforms on News and Journalistic Content*, Sydney: University of Technology Sydney, https://www.accc.gov.au/system/files/ACCC%20commissioned%20report%20-%20The%20impact%20of%20digital%20platforms%20on%20news%20and%20journalistic%20content%2C%20Centre%20for%20Media%20Transition%20%282%29.pdf.

Winseck, Dwayne (2021), 'Vampire Squids, the "broken internet" and platform regulation', *Journal of Digital Media & Policy*, 11, p. 3, https://doi.org/10.1386/jdmp_00025_1.

Zhang, Jane (2022), 'Alibaba, ByteDance share details of prized algorithms with Beijing for first time', *Bloomberg Asia Edition*, 15 August, https://www.bloomberg.com/news/articles/2022-08-15/tech-giants-share-details-of-prized-algorithms-with-beijing.

2

The Contemporary Policy Context: Plurality, Diversity and Automated Curation

Derek Wilding and Tim Dwyer

This chapter begins by looking at different understandings of media pluralism and media diversity, and how contemporary policy needs to embrace the impact of digital platforms and algorithmic content delivery on the state of the public sphere. But it also steps back from these most recent developments in content distribution to analyze the Australian policy and regulatory framework for media pluralism, exploring evolutions in policy and scholarly thinking since the core regulatory settings were developed 30 years ago. Our aim here is to emphasize how the regulatory and institutional frameworks that have developed over many decades continue to affect the availability of media content, even if the methods of distribution and access have changed dramatically.

This exploration of policy and regulatory tools includes international comparative analysis of Australia and the United Kingdom. We focus on the United Kingdom for the following reasons: it is the jurisdiction with the closest structural similarities to Australia, in terms of the role of a multi-platform public broadcaster that does not accept advertising; the UK regulator has a similar converged communications remit; ownership and control is regulated via a few sector-specific rules complemented by competition law; and aspects of quality and news standards are regulated by separate content rules. A recent review of international approaches to measurement of media diversity by the Australian Communications and Media Authority (ACMA 2020) – which we consider further in Chapter 3 – highlighted some interesting features of the South Korean, United States and Canadian environments but essentially confirmed the added relevance for Australia of the UK approach. There are, however, some significant differences between Australia and the United Kingdom, so the review of the current policy and regulatory environment that begins this chapter includes an outline of the basic features of Australian media regulation insofar as it affects media pluralism. As a key part of the analysis of the regulatory framework concerns the interplay between competition law and media regulation, the chapter then considers the place of a public interest test for media mergers. In our view, the diagnosis offered here in relation to Australia contains elements that will resonate with a variety of jurisdictions grappling with formulating responses to increasing media concentration.

Conceptualizing media pluralism

Before looking in more detail at existing media ecosytems and how contemporary concerns such as the role of algorithmic distribution sit with longstanding public policy issues such as media concentration, it is important to explain how the conceptual framework offered by media pluralism can embrace these and other concerns. Specifically, it is necessary to consider the dimensions of 'media pluralism' and how this term is used in relation to 'media diversity' (or, to use the term adopted in UK regulation, 'media plurality'). The need to sketch this scene in advance arises from the different ways in which these terms are used within both academic and policy literature and across different jurisdictions. As Helberger et al. (2018: 193) observe: 'Despite decades of debate on diversity as a policy objective [...] there is no consensus on a generally accepted, consistent definition of what constitutes "diversity" or "pluralism".'

The reason why it remains difficult to achieve a comprehensive and universally accepted definition is evident in a statement from the European Parliament's Committee on Civil Liberties (2018: 31) that underlines the breadth of the concept.

> Media pluralism embraces many aspects, including merger control rules, content requirements in broadcasting licensing systems, transparency and limited concentration of media ownership, the establishment of editorial freedoms, the independence and status of public service broadcasters, the professional situation of journalists, the relationship between media and political actors, as well as economic actors, the access of women and minorities to media content, diversity of opinions, etc.

Many attempts have been made at drawing these various elements into a unifying concept, including the matrix adopted in the EU's Media Pluralism Monitor (discussed below) that identifies four general 'areas' of media pluralism each with five 'indicators' (Centre for Media Pluralism and Media Freedom 2022: 11). For example, the area of 'market plurality' uses indicators of 'transparency of media ownership' and 'news media concentration'. In formulating an approach for this volume – one that embraces traditional concerns such as the concentration of ownership as well as contemporary problems such as the role of algorithmic recommenders, and which best facilitates international comparative assessments involving Australia – we have been guided by two principles. The first is that 'media pluralism' is a more expansive term with many dimensions and with a normative element that emphasizes the *desirability* of achieving a pluralistic media environment. The second is that 'diversity' is useful as a more specific sub-concept that is qualified in terms of diversity of supply, content or exposure. Although we could easily have substituted 'plurality' for 'diversity', as is the case in the United Kingdom, we have chosen 'diversity' on account of its prevalence in Australia, recognizing also its take-up in the United States.

In adopting this approach, we draw on the work of our co-researcher on the 'Media Pluralism and Online News' project (and contributor to this volume) Kari Karppinen (2013: 3–4) who has observed:

> Media diversity is understood in a more neutral, descriptive sense, as heterogeneity on the level of contents, outlets, ownership or any other aspect of the media deemed relevant; whereas media pluralism, as a broader socio-cultural and evaluative principle, is understood as referring to the acknowledgement and preference of such diversity, which also required some schematization of its relationship to democracy or other social values.

This 'broader sociocultural and evaluative principle' means that media pluralism embraces more than just political pluralism. As Valcke et al. (2015: 5) note, in addition to political pluralism, it includes cultural and geographic dimensions (as well as aspects of content and format). Doyle (2002) also distinguishes between political pluralism and cultural pluralism.

In identifying the various aspects of diversity within this larger concept of pluralism, we have had regard to the well-established categorization of source diversity (e.g., concentration of ownership), content diversity (e.g., range of viewpoints) and exposure diversity (i.e., what people actually experience) advanced by Napoli (1999). Napoli's formulation remains useful, even in a digital platform environment, on account of its recognition of the importance of methods of delivery and reception of media content, while still emphasizing that supply is a critical component.

Within the category of content diversity – and acknowledging that we are mostly concerned here with its contribution to the dimension of political pluralism – we place particular importance on content that can be described as 'public affairs content'. This has a connection with, but is not the same as, 'public interest journalism' – a form of content that has acquired a renewed focus in policy literature (e.g., in the Cairncross Review in the United Kingdom: Cairncross 2019) as its viability becomes more fragile in a platform environment that threatens the business model of traditional news producers. One of the key aims of the 'Media Pluralism and Online News' project is to apply a method of computationally evaluating media pluralism in a multi-platform news ecosystem. The concept of 'public affairs' allows us to separate out and identify the categories of content that contributes to media pluralism (at least in the dimension of political pluralism). Our view is that this term is useful in showing the news content that should be valued; that is, media content which is constitutive of a *news* public good, and for which the business model is in a state of crisis.

Classifying content as 'public affairs' is therefore a mechanism for identifying material that might be the subject of public subsidy, philanthropy or some form of regulatory intervention. It avoids the traditional distinction between 'hard news' and 'soft news', which can be important when material that is usually seen as soft news has a public affairs angle. For example, a sports article might be about the need for public funding, health or corruption in sport. Even articles apparently about celebrities can have some kind of pro-social or civic function. It also avoids the need to distinguish between 'news', on the one hand, and comment/analysis/current affairs on the other (Media Pluralism Project 2019).

Making a distinction between public affairs and non-public affairs content is not meant to suggest non-public affairs has no value – it might, for example, be important in maintaining a sense of community – but it does allow us to identify material that is part of news media's role in contributing to government, public administration and civic society.

We define *public affairs* (relative to *non-public affairs*) in the following way:

Public affairs reporting conveys timely, factual and opinion-based information about events and issues in government, politics, business and public administration. This will include education, health, science and other matters that have broad social significance. Examples are items that cover contentious public debates on climate change, immigration and land use.

Non-public affairs reporting conveys timely, factual and opinion-based information about topics of entertainment, art and culture, leisure and lifestyle. This will include sport, well-being, fashion and music. A sports article that just gives sports results or commentary, for example, will be non-public affairs, unless it has a public affairs angle such as government funding or health concerns.

It should also be noted that public affairs content is different from 'public interest journalism', although the two will often overlap. We think 'public interest journalism' is a very useful term to describe certain public-focused activities and the content that results. Public affairs content is any content, produced by news media, that has some public affairs angle. In the example given above, it would cover an article that is largely about sports results if the article also dealt with the lack of suitable facilities at a sports ground. While such a report is included in some definitions of 'public interest journalism', it is excluded from others. We recognize that these definitions are still in development and over time they may coalesce further.

We return to the concept of public affairs content as a part of our analysis in the following chapter of tools for measuring media pluralism. Such a tool could be used to establish a baseline measure of media pluralism or to chart change over time, but it could also be used in assessing media mergers if it can identify the most important sources of public affairs content in a market, ahead of a proposed merger. Much of this current chapter is dedicated to the ongoing relevance of this aspect of source diversity, as we consider the current media ownership rules and the regulation of media mergers. In emphasizing the continuing importance of ownership, we do not mean to suggest that media ownership is always a defining point of source diversity. Further, we acknowledge, as others have done (e.g., Levy 2015; Collins and Cave 2013), that it can be difficult to establish a direct link between a multiplicity of owners and viewpoint diversity. However, ownership remains of concern in an environment where the most popular online news sites – sources in themselves as well as suppliers of content on digital platforms – are often the digital outlets of long established print and broadcast media.

Finally, a crucial consideration in the assessment of media pluralism in contemporary media ecosystems is the role of algorithms in delivering news to consumers and the control of these algorithms by digital platforms. As Natalie Helberger (2018: 156), has explained:

> The true source of digital dominance is the ability to control the way people encounter and engage with information and the ability to steer their choices through the sheer knowledge about their interests and biases. More than ever, diversity has become the result of social dynamics, dynamics that are carefully orchestrated by one or few platforms.

Governments in many different jurisdictions are attempting to regulate the operations of digital platforms – for example, the Digital Services Act and the Digital Markets Act in the EU; the Online Safety Bill in the United Kingdom; or the Online Safety Act 2021 in Australia. Some of this will contribute indirectly to media pluralism, and there are some novel forms of regulation that do not easily fit into established regulatory approaches – specifically, the frequently applied distinction between 'structural regulation' and 'content regulation'. Media ownership rules along with licensing rules, for example, are generally regarded as 'structural regulation', to be contrasted with content regulation, such as rules about accuracy, fairness and representation (see Hitchens 2006). Australia's News Media Bargaining Code (technically, Part IVBA of the Competition and Consumer Act 2010) is largely an exercise in structural regulation, aimed at redirecting advertising revenue from digital platforms to news businesses. However, there is also a requirement – assuming the statutory scheme actually comes into effect (see discussion of this point in Chapter 1 above) – that platforms inform news businesses of changes to algorithms that are likely to have a significant effect on referral traffic (see s 52S). Although it is perhaps best characterized as structural regulation insofar as it is concerned with the actions of one sector of the industry in relation to another, it edges closer to a form of contemporary content regulation in that it could have a direct impact on what consumers are exposed to.

This is only one of the complexities involved in promoting media pluralism in a platform environment but it shows why the interplay of algorithms and the role of curated content need careful consideration. It also helps in endeavours to prise open the 'black box' of algorithms and to address difficult questions about causal responsibility where automated processes are involved. We explore this and other aspects of algorithmic content delivery in the section below, before returning to the enduring problem of ownership concentration.

Automated curation and ethics

Inevitably discussion around the urgent need for monitoring and auditing algorithms in news media contexts bumps up against more fundamental ethical philosophy questions regarding the use of artificial intelligence or machine learning in society more generally, within and beyond the algorithmic media landscape. The dialogic characteristics of these processes prompts further consideration, as Bucher explains: 'questioning the ways in which algorithms shape life also requires us to question how life shapes algorithms'. The 'If … then' in the title of her book refers to the conditional rules in algorithmic statements which have malleable consequences depending on both the 'if' and 'then' presuppositions (Bucher 2018). In the context of code that makes certain news articles visible, but not others, she notes that this will be based on the material arrangements that inform the algorithms. This circularity infers a responsibility on the part of the software coders but also draws attention to ongoing human and machine relations in the curation of platform visible news, and indeed the ubiquity and 'productivity' of these processes. Bucher refers to this framing as an 'ontological politics of algorithms':

> Based on the manner in which notions of the machine, software and artificial intelligence are bound up in and entangled with sociality, subjectivity and social issues, the ontological politics of algorithms refers to the ways in which these categories are made differentially relevant and available as part of specific configurations.
>
> (Bucher 2018: 151)

Agency and politics merge into a question of the 'when' of algorithms, in terms of *when* and *how* they are mobilized and for which purposes. In the case of news articles surfacing on a platform the question might be asked: when did the article appear and how is it linked to particular material and discursive conditions? At a higher level, knowledge production itself has become dependent on 'tools that are driven by the hodgepodge commercial logic of a fragmented industrial space for information' (Finn 2018: 195).

In a working paper by the group Algorithm Watch, *Ethics and algorithmic processes for decision making and decision support*, the observation is made that contemporary ethical debates about the consequences of automation – and, algorithmic processes as the main component of automation – need to be seen in the first instance for their collective dimension (Jaume-Palasi and Spielkamp 2017).

For the authors, machine learning, digital publicness and privacy require more complicated ethical and legal frameworks of analysis: they argue that digital platforms constitute 'a kind of societal frame'. Questions of 'machine agency' or machines as subjects capable of responsibility or harm are, however, problematic. The authors suggest that while initial automated decision making may be by means of algorithmic processes (e.g. the ranking of postings in a news feed):

> these decisions are the result of a combination of the intentions of various actors who (co-) design the algorithmic processes involved: the designer of the personalization algorithm, the data scientist who trains the algorithm with specific data only and continues to co-design it as it develops further and, not least, the individual to whom this personalization algorithm is directed and to whom it is adapted. All these actors have an influence on the algorithmic process.
>
> (Jaume-Palasi and Spielkamp 2017: 19)

Attributing causal responsibility to an automated procedure is situated in an ethically grey zone. Contextual factors and various actors are 'entangled' by those co-shaping the algorithms. Yet in pragmatic regulatory contexts, typically the corporation is inevitably held accountable for the sum of these actors' work.

The concept of human rights by design informs the approach taken by Australia's former Human Rights Commissioner, Ed Santow, in the *Human Rights and Technology Final Report 2021* (Australian Human Rights Commission 2021). The report is part of growing body of literature that examines the human costs of AI and opaque machine reasoning more generally. Santow argues that if judges must explain their reasons behind a decision, then computers must as well, and that the blackbox of computer reasoning is coming to an end (Davidson 2021). Further, the argument is made in the report that the government should 'approach new and emerging technologies by being consultative, inclusive and accountable, with robust human rights safeguards' (AHRC 2021).

As Finn argues, our usage of virtual spaces that have idealistically been referred to as a 'new public square' or perhaps more accurately a 'post public sphere' calls to be re-imagined:

> The private life of the average citizen becomes public, commercially accessible to data brokers, social media companies, and others who trade access to the newly privatized sphere of online community (though sites like Facebook and Twitter) in exchange for commercial access to users' private lives.
>
> (Finn 2018: 173)

News and information are now entrenched within the computational realm of 'programmable culture' and datafication underpins a logic for platforms to be privatized. We therefore need to consider the way that the term 'engagement' is now valorized to describe our interactions with news and other informational content on social media platforms; we are witnessing a process of 'normalizing' our own commodification (Dwyer 2016).

Algorithmic auditing

The executive director of Reset Australia, a public policy advocacy group, commented at the time Facebook went dark at the climax of negotiations over the News Media Bargaining Code: 'Facebook is not a neutral platform or democratic public square, but a curated space where algorithms supercharge sensational and conspiratorial content to keep audiences engaged for longer' (Reset Australia 2021a: n.pag.).

Many experts have called for social media platforms to be subject to an audit process to assess the priorities and impacts of algorithms. In their submission to the Senate inquiry on the News Media Bargaining Code, Reset Australia recommended that the Australian government: 'Institute an audit authority under an independent regulator to both verify the provisions set out under the Minimum Standards of this Code, and empowered to investigate/audit the impact of algorithmic amplification on Australian society' (Reset Australia 2021b: 1).

They argued that the Government not 'lose sight of the real goal: of ensuring a diverse and pluralistic media landscape' (Reset Australia 2021b: 2). Reset Australia made public their criticisms of the legislative mechanisms around vague minimum standards of notifications for changes to algorithms or other platform practices and the 'significant effect' this may have on referral traffic to news publishers' sites. The need for clarity in relation to minimum standards for notifications goes to their key recommendation: verification of information provided by platforms and the institution of an audit authority. They make the point that without such verification and auditing, the whole purpose of the new mandatory bargain code law is made redundant. In their submission, Reset Australia elaborated on the details for the establishment of an audit authority to work for broader public interests. They argued:

> harms caused by the digital platforms, ranging from foreign interference to disinformation, needs a holistic approach and the remit of this authority should expand to provide insights into bigger questions – such as how platform curation algorithms open up risk and create harm to the public.
>
> (5)

The argument is made that in having a remit to investigate bigger public interest questions the audit authority must go beyond narrow commercial considerations to investigate 'systematic impacts of algorithmic amplification'. This refers to the way content is routinely promoted and demoted according to algorithmic prioritization of platforms. A key area to audit would be 'unilateral algorithmic curation and amplification' since this has 'an outsized impact on harming the Australian public and our democracy', and therefore should not be limited to the manipulation of news content.

Reset Australia note that these kinds of auditing processes have been proposed in the EU Digital Services Act (DSA) and represent a clear model that is worthy to emulate. They explain that such an audit authority reviews the 'curation systems of the digital platforms which display news media content'. It would provide capacity to assess anti-competitive aspects in addition to the general online harms arising for society and democracy, including disinformation and foreign interference (6).

They observe that although such investigations could sit within the Australian Competition and Consumer Commission (ACCC), the agency should also have the appropriate powers to instruct independent experts to undertake an audit on its behalf – citing examples from aviation to drug therapeutics.

The ACCC (2019) in its Digital Platforms Inquiry (DPI) final report observed that:

> The profound impact of digital platforms on media markets requires careful consideration. News and journalism generate important benefits for society through the production and dissemination of knowledge, the exposure of corruption, and holding governments and other decision makers to account […] the ACCC considers that commercial news media businesses perform a central role in providing journalism and contributing to media plurality.
>
> (1)

The inquiry's final report had a global impact on how platforms operate in online news ecosystems. It found that in the supply of news content, digital platforms are more than just mere distributors or 'pure intermediaries' for news content commenting:

Digital platforms in Australia are actively involved in the publication, distribution and/or broadcast of news online including through performing some functions that overlap with those of news media businesses such as: selecting and curating content, evaluating content, and ranking and arranging content.

In commenting on Meta's own practices, its then head of newsfeed argued:

> Facebook uses algorithms that consider thousands of data points regarding the available inventory of stories to surface and rank the most relevant content on the Facebook News Feed for its users, including consideration of factors such as Facebook's predictions on how likely a user is to comment on a story or share it with a friend.
>
> (Mosseri 2018: n.pag.)

In practice, these curatorial activities involve layers of machine-learning decisions around the kinds of news coverage that platforms allow to become visible for audiences. A key differentiating aspect of this news content provision is algorithmic personalization based on the likelihood of engagement that takes account of past (click, like, commenting and share) usage patterns (Akos et al. 2021). The sifting and ranking and general organizing of relevant 'candidate' stories based on readers' personal data points or signals are then made visible in newsfeeds.

An important recommendation from the ACCC report was directed at the Government:

> A specialist digital platforms branch be established within the ACCC to build on and develop expertise in digital markets and the use of algorithms, with the purpose of: proactively monitoring and investigating instances of potentially anti-competitive conduct and conduct causing consumer harm by digital platforms, which impact consumers, advertisers or other business users (including news media businesses).
>
> (Rec. 4: 31)

This recommendation was one that the Government said it was 'immediately committed to implement' (Australian Government 2019). The ACCC has since established a Digital Platforms Branch and, in accordance with a direction from government, commenced a five-year Digital Platform Services Inquiry to examine platforms' digital advertising services and the data practices of platforms and data brokers. It should be noted, however, that these responses do not go as far as those recommended by Reset Australia, nor by the ACCC itself in its preliminary report where it floated the idea of 'a regulatory authority [that has] the power to monitor, investigate and report on the ranking of news and journalistic content by digital platforms and the provision of referral services to news media businesses' (ACCC 2019: 252). In its Final Report, after 'strong submissions' in response to this recommendation in the preliminary report (ACCC 2019: 141) the ACCC backed away from the idea of an algorithms regulator and instead proposed its own Digital Services Branch. For the reasons outlined above, this can be regarded as unfinished business; it is a topic we return to in the following chapter that deals specifically with media pluralism policy.

At around the same time, these events were being investigated in other jurisdictions, including in the UK's *Unlocking Digital Competition. Report of the Digital Competition Expert Panel* (The Furman Report). Framed within a competition (or anti-trust) policy approach, the Furman Report recognized the harms that could be caused by the excesses of platform power in terms of increased reliance on algorithmic decision making. The report recommended the establishment of a 'Digital Markets Unit' that should be well-resourced and 'tasked with securing competition, innovation, and beneficial outcomes for consumers and businesses' (UK Government, Strategic Rec. A. 2019). It further recommended that such a unit was to be appropriately skilled with interdisciplinary mix of expertise, drawn from economics, law, computer science and competition policy.

The Furman panel noted that, 'As the scale and use of algorithms by businesses continues to grow, the government, the Competition and Markets Authority (CMA) and Centre for Data Ethics and Innovation (CDEI) should continue to monitor markets closely'. It made the argument that:

authorities should have proportionate information gathering powers to enable them to carry out their functions in the digital economy. The CMA would likely need additional information gathering powers to enable it to effectively audit algorithms and government should consider the case for providing these [...] The Panel considers as a general principle that businesses who use algorithms should take all reasonable steps to understand, and be prepared to explain, how their algorithms work, how they interact with other firms' algorithms, and how they have mitigated against any potential biases or anti-competitive consequences.

(UK Government, 3.170-1: 112)

Therefore, it can be seen that a number of developments in various jurisdictions have advanced the position for the increased need of algorithmic auditing within the automated news space. As we mentioned in the opening chapter, the Digital Regulation Cooperation Forum (2022a; 2022b) in the United Kingdom is pursuing this problem in multi-disciplinary teams and across regulatory bodies.

This shows that the industrial context of digitization as a post public sphere has intensified over the past decade. As Natalie Fenton et al. (2020) have argued, the 'emergence of platform monopolies in search and social media, and excessive content provision, decimates the public value of the internet commons and exacerbates digital divides in access to diverse and credible sources of news and information' (112). They advocate for legislated and broader community responses to protect the public interest, and we agree that media and data systems need to be rebuilt with mechanisms for inclusive citizen participation and democratic control.

The problem, at least from the perspective of our current inquiry, is that questions about the effect of digital platforms and their algorithmic re-formulation of public affairs content are often seen – at least in public policy terms – as quite separate from concerns about media pluralism. At least some national governments, including Australia's, appear to have moved on to tackle the very real challenges of platforms and algorithms without having addressed the residual problem of low levels of media pluralism. Both are issues critical to the maintenance of a healthy public sphere. In our view, it is important to trace back the policy and regulatory settings affecting media pluralism; to repair and modernize them for the platform environment. We begin this process by looking at the regulatory framework in both Australia and the United Kingdom, including how media mergers have been assessed in the past and how – at least in Australia – this might be improved, before moving on in the following chapter to consider how we might develop a more contemporary approach to measuring media pluralism.

The Australian policy and regulatory settings for media pluralism

There are two aspects of sector-specific – 'structural' – regulation that significantly shape media pluralism in Australia: the broadcast licensing arrangements that establish various categories of service, and the media ownership and control rules. These are both described in more detail here, although the second has much more significance than the first. These two sets of rules are aside from other rules – 'content regulation' – dealing with news standards (such as accuracy and fairness), as well as from cross-sector competition (anti-trust) laws that aim to protect against mergers and acquisitions that create, or are likely to create, a substantial lessening of competition in a market. The news standard content rules for commercial media are set out in codes of practice formulated by industry and registered with and enforced by the ACMA under Part 9 of the Broadcasting Services Act 1992, while the merger laws are set out in the Competition and Consumer Act 2010 (the most important being s 50 of that Act).

Licensing categories of service

The licensing arrangements are established in Part 2 of the Broadcasting Services Act 1992, responding to one of the objects of that Act: section 3(1)(a) aims to promote the availability to audiences throughout Australia of a diverse range of radio and television services offering entertainment, education and information. The licensing scheme in Part 2 of the Act then creates different categories of broadcasting service – recognizing for example, not-for-profit community services as well as private, commercial services and public service broadcasting – along with the reservation of radiofrequency spectrum for those services. This statutory form of regulation attempts to produce a level of diversity in industry structure.

As Hitchens (2006) observed, this structural scheme can be regarded as a contributor to some aspects of pluralism within the Australian media environment but it is of limited value. Historically, the number of licences issued to commercial television and radio services (and to the less commercial but for-profit 'open narrowcasting' category) was constrained by both spectrum scarcity and concerns about the viability of relatively small commercial markets (Given 2003). Despite some known additional spectrum capacity, s 37A of the Act maintains a 'moratorium' over the issuing of new commercial television licences. Further, pay TV (in its 'subscription broadcasting' form at least, so not allowing for online-only services or niche satellite services) was not introduced into Australia until 1995 and, after the demise of both a national competitor and a complementary regional service, is now solely provided by Foxtel, controlled by News Corporation.

Australia is by no means unique in not having updated its communications regulatory framework to reflect new distribution and delivery mechanisms for audio-visual content – including digital platforms – even though a forward-looking model was presented a decade ago by the Convergence Review (2012) for a new regulatory regime based on the concept of a 'content service enterprise'. Although there have been signals from Australia's Labor Government (elected in May 2022) that regulatory reform is part of the policy agenda, initiatives to date have targeted specific issues. For example, discussion papers were issued in late 2022 on possible changes to the 'anti-siphoning' list that restricts pay-TV exclusive access to some marquee sports events, and on the possible introduction of rules addressing prominence of Australian services. In early 2023, in a positive sign of government interest in media diversity, the media regulator issued a follow-up to its 2020 paper on the development of a measurement framework for media diversity (ACMA 2023), although this is unlikely to result in short-term regulatory change. An important decision made in the second half of 2022 offered an indication that more holistic regulatory reform is likely to be deferred to a second term of the Labor government: in September, the Minister for Communications (Rowland 2022) renewed for five years a legislative instrument that excludes online services including streaming video-on-demand and broadcast video-on-demand from the legislative definition of 'broadcasting service'.

Media ownership and control in Australia

Successive rounds of legislative amendments have repealed all but three of Australia's media ownership laws, with much confidence placed in the role of competition law. The removal of sector-specific media ownership rules is not unique to Australia; deregulation has been widely practised in Europe, although some countries such as Italy and Germany along with the United States and the United Kingdom retain some rules (Van der Burg and Van den Bulck 2015: 5). It should also be acknowledged that in addition to repeal of sector-specific laws, failure to update them has rendered some of them obsolete. Napoli (2019: 153), for example, has noted the failure of US law to adequately deal with the 'large, wide-ranging and impactful' merger of AT&T and Time Warner in 2016. As a result of the Federal Communications Commission's remit being tied to legacy media, Time Warner was able to by-pass the application of a public interest test by selling its sole terrestrial TV licence, leaving the merger to be considered – and approved – under competition law.

This growing obsolescence is easily seen in the objects of broadcasting legislation in Australia. Diversity in ownership is one of the objects of the Broadcasting

Services Act – section 3(1)(c) seeks 'to encourage diversity in control of the more influential broadcasting services' – but the media ownership rules that give effect to this object (found in Part 5 of the Act) apply only to commercial television, commercial radio and newspapers 'associated with' the licence areas of these categories of service. In the transition from analogue to digital television, an object (in s 3(1)(n)) was added to the Act 'to ensure the maintenance and, where possible, the development of diversity, including public, community and indigenous broadcasting' but implementation of this goal was limited to the addition of multi-channelling on existing services and the ill-fated creation of the category of 'datacasting services'. Even before the emergence of digital TV and online news, the exclusion of pay TV from this scheme was notable, and reflects the foundations of Australia's media ownership regime in the late 1980s. At this time, a prohibition on the formation of television networks from licences held in more than two capital cities was replaced by a national '75 per cent reach rule' that effectively required separate commercial television networks in regional and metropolitan areas, along with a prohibition on cross-media ownership in local areas. The new cross-media rule applied to control of more than one of the regulated platforms in a single licence area. Chadwick (1989) provides a detailed analysis of the policy motivations and political manoeuvres involved in the highly charged environment of the late 1980s, noting that 'reform' tended to occur when the interests of political parties aligned with the commercial interests of powerful media proprietors.

These rules commenced in 1986 and, after amendment in 1987, remained intact until the removal of foreign ownership limits and the recasting and scaling back of the cross-media ban so that it permitted control of two of the three regulated platforms, all of which came into effect in 2007. These aspects of deregulation were accompanied by a new 'minimum voices rule' (sometimes referred to as the '5/4' rule) that stops further consolidation, mostly in regional areas, when certain concentration levels in the regulated platforms are reached. Wilding (2003), Dwyer et al. (2006) and Given (2007) have commented on the background to and introduction of these legislative changes. While some of the same features noted by Chadwick (mentioned above) were identified in this round of legislative reform, by the mid 2000s, a persistent theme underpinning calls for repeal of existing laws was the 'game changing' impact of the internet and the assertion that wider access by some consumers to overseas media sources had produced a new level of diversity.

These arrangements remained in place until a further round of legislative change in 2017, which repealed the 'two-out-of-three' cross-media rule and the 75 per cent national reach rule.

Following the most recent round of changes, Australia's media ownership rules are confined to the following:

- the limit of one commercial television licence in a commercial television licence area (with some exceptions for smaller markets);
- the limit of two commercial radio licences in a commercial radio licence area;
- the 5/4 minimum voices rule which established the concept of 'an unacceptable media diversity situation' based on a points scheme (established by way of the Register of Controlled Media Groups) that applies a floor of five points in metropolitan licence areas and four points in regional licence areas, after which transactions resulting in further concentration are prohibited.

As a complement to these ownership rules, Australia's version of a 'fit and proper person' test is found in the 'suitable licensee' test in s 41 of the Broadcasting Services Act 1992. In contrast to the position under the more interventionist regulatory regime that existed prior to 1992, the suitable person test is not routinely applied at the point of licence renewal; it only arises in response to some specific evidence prompting its consideration (see, e.g., ACMA 2006).

Finally, it should be noted that the aspects of structural regulation represented by the categories of services and the ownership and control rules are separate from content requirements relating to news standards (such as accuracy and fairness), as well as broadcast quotas for the provision of local television and radio news and information in regional areas. News standards are a part of co-regulatory codes of practice developed by sections of the industry and registered with the ACMA. These rules respond to the objects of the Act which include encouraging commercial and community broadcasters 'to be responsive to the need for a fair and accurate coverage of matters of public interest' (s 3(1)(g)).

Accordingly, while the Act invokes the concept of 'the public interest', and includes among its objects a recognition of cultural diversity (object 1(e) refers to 'developing and reflecting a sense of Australian identity, character and cultural diversity'), it sidesteps the issues of viewpoint diversity in favour of diversity in control of licences and associated companies. As we note above, although there is no consensus internationally on definitions of diversity or pluralism, content (or viewpoint) diversity and exposure (or consumption) diversity have long been recognized as important dimensions of diversity (see, e.g., Napoli 1999).

In relation to diversity of viewpoints, there is a legislative objective that uses the related concept of quality in its encouragement of commercial and community broadcasters to be 'responsive to the need for fair and accurate coverage of matters of public interest' ((3(1)(g)), and this objective is addressed in co-regulatory codes of practice that include references to viewpoints presented in news and/or current affairs programs. However, the codes for commercial TV and commercial radio do not require inclusion of a range of viewpoints while the public service broadcasters explicitly have this requirement; instead the commercial codes provide a protection against 'false balance' by stating explicitly that programs are not required 'to allocate equal time to different points of view or to include every aspect of a person's viewpoint' (Commercial Television Industry Code of Practice 3.4.2; Commercial Radio Code of Practice 3.9). These differences between the schemes operated by public service broadcasters and commercial broadcasters were noted in the report of a recent parliamentary inquiry into Media Diversity in Australia, with the public standards schemes being seen to represent 'a higher level of accountability' (Senate, Environment and Communications References Committee 2021: 65).

There is no recognition at all of *exposure* diversity in Australian media regulation, despite the attention it has gained in recent years (see, e.g., Helberger 2018) as a result of concerns over the role of digital platforms. As Helberger et al. (2020) note in their recent work for the Canadian Government, a dimension of exposure diversity has emerged to address the ways in which recommenders and algorithms structure the delivery of content in an environment featuring an overabundance of information. While noting the importance of consumption or exposure diversity, their research has observed the continuing need to recognize the role of source diversity:

> [T]he possibility of exposure diversity depends on the availability of content in the pool. If the quality and diversity of the pool is low, recommenders have insufficient options to provide good recommendations. That means exposure diversity ultimately is dependent on external diversity.
>
> (Helberger et al. 2020: n.pag.)

The impacts of these rules

The extent to which these rules protect – or rather, fail to protect – media diversity has been described elsewhere (see e.g., Dwyer et al. 2021; Brevini and Ward 2021; Papandrea and Tiffen 2016; Hitchens 2015). However, three aspects are worth highlighting here. The first is the relatively small base of local news producers. Across Australia's eight state and territory capital cities, there are ten metropolitan daily newspapers and two national dailies. Sydney and Melbourne each have two daily newspapers; the other capital cities have one. There are three commercial television networks that compete for digital terrestrial television in capital cities (with affiliates in regional areas) and two public service broadcasters, and there are a few local online-only offshoots of international brands such as *The Guardian* and the *Daily Mail* as well as several radio networks and some smaller independent newspaper groups and local online-only news sites.

The second noteworthy aspect is the level of concentration. Eleven of the twelve newspapers are owned by the largest three media companies, News Corp Australia,

Nine Entertainment, and Seven West Media. Nine and Seven own one each of the three metropolitan commercial television networks, while News Corp owns the single pay TV subscription broadcaster, Foxtel. In the digital environment, these three companies control six of the top ten digital news sites (Mediaweek 2021). News Corp also owns a sufficient number of regional and suburban news titles to give it a 59 per cent share of newspaper readership in Australia (Brevini and Ward 2021: 51) as well as one of two leading local media streaming services, Binge. Nine owns the other leading streaming service, Stan. News Corp and Nine own the two national daily newspapers, *The Australian* and *The Australian Financial Review*, respectively. National newspapers, online news sites and streaming services are all excluded from the ownership and control rules. Apart from the work of the non-profit Public Interest Journalism Initiative, there is no monitoring and charting of news sources that also takes into account digital start-ups, the public service broadcasters, community radio etc.

Accordingly, it is well established that Australia's media market is highly concentrated; that neither its media ownership laws nor competition regulation has been effective in addressing concentration at the point when transactions have been proposed; and that there are no formal mechanisms for monitoring and assessing levels of media diversity at a local, regional or national level. It is for this reason that the experience of other jurisdictions, and in particular the United Kingdom, may be helpful in considering a more effective approach to promoting media pluralism.

Yet the unfolding structural trend to media concentration in media markets is a global phenomenon that various expert commentators have noted continues to have a deleterious impact on democratic processes. For example, Jolly and Pickard have recently argued that, 'While a few dominant firms further concentrate their media power, the press withers and public trust recedes. As newsrooms shudder, communities lose vital sources of locally relevant information and democratic culture' (Jolly and Pickard 2021: n.pag.). These authors argue that factors including the convergence of previously distinct media technologies over digital networks have accelerated the concentration of power, and the continuing centrality of advertising in media markets requires an 'enlivened' policy program.

Media ownership and control in the United Kingdom

Media ownership rules

Several aspects of policy and regulation distinguish the United Kingdom from Australia. The United Kingdom has a cross-media rule (in Schedule 14 of the

Communications Act 2003) which operates at a national level and prohibits a newspaper operator with a national market share of 20 per cent or more from holding a Channel 3 licence or a stake in a Channel 3 licensee company that is greater than 20 per cent, and prohibits a Channel 3 licensee from acquiring an interest of 20 per cent or more in a newspaper operator with a national market share of 20 per cent or more. This is the key ownership rule aimed at plurality but it is accompanied by rules relating to the independent supply of national news services by Channel 3 licensees; rules that disqualify certain persons and groups (such as advertising agencies and political associations) from holding licences; and the Media Public Interest Test applied in relation to mergers (see below). In the United Kingdom, there is also a 'fit and proper person' test which applies to the holders of broadcasting licences: Broadcasting Act 1990 s3(3) and Broadcasting Act 1996 s3(3). This test has been applied by Ofcom in recent media mergers.

In its consultation document published in June 2021 as part of its periodic review of the operation of these rules, Ofcom (2021b) proposed recommending to the Secretary of State that except for some aspects of the disqualified persons provisions, all these rules should be retained and that one feature (the public interest test) should be enhanced. The details concerning the public interest test are addressed in the next section.

Media mergers

Ofcom and its predecessors have long held responsibilities for monitoring and regulating media ownership and control. Aside from Ofcom's decisions on media ownership laws, in 2003, plurality became a 'public interest consideration' included in the Enterprise Act 2002. Section 58 sets out the public interest considerations, while s 42 gives the Secretary of State the power to issue an 'intervention notice' if one or more of the public interest grounds in section 58 is activated. The arrangements only apply to licensed broadcasters and print newspapers. In practice, Ofcom may be asked to provide an initial assessment in accordance with the intervention notice and then this assessment, depending on its findings, might support a subsequent referral by the Secretary of State to the Competition and Markets Authority (CMA) for a more comprehensive assessment. The CMA can consider both the plurality aspects and the competition aspects. In its review of the application by 21st Century Fox for the remaining share of Sky Plc in 2017/2018 (see below), the CMA explained that it takes Ofcom's framework as 'an appropriate starting point' (CMA 2018: 97) in the plurality analysis; however, it notes that there is limited external guidance on the subject and that the framework does not establish a benchmark for what is a 'sufficient' level of plurality (13).

Although newspapers and broadcasting services are treated separately, the 'sufficient plurality' test applies to both. For newspapers, this is (where reasonable and practicable) 'a sufficient plurality of views' (s 58(2B)), whereas for radio and television, it is 'a sufficient plurality of persons with control of the media enterprises serving that audience' (s 58(2C)(a)). And in a demonstration of the ways in which plurality, quality and standards are interwoven, the Secretary may also issue an intervention notice in relation to: accurate presentation of news and free opinion in newspapers (s 58(2A)); a wide range of broadcasting services 'of high quality and calculated to appeal to a wide variety of tastes and interests' (s 58(2C)(b)); and a genuine commitment to broadcasting standards (s 58(2C)(c)).

An intervention notice was issued on the grounds in s 58(2A) in 2019 in relation to the acquisition by Saudi interests (through companies in the Cayman Islands) of a stake in the companies that controlled *The Evening Standard* newspaper and the website of *The Independent*. The notice required consideration by Ofcom of the likely impact on accurate reporting of news and possible editorial interference. Although Ofcom concluded there was not cause for a reference by the Secretary of State for further consideration by the CMA (and in any event it was complicated by problems around compliance with the statutory timeframes), the matter is of interest because it shows how Ofcom will consider the way commercial factors influencing investment in the media source may affect its news coverage (see Ofcom 2019: 27–28). This included a review of the employment of journalists and an analysis of content over an extended period (Ofcom 2019: 36–41).

In its most recent periodic review of the media ownership rules, Ofcom (2021c: 26) identified the limited application of the public interest test (the 'Media PIT') to broadcasters and print newspapers, noting the significant changes in the way in which people access news since the rule was introduced in the early 2000s, meaning there was a need to capture online news providers. It has recommended to the Secretary of State that the test is reformulated to capture 'news creators' which would include online news sources as well as wholesale news providers and relevant magazines – in other words, 'all entities who have editorial control over the creation and publishing of news material by journalists, irrespective of platform' (2021c: 29). This would involve amendments to some of the specific provisions applying to the 'sufficient plurality' measure. For example, 'a sufficient plurality of views in newspapers' in s 58(2B) of the Enterprise Act would become 'a sufficient plurality of views created by news creators' (see Ofcom 2021c: 31). A similar change would apply to controllers of news creators in s 58(2C)(a). An accompanying change from news 'markets' to news 'platforms' is said to allow for Ofcom to examine the public interest aspects 'on a sector by sector, as well as overall level' (2021c: 31). While urgently needed, it should be noted that the proposal to expand the public interest test beyond broadcasters and print newspapers is hardly revolutionary, and the need for such an approach was advanced by Hitchens over 15 years ago (2006: 210–11).

In 2021, Ofcom concluded that online intermediaries should not, at that time, come within the test on the basis that there is no agreement on metrics for online consumption of news other than via direct news sources (see Ofcom 2021b: 24) and that they would in any event be covered by the public interest test if they acquired a news creator (Ofcom 2021c: 27). Ofcom said that this approach may change in future media ownership reviews (2021c: 29) and that the significant changes to news production and consumption have prompted it to further consider whether there are concerns for maintaining media plurality and how to address these (Ofcom 2021c: 43). In a discussion document released the following year, Ofcom took up the question of on how to account for online news and the role of intermediaries (Ofcom 2022); we consider aspects of this work in Chapter 3.

Monitoring and assessing plurality

Ofcom's role in media mergers follows from the guiding statement of its obligation towards media plurality, found in s 3(2)(d) of the Communications Act 2003 (UK): 'Ofcom is required to secure the maintenance of a sufficient plurality of providers of different television and radio services'. This is quite unlike the Australian legislative objects set out in the Broadcasting Services Act 1992, and the accompanying functions of the ACMA set out in the Australian Communications and Media Authority Act 2005, which contains no reference to media diversity. This overall maintenance role is supplemented by the responsibility, found in s 391 of the UK Communications Act 2003, to review media ownership rules at least every three years. Its latest review, commenced in June 2021, is notable for the breadth of its inquiry. Citing the significant change in patterns of media use since the commencement of the Act in 2003, Ofcom, announced that in its latest review it will seek to understand 'what media plurality means in the 21st century, looking beyond existing media ownership rules' (2021b: 3).

While these reviews assess the operation, effectiveness and relevance of the rules, not the state of plurality per se, Ofcom has conducted extensive work at the request of government. In its 2012 advice to the Minister on measuring plurality, Ofcom (2012) responded to specific questions on how a plurality review might be triggered in the absence of a merger. It identified two types of triggers for a plurality review outside of a merger environment, which would be able to take account of organic growth and other developments, not simply propose transactions. These comprised:

A metric-based trigger, which would require a plurality review to be carried out if organic growth resulted in a specific metric being breached.

A time-based trigger, which would require a plurality review to be carried out automatically on a periodic basis.

(Ofcom 2012: 28)

For reasons that include the difficulty of developing a metric-based trigger and the additional certainty provided to industry participants through the use of a time-based metric, Ofcom favoured the latter. This position was echoed by the House of Lords Select Committee on Communications (2014) in its report on media plurality, which recommended a statutory periodic review by Ofcom every four to five years. Finally, in its own consultations on the development of a measurement framework, the Department of Culture, Media and Sport (2014) explicitly recognized the need for a 'baseline market assessment of media plurality in the UK'.

This policy work resulted in the Measurement Framework for Media Plurality (Ofcom 2015) considered more fully in Chapter 3. Although in theory it supports the kind of baseline assessment of media plurality that could be adopted in Australia, Ofcom itself has noted that in practice it will largely be a test for media mergers (Ofcom 2015: 1). For this reason, some of the explanation in the next section of the elements of the framework relates to specific merger proposals: the ultimately unsuccessful bid by 21st Century Fox for the remaining share of Sky Plc in 2017/2018, referred to here as 'Sky/21C Fox' (see Ofcom 2017; CMA 2018); the acquisition by Trinity Mirror PLC of Northern and Shell Media Group in 2018, which brought together *The Daily Mirror* and a large number of regional titles (Trinity Mirror) and *The Daily Express* and *The Daily Star* (Northern and Shell) into a group now known as 'Reach' (see Ofcom 2018a); the acquisition of a 30 per cent stake by Saudi interests in *The Evening Standard* and the *Independent* (see Ofcom 2019); and the acquisition by DMG Media Limited of JPI Media Publications Limited that involved the *i* UK national newspaper and website, which Ofcom was asked to consider in 2020 (Ofcom 2020). Although the Sky/21C Fox matter raised plurality concerns for Ofcom, the others did not. These various matters engaged different aspects of the public interest factors spelled out in the Enterprise Act 2002. For example: the Sky/21C Fox merger concerned a sufficient plurality in control of media enterprises and the attainment of broadcasting standards per s 58(2C)(a) and (c); the '*i* news' matter concerned a sufficient plurality of views in newspapers per s 58(2B); and *The Evening Standard* and *Independent* matter concerned the accurate reporting of news and free expression of opinion in newspapers per ss 58(1) and (2).

Can the UK approach be adapted for media mergers in Australia?

Media markets and diversity

While on one level, it is unreasonable to expect competition law – largely based on economic principles – to fulfil parallel social objectives, the removal of sector-specific media diversity rules makes it necessary to test just how far competition law can go towards this end. One useful starting point is the identification of relevant markets.

In Australia, with media mergers, as with transaction in other industries, the ACCC applies the test in s 50 of the Competition and Consumer Act 2010 and considers whether an acquisition of shares or assets has the effect or likely effect of 'substantially lessening competition in a market'. It has long been recognized that media markets are 'two-sided' – one side addressing the relationship between an advertiser and a news organization, and the other the relationship between the news organization and the consumer (Gabszewicz et al. 2015: 6; Doyle 2013: 13). There are two forms of market definition – the relevant product market and the relevant geographic market, although they are not always totally separate exercises (Bjorkroth and Gronlund 2015: 307, 313) – and there may be various sub-markets, for example, tabloid and quality newspapers (Bjorkroth and Gronlund 2015: 312).

The importance competition law places on the one side of this two-sided market – the relationship between the news organization and the advertiser rather than the news organization and the reader of news – was a point signalled clearly by the Productivity Commission (2000) in its Broadcasting inquiry report. The Commission argued that in cross-media mergers, in particular: 'the normal approach to competition policy with the current definition of media markets does not appear to provide a sufficiently robust framework to prevent concentration in diversity of information and opinion' (2000: 351). This point is also made in the academic literature (e.g., Baker 2007: 56–76; Humphreys and Simpson 2018: 146) and in international policy reviews (e.g., House of Lords Communications Committee 2014: 9). And it is essentially the position adopted by the ACCC in its *Media Merger Guidelines* (ACCC 2017: 6) which describes competition and diversity as 'interlinked'. Former ACCC Chair, Rod Sims, argued:

> Our merger laws are aimed at competition, and that will help. If you want additional things for diversity, that's where you go to the ACMA laws. There are still remaining ACMA laws – not many now, but some – that do go to that diversity issue.
>
> (Senate Hansard 12.03.21: 19)

In applying the 'substantial lessening of competition' test, the ACCC will look at, among other things, the substitutability of one product or service for another in order to assess whether the merged entity is likely to be able to exercise market power – for example in the form of increased prices. But this is not always a good fit for media markets, or at least for media audiences. Competition law has long asserted that TV, radio and print are not close substitutes and are therefore in different markets, meaning that acquisitions across media platforms will not lead to a potential lessening in competition. The consequence of this approach is highlighted by the approval of the Sky/21C Fox transaction under European Competition law before it was closely examined (as noted earlier) under the UK public interest test. And despite the recognition that treating cross-media assets as being in different markets could change at some point as a result of media convergence (see, e.g., ACCC 2017: 4), that has not yet eventuated – as evidenced in the decision to not oppose the merger of Nine Entertainment and Fairfax Media in 2018 (ACCC 2018). Even if it did evolve in this way, the expanded number of providers in the larger market for, say, the supply of advertising opportunities might lead the ACCC to conclude that there is unlikely to be a substantial lessening of competition, even where there might be a reduction in diversity (Hitchens 2006: 265).

There appears to be some scope for competition law to deal with risks to diversity through its recognition of discourses of 'quality' but again there are limitations. In New Zealand – where there are no sector-specific ownership rules but competition law is modelled on Australian law – an application for authorization of a transaction involving NZME and Fairfax New Zealand was rejected by the New Zealand Commerce Commission in 2017 (with the decision upheld on appeal in NZME Limited v Commerce Commission [2018] NZCA 389). The Commerce Commission took into account non-economic criteria including the key detriments of loss of plurality and reduction in quality (Commerce Commission 2017: 12–13). Berry and Spittle explained that aspects of the reduction in quality (such as variety, diversity and volume of news) were identified in the 'clearance phase' of the two-step regime, during which there was an assessment of the likely substantial lessening of competition, while the effects on media plurality were considered under the second, 'authorization phase', explaining that it was the combination of these two elements that resulted in the rejection of the transaction 'by no small margin' (2019: 108).

Despite this approach taken in New Zealand, in Australia, there has been very limited exploration of how the concept of quality plays out in relation to media mergers. An ACCC official told the Senate Inquiry into Media Diversity in Australia that in the Digital Platforms Inquiry (ACCC 2019) the ACCC considered the following three measures of quality: number of news sources, number of journalists, presence of different types of reporting such as local court and local government reporting (Senate Hansard 12.03.21: 24). However, this is difficult to identify in practice in media mergers, and other commentary from the ACCC suggests the approach to plurality demonstrated in New Zealand might not be followed in Australia. Rod Sims, for example, has said, 'I am opposed to introducing broader public interest considerations into the core of competition law enforcement' (2018: 9).

Internationally, Van der Burg and Van den Bulk (2015: 4) have observed that competition law considers quality through the application of the consumer welfare standard which also takes account of cheaper prices and product variety. In their review of Belgian and Dutch competition authorities' merger decisions, these authors found that economic factors far outweighed non-economic and that even when other factors were present, 'it remains unclear what exactly the notions of content, diversity and quality entail, and how they should be safeguarded' (2015: 13).

In addition to these limitations, the ACCC's approach to the geographic boundaries of media markets means that broader public interest aspects are unlikely to play out. In 2016, News Corp Australia acquired the Australian Regional Media (ARM) division of APN News and Media Limited. ARM owned ten paid daily newspapers, fourteen paid non-daily newspapers and 32 free non-daily community newspapers circulating in the state of Queensland and in the northern area of the state of New South Wales. News Corp owned *The Courier Mail* (and its Sunday equivalent), a major daily paid newspaper based in the Queensland capital, Brisbane, and circulating throughout much of the state. In Queensland and northern New South Wales, News Corp also owned three paid regional dailies, seventeen free community newspapers and what the ACCC described as 'a number of small paid non-daily and free publications circulating in Cairns and Townsville' (ACCC 2016a: 5). In this matter, the ACCC's geographic market-by-market analysis of a transaction involving only print/online media resulted in a decision (ACCC 2016b) that allowed News Corp to acquire ARM so that it now owned all the daily newspapers up the coast of Queensland, placing it in a position of considerable influence over the whole state.

The ACCC's position that, for a business in a regional town, state or national media will seldom be a substitute for local advertising, does of course make sense. However, substitutability alone is not an adequate measure of the *whole of the public interest* in whether a merger should proceed, and the consequences for citizens in a democratic society have been widely acknowledged. For example, in its report, 'Media Plurality' (2014: 77), the UK House of Lords Select Committee on Communications called for a rebalancing of citizen interests against consumer interests expressing the view that 'a democratic and informed society should have greater importance than at present when weighed against the cost of advertising' (66).

Options for a public interest test

So far this analysis has shown that cross-sector competition law is not designed to protect media diversity and, in practice, has not done so. Despite this, existing protections for media diversity in sector-specific broadcasting regulation have been severely reduced, and there are further calls from industry in Australia for the removal of the remaining media ownership rules (e.g. Prime Media Group et al. 2020).

The remainder of our analysis is based on the assumption that public policy can and should remedy this situation by way of new legislative protections. While it does not rule out calls for the reinstatement of 'bright line' ownership and control limits, it turns to a solution that builds on existing regulatory approaches in competition and communications law and has the benefit of serious consideration in previous policy reviews; namely, the development of a media-specific public interest test. In the United Kingdom, as Hitchens (2006: 209–10) observed, this was explicitly recognized almost twenty years ago as the introduction of a public interest test into the Enterprise Act 2002 and was directly related to the removal of the sector-specific ownership rules: 'it was an express acknowledgement that competition law could not be relied upon to protect the marketplace of ideas.'

In developing a public interest test for Australia, there are three key issues that need to be addressed: what kind of public interest test should be used and whether there would be any exemptions; the scope of the test's application to existing and emerging media businesses; and the allocation of the test to the media regulator or the competition regulator.

(i) What kind of public interest test?

Proposals for some form of public interest test have emerged from three previous policy reviews or attempts at legislative reform. In addition to the Productivity Commission's inquiry into broadcasting in 2000, the issue was considered in some detail by the Convergence Review in 2012, and in a package of legislation tabled (but subsequently withdrawn) by the Gillard Labor Government in 2013. The package, including the Broadcasting Legislation Amendment (News Media Diversity) Bill 2013, was developed as a response to the Independent Media Inquiry (the 'Finkelstein' inquiry) and the Convergence Review, both of which reported in 2012.

The description of what constitutes the public interest varied across these three schemes. In the Productivity Commission's 'not contrary to' test, the public interest was described in terms of 'the public interest in a diversity of sources of information and opinion'. However, the Commission noted that other elements could be considered (2000: 364). For the Convergence Review, it was essentially whether the transaction would 'diminish the diversity of unique owners providing general content services as well as news and commentary at a national level' (2012: 24). In the Media Diversity Bill, it concerned 'any lessening of diversity of control of registered news media voices' (cl 78EC).

Neither of the first two proposals was taken up by Government at the time, and the third faced considerable political and media backlash, as well as independent critique (Fernandez 2013; Flew and Swift 2013; Lidberg and Hirst 2013; Rab and Sprague 2014; Young 2015). However, none of these proposals had the benefit of the work by the ACMA on its News Measurement Framework (considered further in Chapter 3). The framework's various indicators – availability of sources, availability of journalists, number of owners, range of topics, range of viewpoints, local relevance, consumption and impact – could all be used to assist the regulator to assess whether a transaction results in a 'reduction in a diversity' such that the transaction should not be permitted. It could be argued that, in effect, this is what Ofcom does when it applies the public interest test to a proposed transaction. In explaining its approach in the proposed acquisition of the *i* newspaper by Daily Mail and General Trust (DMGT) in 2020, Ofcom noted there would be a slight increase in share of references (discussed in Chapter 3 below) for DMGT but concluded:

> Overall, the transaction does not substantially change the distribution of share of reference and we do not consider that the small increase in share of reference resulting from the transaction indicates a reduction in plurality of any meaningful extent.
> (Ofcom 2020: 22)

The transaction overall could be assessed taking into account the reduction in diversity along with other relevant aspects of public policy objectives, as discussed previously, in recognition of the fact that decisions on media mergers that do not take account of these interconnecting issues are unlikely to serve the broader public interest in a vibrant and sustainable news media sector. These could include:

- the sustainability of local businesses;
- the encouragement of original and local news content;
- quality of content, in terms of the promotion of professional news standards;
- modes of delivery and consumption, including the 'automated curation' of digital platforms.

The recognition of these factors would also offset the need for a second-stage 'public benefit' exemption that allows transactions to proceed even where they fail the initial diversity test. Both the Convergence Review and the Media Diversity Bill included such an exemption: for the Convergence Review, an increase in localism or the threat of withdrawal of a service from a market could be taken into account, whereas in the Media Diversity Bill, the countervailing benefit was more broadly expressed in terms of 'a benefit to the public [...] [that] [...] would outweigh the detriment to the public of any lessening of diversity'.

A similar approach is taken under the proposed European Media Freedom Act 2022 in the arrangements for member states to introduce requirements for notification and assessment of transactions that might have a 'significant impact on media pluralism and editorial independence'. Article 21 sets out elements that would be taken into account in the making of these assessments, including the impact of the additional concentration on media pluralism, and whether the acquiring and acquired enterprises would remain economically sustainable in the absence of the transaction, and whether there are any alternatives. Sustainability is also recognized at a sector-side level in the EU media pluralism monitor as 'media viability'. In the Australian scheme, there could also be a power to approve transactions that would otherwise fail the test, provided certain action is taken to address the identified problem – as exists at present under the Broadcasting Services Act 1992. A more expansive approach could therefore be taken similar to the one adopted in the United Kingdom where Ofcom considers mitigation measures such as a guarantee to fund a news service for a lengthy period (as in the Sky/21C Fox matter) and to maintain editorial independence. However, we do not favour a test based on a judgment such as 'sufficient plurality'. The state of media concentration in Australia means that any such test is destined for failure from the outset. A pragmatic alternative, as we discuss further in Chapter 8, would be to develop indicative thresholds of what consitites a diverse market, taking into account the factors listed earlier, and based on a more expansive approach to included media sources.

An important advantage of the public interest test is that it would allow for the repeal of the inefficient 5/4 minimum voices rule currently in place under broadcasting regulation. However, the rule preventing common control of the three commercial television licences in a single area provides an important and foundational pillar for the continuing existence of at least three separate commercial media organizations in most areas of Australia; for this reason, it should remain.

(ii) Media sources for inclusion

A further key question for a public interest test involves deciding which of the services in a local area, and nationally, would be subject to the scheme. While the Convergence Review nominated a dual test of revenue and reach – at least $50 million

USD a year in 'Australian-sourced content service revenue' and a reach of 500,000 users per month (Convergence Review 2012: 12) – the Gillard Government's Media Diversity Bill opted for a single reach measure of 30 per cent of the average metropolitan evening television news audience. And in a paper on media ownership produced by the Department of Communications (2014: 42) a 'threshold for regulation' was identified in the following terms:

> Ideally, news media voices subject to regulation would be those with significant reach and impact in terms of informing ideas, opinion and debate in the general population in a given market, and would exclude news outlets targeted to narrow or special interest groups, or outlets with limited audience reach.
>
> (42)

This is approaching but not identical to Nielsen's concept of 'keystone media' which is designed to identify 'the primary provider of a specific and important kind of information – news about local politics – and a medium that enables other media's coverage of this area' (2015: 68). Another approach is evident in the characterisation of 'core news content' as the content qualifier for a 'news media business' under Australia's News Media Bargaining Code. However, if the News Measurement Framework was in place, there would be no need for such a mechanism as all sources that contribute to the provision of news and current affairs could be taken into account by the regulator. Some – such as a local print or online newspaper that employs its own journalists and which is itself a source for other local information providers – would be seen to provide a more substantial contribution than others.

As we have discussed earlier in the chapter, our term 'public affairs content' from the Media Pluralism Project (2019) could also make a valuable contribution in this context, being both more inclusive than 'core news content' and less expansive than 'covered news content'. It would fit with an approach like the one recently proposed by Ofcom to consider 'news creators' when applying the media PIT, rather than just broadcasters and print newspapers. And it would also allow for the consideration of the 'social media news influencers' we discuss in Chapter 5, assessed on the basis of what they do rather than the platform they use. In its statement on the future of media plurality (Ofcom 2021b), Ofcom rejected calls for greater clarity on the scope of 'news creators', saying that 'the term should be broad enough to encompass all entities who have editorial control over the creation and publishing of news material by journalists, irrespective of platform' (Ofcom 2022: 29). It offered the examples of online-only news outlets such as Vice, as well as the online sites of current or former print publishers (26–27). Meanwhile, the scope of the news market remains an active point of consideration in ACMA's consultations on the design of an Australian measurement framework (ACMA 2023: 6), which we discuss in Chapter 3.

(iii) Which Act and which regulator?

In principle, either the competition regulator (the ACCC) or the media regulator (the ACMA) could apply the public interest test. However, as Kari Karppinen explains in Chapter 4, decisions around problem definition – for example, whether the problem to be addressed is one of competition law or media regulation – can have important consequences for both the regulatory approach and the range of outcomes.

In commenting on arrangements in the United Kingdom, Humphreys (2015: 163) observed that it is important that this task is given to a 'dedicated and politically independent media pluralism monitoring body'. These points also have a connection to an argument made by Robert Picard (2020: 33–34) who emphasizes the need for agency competency on the part of the regulator but also notes the potential for policy competition between agencies that share some functions or aspects of expertise.

There are two reasons why it would be preferable for this task, in Australia, to be performed by the media regulator. First, the ACCC has expressly stated that it wishes to avoid the importation of public interest considerations into competition law. Rod Sims has said:

> I think, once you put public interest in there in trying to get us to consider a broader range of issues, in the end it will probably kill what we try to do [...] I think we're best targeted at competition, and let us do that. If there are other objectives, then they should be done through other instruments and other bits of legislation, just like we deal with equity through the tax and social welfare system; it's not our remit. I'm very happy for other laws to deal with it but they're not ours.
>
> (Senate Hansard 12.03.21)

Second, an assessment of media diversity levels and application of the public interest test would be consistent with its other functions that involve monitoring media businesses and maintaining registers (including the Register of Controlled Media Groups under the Broadcasting Services Act 1992 and, more recently, for the register for the News Media Bargaining Code under the Competition and Consumer Act 2010); with administering the existing media ownership laws and conducting investigations (under Part 5 and Schedule 1 of the Broadcasting Services Act 1992) into control of media companies and broadcasting licences; and with developing and enforcing media content rules. The ACMA could then maintain a database of news media businesses and would have an ongoing monitoring and reporting role, with a periodic national review conducted at least every five years based on the News Measurement Framework. Changes would be needed to both the objects set out the Broadcasting Services Act 1992 and the functions of the ACMA enumerated in the Australian Communications and Media Authority Act 2005, but both Acts are, in any event, in need of modernization.

The application of this kind of approach in Australia would differ from the United Kingdom in the nature of the task given to the media regulator. In the United Kingdom, Ofcom provides advice to the Secretary of State on the public interest test but this is essentially a preliminary step to a reference by the Secretary to the Competition and Markets Authority on the same aspect (although the CMA's inquiries also involve competition grounds). Ofcom representatives have described it as 'quite a low bar' to proceed to a recommendation for referral to the CMA; this initial investigation must be completed within 40 days and while it might be a rather intense period, there is limited scope for information-gathering (Ofcom 2018b). In the Australian context, where it would be preferable to keep the competition and diversity tests separate, it would be the ACMA that conducts the substantive test. As noted above, rather than complicating matters, this would easily be accommodated within the ACMA's existing procedures.

This approach would have the added benefit of avoiding ministerial involvement. In addition to his point mentioned above about the need for a dedicated and politically independent pluralism monitoring body, Humphreys (2015: 163) stresses the importance of avoiding ministerial discretion in decision making. Interestingly, this was a point made in 2022 by Pablo Rodriguez, the minister of Canadian Heritage, in relation to that country's adaptation in Bill C-11 of the Australian News Media Bargaining Code. Rodriguez (Turvill 2022: n.pag.) observed that the replacement of a ministerial discretion over designation of digital platforms by a decision of the independent regulator based on clear criteria as an improvement on the Australian model. In the context of media regulation, the point has also been made by Hitchens (2006: 211), Schlosberg and Freedman (2020: 120) and more recently, by Rachel Craufurd Smith (2021: 6) in her submission to Ofcom's consultation on 'the future of media plurality in the United Kingdom (Ofcom 2021b).

Finally, the fact that Ofcom has never conducted a baseline assessment of media plurality as a result of never having been requested to do so by the Secretary of State (Ofcom 2021c) indicates that such a task should not be left to ministerial discretion but should be inserted into legislation, much as the ACMA's predecessor (the Australian Broadcasting Authority) was required, after the commencement of the Broadcasting Services Act in 1992, to conduct a nationwide spectrum planning exercise. A key requirement for that work is having detailed and up-to-date information about media interests. The recent Recommendation of the European Commission provides an example of a more comprehensive approach to media ownership transparency (Recommendation 2022/1643: Section III); this would address some of the deficiencies under the Broadcasting Services Act 1992. As Elda Brogi, Scientific Coordinator with the Centre for Media Pluralism and Media

Freedom, explained to a committee hearing of the European Parliament, transparency measures benefit the public as well as regulators: 'the EMFA asks for more transparency regarding ownership of media companies [...] it helps media users to understand how ownership may influence the content' (Brogi 2023: n.pag.).

Conclusion

After looking at the various dimensions of 'media pluralism' and explaining how, in a contemporary media ecosystem, this needs to take account of the automated curation of content by digital platforms, this chapter considered how to develop an effective test for media mergers. Such a mechanism needs to be seen as one half of a two-part framework for regulating for media diversity – the other side being an effective measurement tool. In the following chapter, we move on to consider this second element, a measurement framework for media diversity and pluralism, again comparing policy developments in Australia and the United Kingdom.

In closing the initial comparison in this chapter of regulatory arrangements in Australia and the United Kingdom, it is helpful to note that an important issue connecting the work of ACMA and Ofcom is the recent recognition by ACMA of 'influence'. This is expressed explicitly by Ofcom in its identification of two core elements of media plurality: diversity in viewpoints both across and within media enterprises, and 'preventing any one media owner, or voice, from having too much influence over public opinion and the political agenda' (Ofcom 2015: 6). Foster (2012: 5) expressed the same idea in terms of having both diverse media content and a system that disrupts the dominance of communicative power. And it is worth noting that this is not a new concept, either for the United Kingdom or Australia. In 1981, the Norris Report into newspaper ownership in Victoria drew on the observations of a British Royal Commission of 1947–49 to observe that:

> The two major dangers associated with the concentration of ownership are, first, loss of diversity in the expression of opinion and, second, the power of a very few men to influence the outlook and opinions of large numbers of people, and consequently the decisions made in society.
>
> (Norris 1981: 84, 217)

Some of the questions considered in this chapter have been simmering for at least twenty years; the observation from the Norris Report shows the call for adequate regulation has been left unanswered for far longer.

REFERENCES

ACCC (2016a), 'Statement of issues: News corporation – proposed acquisition of APN News & Media Limited's Australian Regional Media Division', 6 October, Canberra: ACCC, https://www.accc.gov.au/public-registers/mergers-registers/public-informal-merger-reviews/news-corporation-proposed-acquisition-of-apn-news-media-limiteds-australian-regional-media-division-arm. Accessed 5 September 2021.

ACCC (2016b), 'News corporation: Proposed acquisition of APN News & Media Limited's Australian Regional Media Division – ARM', ACCC, 8 December, https://www.accc.gov.au/public-registers/mergers-registers/public-informal-merger-reviews/news-corporation-proposed-acquisition-of-apn-news-media-limiteds-australian-regional-media-division-arm. Accessed 5 September 2021.

ACCC (2017), *Media Merger Guidelines*, Canberra: ACCC, https://www.accc.gov.au/publications/media-merger-guidelines-2017. Accessed 11 January 2019.

ACCC (2018), 'Nine Entertainment Co Holdings Limited (Nine): Proposed merger with Fairfax Media Limited (Fairfax)', ACCC, 8 November, https://www.accc.gov.au/public-registers/mergers-registers/public-informal-merger-reviews/nine-entertainment-co-holdings-limited-nine-proposed-merger-with-fairfax-media-limited-fairfax#:~:text=Summary,shareholders%20owning%20the%20remaining%2048.9%25. Accessed 5 May 2019.

ACCC (2019), *Digital Platforms Inquiry: Final Report*, Canberra: ACCC, June, https://www.accc.gov.au/focus-areas/inquiries-finalised/digital-platforms-inquiry-0. Accessed 3 June 2020.

ACMA (2006), *Investigation into the Control of Commercial Radio Broadcasting Licences Held by Elmie Investments Pty Ltd: Final Report*, Sydney: ACMA, November, https://www.acma.gov.au/publications/2019-11/report/investigation-control-commercial-radio-broadcasting-licences-held-elmie-investments-pty-ltd. Accessed 30 January 2023.

ACMA (2020), *News in Australia: Diversity and Localism – International Comparisons*, Melbourne: ACMA, December, https://www.acma.gov.au/publications/2020-12/report/news-australia-diversity-and-localism. Accessed 4 February 2021.

ACMA (2023), 'A new framework for measuring media diversity in Australia: Consultation paper', Melbourne: ACMA, January, https://www.acma.gov.au/consultations/2023-01/new-framework-measuring-media-diversity-australia. Accessed 19 January 2023.

Australian Government (2019), *Regulating in the Digital Age: Government Response and Implementation Roadmap for the Digital Platforms Inquiry*, 12 December, https://treasury.gov.au/publication/p2019-41708. Accessed 22 April 2020.

Australian Human Rights Commission (2021), *Human Rights and Technology. Final Report*, Australia: Australian Human Rights Commission, https://humanrights.gov.au/our-work/rights-and-freedoms/publications/human-rights-and-technology-final-report-2021. Accessed 30 January 2023.

Baker, C. Edwin (2007), *Media Concentration and Democracy: Why Ownership Matters*, New York: Cambridge University Press.

Berry, Mark and Spittle, George, (2019), 'Media mergers and the critical impact of non-price considerations: A New Zealand case study', *Journal of European Competition Law and Practice*, 10:2, pp. 101–08.

Bjorkroth, Tom and Gronlund, Mikko (2015), 'Media economics in competition law', in R. G. Picard and S. S. Wildman (eds), *Handbook on the Economics of the Media*, Cheltenham: Edward Elgar, pp. 302–27.

Brevini, Benedetta and Ward, Michael (2021), *Who Controls Our Media? Exposing the Impact of Media Concentration on Our Democracy*, Surry Hills: GetUp!.

Brogi, Elda (2023), 'Oral evidence to European Parliament, Committee on Education and Culture', Hearing on 6 February, https://multimedia.europarl.europa.eu/en/webstreaming/cult-committee-meeting_20230206-1500-COMMITTEE-CULT. Accessed 8 February 2023.

Bucher, Taina (2018), *If… Then: Algorithmic Power and Politics*, New York: Oxford University Press.

Cairncross, Frances (2019), *Cairncross Review: A Sustainable Future for Journalism*, London: Department for Digital, Culture, Media & Sport https://www.gov.uk/government/publications/the-cairncross-review-a-sustainable-future-for-journalism. Accessed 4 March 2020.

Centre for Media Pluralism and Media Freedom (2022), *Monitoring Media Pluralism in the Digital Era: Application of the Media Pluralism Monitor in the European Union, Albania, Montenegro, the Republic of North Macedonia, Serbia and Turkey in the Year 2021*, Fiesole FI: European University Institute, https://cadmus.eui.eu/handle/1814/74712. Accessed 30 January 2023.

Chadwick, Paul (1989), *Media Mates: Carving up Australia's Media*, South Melbourne: Macmillan.

Collins, Richard and Cave, Martin (2013), 'Media pluralism and the overlapping instruments needed to achieve it', *Telecommunications Policy*, 37:4&5, pp. 311–20.

Commerce Commission (NZ) (2017), *Determination: NZME Limited and Fairfax New Zealand Limited*. Wellington: Commerce Commission.

Competition and Markets Authority (2018), *21st Century Fox, Inc and Sky Plc: A Report on the Anticipated Acquisition by 21st Century Fox, Inc of Sky Plc*, London: CMA, May, https://www.gov.uk/government/publications/cma-phase-2-report. Accessed 30 January 2023.

Convergence Review (2012), *Convergence Review Final Report*, Australia: Department of Broadband, Communications and the Digital Economy.

Craufurd Smith, Rachel (2021), *Submission to Ofcom: The Future of Media Plurality in the UK Including Ofcom's Consultation on the Media Ownership Rules Review*.

Davidson, John (2021), 'Zen and the art of transparent machine reasoning', *Australian Financial Review*, 30 May, https://www.afr.com/technology/zen-and-the-art-of-transparent-machine-reasoning-20210521-p57tvf. Accessed 30 January 2023.

Department of Communications (2014), *Media Ownership and Control: Policy Background Paper No. 3*, Canberra: Department of Communications.

Department for Culture, Media and Sport (UK) (2014), *Media Ownership & Plurality Consultation Report: Government response to the House of Lords Select Committee on Communications Report into Media Plurality*, London: DCMS.

Doyle, Gillian (2002), *Media Ownership: The Economics and Politics of Convergence and Concentration in the UK and European Media*, London: SAGE.

Doyle, Gillian (2013), *Understanding Media Economics*, 2nd ed., London: SAGE.

DRCF (2022a), 'Auditing Algorithms: The existing landscape, the role of regulators and future outlook', 28 April, London: DRCF, https://www.gov.uk/government/publications/findings-from-the-drcf-algorithmic-processing-workstream-spring-2022/auditing-algorithms-the-existing-landscape-role-of-regulators-and-future-outlook. Accessed 21 September 2022.

DRCF (2022b), 'The benefits and harms of algorithms: A shared perspective from the four digital regulators', 28 April, London: DRCF, https://assets.publishing.service.gov.uk/government/uploads/system/uploads/attachment_data/file/1071221/DRCF_-_Algorithmic_Harms_and_Benefits_Paper.pdf. Accessed 21 September 2022.

Dwyer, Tim (2016), *Convergent Media and Privacy*, Basingstoke: Palgrave Macmillan.

Dwyer, Tim, Wilding, Derek and Koskie, Tim (2021), 'Australia: Media concentration and deteriorating conditions for investigative journalism', in J. Trappel and T. Tomaz (eds), *The Media for Democracy Monitor 2021: How Leading News Media Survive Digital Transformation*, vol. 1, Gothenburg: Nordicom, University of Gothenburg, pp. 59–94.

Dwyer, Tim, Wilding, Derek, Wilson, Helen and Curtis, Simon (2006), *Content, Consolidation and Clout: How Will Regional Media Be Affected by Media Ownership Changes?*, Melbourne: Communications Law Centre.

European Commission (2022), *Commission Recommendation (EU) 2022/1643 of 16 September 2022 on internal safeguards for editorial independence and ownership transparency in the media sector*, https://eur-lex.europa.eu/legal-content/EN/TXT/?uri=CELEX:32022H1634. Accessed 30 January 2023.

European Parliament Committee on Civil Liberties, Justice and Home Affairs (2018), *Report on Media Pluralism and Media Freedom in the European Union*, Document A8-0144/2018, Brussels: European Commission, https://www.europarl.europa.eu/doceo/document/A-8-2018-0144_EN.html. Accessed 30 January 2023.

Fenton, Natalie, Freedman, Des, Schlosberg, Justin and Dencik, Lina (2020), *The Media Manifesto*, Cambridge: Polity.

Fernandez, Joseph M. (2013), 'The Finkelstein inquiry: Miscarried media regulation moves miss golden reform opportunity', *The West Australian Jurist*, 4, pp. 23–60.

Finn, Ed (2018), *What Algorithms Want: Imagination in the Age of Computing*, Cambridge: The MIT Press.

Flew, Terry and Swift, Adam (2013), 'Regulating journalists? The Finkelstein Inquiry, the convergence review and news media regulation in Australia', *Journal of Applied Journalism and Media Studies*, 2:1, pp. 181–99.

Foster, Robin (2012), *News Plurality in a Digital World*, Oxford: Reuters Institute for the Study of Journalism.

Gabszewicz, Jean J., Resende, Joanna and Sonnac, Nathalie (2015), 'Media as multi-sided platforms', in R. G. Picard and S. S. Wildman (eds), *Handbook on the Economics of the Media*, Cheltenham: Edward Elgar, pp. 3–35.

Given, Jock (2003), *Turning off the Television: Broadcasting's Uncertain Future*, Kensington: UNSW Press.

Given, Jock (2007), 'Cross-media ownership laws: Refinement or rejection?', *University of New South Wales Law Journal*, 30:1, pp. 258–68.

Helberger, Natali (2018), 'Challenging diversity: Social media platforms and a new conception of media diversity', in M. Moore and D. Tambini (eds), *Digital Dominance: The Power of Google, Amazon, Facebook, and Apple*, New York: Oxford University Press, pp. 153–75.

Helberger, Natali, Karppinen, Kari and D'Acunto (2018), 'Exposure diversity as a design principle for recommender systems', *Information, Communication and Society*, 21:2, pp. 191–207.

Helberger, Natali, Moeller, Judith and Vrijenhoek, Sanne (2020), 'Diversity by design: Diversity of content in the digital age', *Discussion Paper for the Government of Canada*, February, https://www.canada.ca/en/canadian-heritage/services/diversity-content-digital-age/diversity-design.html. Accessed 30 January 2023.

Hitchens, Lesley (2006), *Broadcasting Pluralism and Diversity: A Comparative Study of Policy and Regulation*, Portland: Hart Publishing.

Hitchens, Lesley (2015), 'Reviewing media pluralism in Australia', in P. Valcke, M. Sukosd and R. Picard (eds), *Media Pluralism and Diversity: Concepts, Risks and Global Trends*, London: Palgrave Macmillan, pp. 252–66.

House of Lords Select Committee on Communications (2014), *Media Plurality*, 1st Report of Session 2013–14, London: House of Lords.

Humphreys, Peter (2015), 'Transferable media pluralism policies from Europe', in S. Barnett and J. Townend (eds), *Media Pluralism and Plurality, From Hyperlocal to High-Level Policy*, London: Palgrave MacMillan, pp. 151–69.

Humphreys, Peter and Simpson, Seamus (2018), *Regulation, Governance and Convergence in the Media*, Cheltenham: Edward Elgar.

Karppinen, Kari (2013), *Rethinking Media Pluralism*, Oxford: Oxford University Press.

Jaume-Palasi, Lorena and Spielkamp, Matthias (2017), *Ethics and Algorithmic Decision Making and Decision Support. Algorithmic Working Paper No. 2*. Algorithm Watch, 1 June, https://algorithmwatch.org/wp-content/uploads/2017/06/AlgorithmWatch_Working-Paper_No_2_Ethics_ADM.pdf. Accessed 30 January 2023.

Jolly, Sanjay and Pickard, Victor (2021), *Towards a Media Democracy Agenda: The Lessons of C. Edwin Baker. LPE Project*, https://lpeproject.org/blog/towards-a-media-democracy-agenda-the-lessons-of-c-edwin-baker/. Accessed 30 January 2023.

Lada, Akos, Wang, Meihong and Yan, Tak (2021), 'How does News Feed predict what you want to see?', *Facebook Newsroom*, 26 January, https://about.fb.com/news/2021/01/how-does-news-feed-predict-what-you-want-to-see/. Accessed 30 January 2023.

Levy, Jonathan D. (2015), 'Economic analysis in media policy making', in R. G. Picard and S. S. Wildman (eds), *Handbook on the Economics of the Media*, Cheltenham: Edward Elgar Publishing, pp. 277–301.

Lidberg, Johan and Hirst, Martin (2013), 'In the shadow of phone hacking: Media accountability inquiries in Australia', *The Political Economy of Communication*, 1:1, pp. 111–21.

Media Pluralism Project Website (2019), 'The role of a pluralistic media in Australia's democracy', 13 May, https://mediapluralism.org.au/2019/05/the-role-of-a-pluralistic-media-in-australias-democracy/. Accessed 30 January 2023.

Mediaweek (2021), 'ABC News websites continue to top digital news rankings as nine overtakes news.com.au', 13 January, https://www.mediaweek.com.au/abc-news-websites-continue-to-top-digital-news-rankings-as-nine-overtakes-news-com-au/. Accessed 30 January 2023.

Mosseri, Adam (2018), 'News feed ranking in three minutes flat', *Facebook Newsroom*, 22 May, https://about.fb.com/news/2018/05/inside-feed-news-feed-ranking/. Accessed 30 January 2023.

Napoli, Philip M. (1999), 'Deconstructing the diversity principle', *Journal of Communication*, 49:4, pp. 7–34.

Napoli, Philip M. (2019), *Social Media and the Public Interest: Media Regulation in the Disinformation Age*, New York: Columbia University Press.

Nielsen, Rasmus Kleis (2015), 'Local newspapers as keystone media: The increased importance of diminished newspapers for local political information environments', in R. K. Nielsen (ed.), *Local Journalism: The Decline of Newspapers and the Rise of Digital Media*, London: I.B. Tauris & Co. Ltd, pp. 51–72.

Norris, Hon. John Gerald (1981), *Report of the Inquiry into the Ownership and Control of Newspapers in Victoria: Report to the Premier of Victoria*, Melbourne: Government of Victoria.

NZME Limited v. *Commerce Commission* (2018), NZCA 389.

Ofcom (2012), 'Measuring media plurality Ofcom's advice to the Secretary of State for Culture, Olympics, Media and Sport', 19 June, https://www.ofcom.org.uk/consultations-and-statements/category-1/measuring-plurality. Accessed 30 January 2023.

Ofcom (2015), 'Measurement framework for media plurality: Ofcom's advice to the Secretary of State for Culture, Media and Sport', 5 November, https://www.ofcom.org.uk/consultations-and-statements/category-1/media-plurality-framework. Accessed 30 January 2023.

Ofcom (2017), 'Public interest test for the proposed acquisition of Sky plc by 21st Century Fox, Inc: Ofcom's Report to the Secretary of State', 20 June, https://www.ofcom.org.uk/consultations-and-statements/category-3/public-interest-test-sky-fox. Accessed 28 November 2021.

Ofcom (2018a), 'Public interest test for the acquisition by Trinity Mirror Plc of the publishing assets of Northern and Shell Media Group Limited: Ofcom's Advice to the Secretary of State', 31 May, https://www.gov.uk/government/news/statement-merger-between-trinity-mirror-plc-and-northern-shells-publishing-assets. Accessed 30 January 2023.

Ofcom (2018b), interview with Jonathan Mackay, London, 7 November.

Ofcom (2019), 'Public interest test on the completed acquisitions by international media company of shares in Lebedev Holdings Limited and by Scalable Inc of Shares in Independent Digital News and Media Limited: Ofcom's Advice to the Secretary of State', 21 August, https://www.gov.uk/government/publications/ofcom-report-to-dcms-lhm-and-idnm-21-august-2019. Accessed 21 November 2021.

Ofcom (2020), 'Public interest test on the completed acquisition by *Daily Mail* and General Trust pie of JPI Media Publications Limited and thus the "I" Newspaper: Ofcom's Advice to the Secretary of State', 10 March, https://www.gov.uk/government/collections/daily-mail-and-general-trust-plc-dmgt-acquisition-of-jpi-media-publications-limited. Accessed 24 August 2021.

Ofcom (2021a), 'The future of media plurality in the UK including Ofcom's consultation on the media ownership rules review', 15 June, https://www.ofcom.org.uk/consultations-and-statements/category-2/future-media-plurality-uk. Accessed 14 November 2021.

Ofcom (2021b), 'The future of media plurality in the UK: Ofcom's report to the secretary of state on the media ownership rules and our next steps on media plurality', 17 November, https://www.ofcom.org.uk/consultations-and-statements/category-2/future-media-plurality-uk. Accessed 14 November 2021.

Ofcom (2021c), 'Freedom of information: Right to know request', 23 March, https://www.ofcom.org.uk/about-ofcom/foi-dp/foi-responses. Accessed 14 November 2021.

Papandrea, Franco and Tiffen, Rodney (2016), 'Media ownership and concentration in Australia', in E. M. Noam (ed.), *Who Owns the World's Media?: Media Concentration and Ownership around the World*, Oxford: Oxford University Press.

Picard, Robert G. (2020), *Media and Communications Policy Making: Processes, Dynamics and International Variations*, Cham: Palgrave Macmillan.

Prime Media Group, Southern Cross Austereo, Win Network, Imparja Television (2020), *Submission to Senate Inquiry into Media Diversity in Australia*, December.

Productivity Commission (2000), *Broadcasting*, Report No. 11, Canberra: AusInfo.

Rab, Suzanne and Sprague, Alison (2014), *Media Ownership and Control: Law, Economics and Policy in an Indian and International Context*, London: Hart Publishing.

Reset Australia (2021a), 'Facebook opts for Australian seeing dangerous, unchecked misinformation, rather than pay for news', 17 February, https://au.reset.tech/news/facebook-opts-for-australians-seeing-dangerous-unchecked-misinformation-rather-than-pay-for-news/. Accessed 30 January 2023.

Reset Australia (2021b), 'Submission on Treasury Laws Amendment (News Media and Digital Platforms Mandatory Bargaining Code) Bill 2020', Submission 54 to Senate Economics

Legisation Committee, 31 January, https://www.aph.gov.au/Parliamentary_Business/Committees/Senate/Economics/TLABNewsMedia/Submissions. Accessed 30 January 2023.

Rowland, Michelle (2022), 'Broadcasting services determination extension', Media Release, 18 September, https://minister.infrastructure.gov.au/rowland/media-release/broadcasting-services-determination-extension. Accessed 30 January 2023.

Schlosberg, Justin and Freedman, Des (2020), 'Opening the gates: Plurality regulation and the public interest', *Journal of Digital Media & Policy*, 11:2, pp. 115–32.

Select Committee on Communications (2014), *Media Plurality – 1st Report of Session 2013–14*, London: House of Lords, The Stationary Office Ltd.

Senate, Environment and Communications References Committee (2021), *Media Diversity in Australia*, Canberra: Parliament of Australia.

Senate Hansard, Environment and Communications References Committee (2021), transcript, 12 March.

Sims, Rod (2018), *Address to the 2018 Annual RBB Economics Conference*, 29 November 2018.

Turvill, William (2022), 'How Canada's Online News Act will differ from Australia's news media bargaining code', *Press Gazette*, 25 February, https://pressgazette.co.uk/news/canada-online-news-act-google-meta-facebook/. Accessed 24 January 2023.

UK Government (2019), 'Unlocking digital competition. Report of the digital competition expert panel', *The Furman Report*, March, https://assets.publishing.service.gov.uk/government/uploads/system/uploads/attachment_data/file/785547/unlocking_digital_competition_furman_review_web.pdf. Accessed 20 December 2019.

Valcke, Peggy, Robert G. Picard and Miklos Sükösd (2015), 'A global perspective on media pluralism and diversity: Introduction', in P. Valcke, R. G. Picard and M. Sükösd (eds), *Media Pluralism and Diversity: Concepts, Risks and Global Trends*, London: Palgrave Macmillan, pp. 1–19.

Van der Burg, Miriam and Van den Bulck, Hilde (2015), 'Economic, political and socio-cultural welfare in media merger control: An analysis of the Belgian and Dutch Competition Authorities' reviews of media mergers', *Information Economics and Policy*, 32, pp. 2–15.

Wilding, Derek (2003), 'The House, the Senate and the Media Ownership Bill: An "Unacceptable Three-Way Control Situation"?', *Media International Australia*, 108:1 pp. 115–24.

Young, Sally (2015), 'Sending a message: The Australian's reporting of media policy', *Media International Australia*, 157, November, pp. 79–90.

3

New Directions in Media Pluralism and Diversity Interventions

Derek Wilding and Tim Dwyer

This chapter explores recently developed tools for measuring media diversity that take account of the contemporary media environment as well as evolutions in policy and scholarly thinking since the core regulatory settings were developed 30 years ago. Building on the approach in the previous chapter where we described the regulatory and institutional settings of Australia and the United Kingdom, in this chapter, we compare the analytical tool developed in the United Kingdom, the Media Plurality Framework (Ofcom 2015), with a recent proposal presented by the Australian regulator, the ACMA (2020a). We also draw on the work of the EU's cross-nation analytical framework, the Media Pluralism Monitor (Bleyer-Simon et al. 2021), and other attempts to set indicators or benchmarks for aspects of media pluralism (e.g., Trappel and Tomaz 2021; Napoli 2015). The research references the literature in this area as well as international comparative policy analysis and interviews with some key figures in the policy field and with leading academic critics of current policy.

After examining the United Kingdom, the chapter turns to the recent proposal for policy reform in Australia. In December 2020, in what is perhaps the most significant attempt at government policy analysis on this topic in three decades, the ACMA released a discussion paper offering a possible model for a News Measurement Framework (ACMA 2020a). In a departure from the United Kingdom, this model brought media localism – most significantly, the provision of local news and current affairs to regional audiences – into the same framework for assessing media pluralism (or 'media diversity' as it is termed in the ACMA's work, an aspect we explore further below). While researchers have, in the past, considered diversity and localism as closely related topics (see, e.g., Napoli 2007), they are more commonly seen as separate issues. Whether ACMA's recent proposal provides a workable model for other territories is debatable but this should not be seen as a limitation; instead it could point to the reasons why the search for a conceptual framework that fits multiple jurisdictions requires innovative thinking.

This chapter does not attempt a complete reformulation of a media pluralism framework (e.g., it does not seek to enumerate the sub-elements of market plurality or political independence, as the EU's Media Pluralism Monitor does), as Australia is some distance back from adopting a finely developed framework. Instead, it attempts to identify the guiding principles and higher level components for such a tool. In doing so, it takes account of the ACMA's attempt to explicitly tie localism to pluralism.

Ofcom's media plurality measurement framework

The Ofcom measurement framework is based on the key elements of availability, consumption, impact and 'contextual factors' (represented in Figure 3.1, Ofcom 2015: 5). 'Market context', meaning the relevant media environment, is also considered. This involves an extensive review of multiple aspects of the national media market. In Ofcom's assessment of Sky/21 C Fox (2017) (described, along with the other matters considered below, in the previous chapter), this included the results of surveys which show relative use of the relevant media platforms (television, radio, newspapers and internet); the average weekly reach of these platforms by age group; cross-platform audience reach; and use of digital intermediaries. Ofcom groups these intermediaries into three categories: aggregators (such as Google News), search engines (such as Google and Yahoo), and social media (such as Facebook and Twitter). If relevant, in this market context review, Ofcom may also include information such as newspaper circulation and advertising revenue across different platforms. In the Trinity Mirror matter that involved newspapers, the market context discussion included information on the overall number of newspapers in the United Kingdom at both a national and local level, and the number of suppliers; the information on the four main platforms and top twenty news sources; as well as information on newspaper circulation, readership and revenue (Ofcom 2018a).

Availability

This quantitative measure of the number of news sources available in the identified market is applied across different platforms. It is described in the framework as 'a count of the number of entities providing news sources' and is assessed using industry data. By analyzing availability at the wholesale level as well as a retail level, the framework provides a picture of content supply by prominent media groups.

Category		Metrics	Description	Source	What it indicates
Availability	Availability and consumption metrics to be calculated at retail and wholesale levels to allow analysis of media ownership. Consumption metrics to also be calculated at intermediary level to reflect use of intermediaries	Number of providers	A count of the number of entities providing news sources	Industry data	An indication of the potential for diversity of viewpoints
Consumption		Reach	By platform – TV, Radio, Newspapers, Internet By provider within platform	Industry measurement systems, consumer research	An indication of the variety of viewpoints disseminated
			Cross platform	Consumer research	As above. Cross media reach establishes the capability for each provider to reach the population regardless of platform
		Share of consumption	By platform – TV, Radio, Newspapers, Internet By provider within platform	Industry measurement systems, consumer research	An indication of the potential concentration in patterns of consumption Note: This would be calculated from time spent for each platform as measured by the industry measurement systems
			Cross platform Cross platform by provider	Consumer research	As above Note: this can be in the form of the share of reference metric that captures the reach and frequency of consumption
		Multi-sourcing	By platform and cross-platform	Consumer research	An indication of the extent to which consumers are sourcing their news from one or a range of sources
Impact		Personal importance	By platform By provider	Consumer research	Provides one proxy for measuring the potential to influence opinion
		Perceived impartiality, reliability and trust and the extent to which a news source helps people make up their minds about news	By platform By provider	Consumer research	Provide additional context to the metric of personal importance
Contextual factors		A range to be considered	A description of the qualitative differences between news sources and organisations	Multiple sources. Examples of relevant factors include, but are not limited to: Internal plurality Internal governance processes Editorial policy Impartiality requirements Market trends and future market developments	Elements relevant to an understanding of plurality that are not able to be quantified by metrics

FIGURE 3.1: Ofcom media plurality measurement framework. Source: Ofcom (2015).

In the ACMA model outlined below, this corresponds to the 'news infrastructure' category, although the ACMA includes elements that are also relevant to localism such as the number of journalists (ACMA 2020a: 51). Some of this could be captured by what Ofcom identifies as 'market context', as discussed earlier.

Ofcom stresses availability is only one measure of plurality and offers an indication only of *the potential* for diversity of viewpoints. In advice to the Secretary of State, Ofcom (2012: 18) described this measure as a reflection of 'the "shelf space" occupied by titles or news organisations'. In pointing to its limitations, Ofcom noted:

> At the most extreme, adopting a count of the number and range of owners of media enterprises, without taking account of their ability to influence opinion would mean that all news and current affairs providers would be included as contributing to plurality simply by being available, regardless of whether they were used by several million or very few consumers.
>
> (19)

Consumption

The consumption measure marks a significant point of departure from traditional ways of assessing plurality, including the approach currently adopted in Australia – although it is one of two elements in 'news engagement' in the ACMA model. It represents a shift away from supply, towards the kind of 'exposure diversity' that has been identified as a crucial factor in a more effective assessment of plurality. Ofcom itself has described consumption metrics as 'the most useful starting point of any plurality assessment' (2015: 12).

In the measurement framework, Ofcom explains that its consumption metrics measure 'the number of people using news sources and the frequency and/or time that they spend consuming it' (2015: 12).

This inquiry first involves the measure of reach used within different sectors of the industry (e.g., the number of people who spent at least five minutes watching television at a particular time; print circulation; the number of 'likes' on Facebook). For example, Figure 3.2, used by Ofcom in its consideration of the acquisition of the *i* newspaper by DMG in 2020, depicts the reach of various national newspaper groups within the United Kingdom, clearly displaying the difference between DMG and JPI (the former owner of *i*) (see Ofcom 2020: 14).

Ofcom has enhanced these results for reach by taking account of time spent watching and consumption across different platforms. It looks at 'multi-sourcing', a measure of the average number of sources a consumer uses across different platforms across a specified period. In moving beyond the measure of reach, Ofcom has developed its own measure known as 'share of references'. Ofcom describes this approach in the following terms (2015):

> Share of references is calculated by asking people which news sources they use and the frequency with which they use them. Each reference is then weighted for the frequency of use, and summed. The share of each source or provider can then be

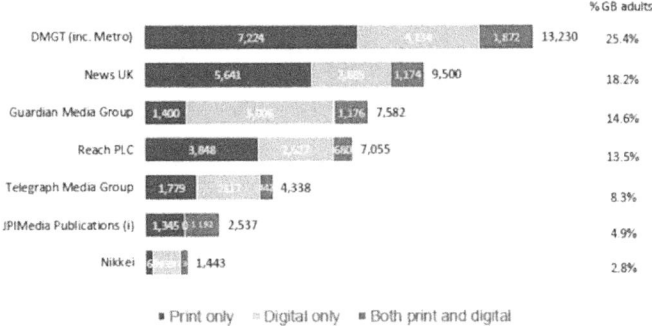

FIGURE 3.2: Ofcom table on weekly readership of UK national newspaper groups.
Source: TouchPoints 2019, GB adults 15+. National titles only.
NR3a: Thinking about specific newspaper titles, please indicate when you last looked at or read each of these titles. Ranked by total weekly readership. [Yesterday/past 7 days].

calculated based on their total number of references as a proportion of all references for all news sources, regardless of the platform or media.

(12)

In a report published as a part of the development of the framework, Ofcom (2012) explained how these various aspects work together to provide an overall picture of consumption:

Share of consumption (using single-sector measurement systems, where this is possible, and bespoke cross-media 'share of references') is a good proxy for measuring influence in the news media market.

Reach (particularly cross-media, using bespoke quantitative research) and multi-sourcing (using the same) are good proxies for diversity of viewpoints consumed.

(21)

Ofcom has used these tools in merger assessments and on occasion in other reporting on media use. For example, in its 2018 *News Consumption in the UK* report (but not in subsequent annual reports), it published a chart on share of references at a retail level, including digital intermediaries (Ofcom 2018b: slide 83). This more sophisticated measure that combines 'use' with 'frequency of use' shows that ITV, for example, has a reach measure of 45 per cent (just over half that of the BBC) but when frequency is added and the results are weighted to give a 'share of references' measure, ITV's share drops to less than one quarter of that of the BBC (7 per cent compared to 32 per cent for the BBC).

In the Trinity Mirror merger assessment (where Ofcom took account of ownership by combining the shares for the separate sources subject to the transaction), this form of analysis was used to show that the print sources subject to the transaction would have a *combined share of references* of 3 per cent (compared to 42 per cent for the BBC) even though they had a *combined reach* of 10 per cent (compared to 77 per cent for the BBC) (Ofcom 2018a: 26–27).

Ofcom offered a note of caution around the use of its share of references measure in its report on DMG's acquisition of the *i* newspaper in 2020. Its analysis represented in Figure 3.3 (Ofcom 2020: 22) showed clearly that DMG's titles accounted for a relatively small share of people's total news consumption. But it also noted that the share of references measure may not accurately represent the number of other news sources consumed. A news consumption survey had shown that *Daily Mail* readers had an average of 10.4 news sources while *i* readers had an average of 13. Ofcom concluded that the 'strength of voice' of both DMG and *i* might therefore be diluted (Ofcom 2020: 15–16).

While Ofcom has not included a share of references measure in its more recent annual news consumption reports, its commissioned research has provided additional important insights. For example, it has disaggregated a result for the question 'which platforms do you use for news nowadays' where results for internet (73 per cent) far outrank those for newspapers (32 per cent). When the responses for 'internet' are broken down and the use of newspaper websites and apps is added to the results for newspapers (as well as being included within the internet results), the overall result for newspapers increased to 49 per cent (see Ofcom 2021a: slides 13 and 14).

There are still some uncertainties with these measures and also, as noted below, some further limitations identified in scholarly critique of the scheme. Ofcom made this point in its recent discussion document on how to account for online news where it raised the idea of a new measure of 'share of attention' which it said might provide a more accuracte guide to the potential influence of a news source (Ofcom 2022: 40–41). (We consider the ideas raised in this paper below, when we explore how a new Australian framework could build on the Ofcom work.) However, the similarities between the UK industry environment and that of Australia – especially the prominence of legacy news media providers in the digital environment, the role of public broadcasters, and the presence of some of the same news organizations (e.g., News Corp, *The Guardian* and *Daily Mail*) – point to clear benefits for Australia in introducing consumption metrics. Although some aspects of these data are available from other sources, there is no source as comprehensive as Ofcom. Roy Morgan does produce a very useful 'cross-platform audience' report (a four-week estimate of Australians who have read or accessed individual newspaper content via print, web,

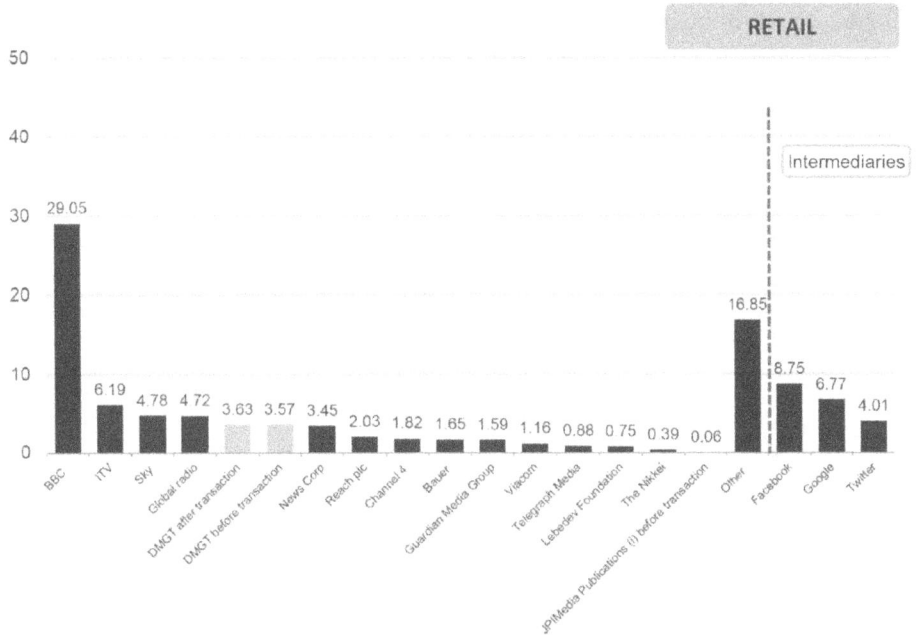

FIGURE 3.3: Ofcom share of reference for retail providers used 'Nowadays' for news.
Source: Ofcom News Consumption Survey 2019.
Question: D2a-8a. Thinking specifically about <platform>, which of the following do you use for news nowadays?
Base: All adults 16+ using TV/Newspapers/Radio/Internet/Magazines for news – 2019=4481, 208=4479
Note: "Google'=Google News + Google + YouTube. 'Other intermediary' includes MSN, Yahoo, AOL, Flipboard, NewsNow. We distinguish between retail news provision (the individual title or brand of each news source that provides content to the user e.g. ITV News) and wholesale news provision (the supply and production of the news for a retail news source e.g. ITN). The information included in this chart is based on the most up to date information we have.

app or Apple News) for some publications. The February 2021 report showed that *The Sydney Morning Herald* had the largest cross-platform audience (Roy Morgan 2021). The reach measure is also to some extent available in the annual reports included in the *Digital News Report* published by the University of Canberra (see, e.g., Park et al. 2021, 2022), but for the purposes of measuring diversity as opposed to news consumption in general, these results are not sufficiently granular. While the 2021 report includes a useful set of two tables showing 'offline news brands accessed' and 'online news brands accessed', it only records access in the previous week at a national level and gives no indication of importance via a measure of time spent (Park et al. 2021: 55). And for the reasons identified above, results showing the growth in social media as a main source of news (53) and which social media platforms are used for news (63) are interesting but need further interrogation as a measure of diversity. That said, other aspects of this work, such as the results for modes of interaction with news (66), political orientation and news use (Chapter 8), and attitudes towards impartiality in news (Chapter 2) demonstrate that there is already a rich source of consumption data in Australia that could be used as the platform for the development of Ofcom-style metrics.

Impact

Impact is designed to extend the measure of consumption and allows for some insight into the influence of a media source. Ofcom acknowledges that influence and impact are difficult concepts to measure and that certain proxy measures should be used to gauge them. Ofcom uses 'personal importance' as a principal measure, complemented with 'perceived impartiality', 'reliability', 'trust' and 'the extent to which sources help make up their mind about the news'.

Referring to one of these measures, Ofcom notes, 'News providers may have a particular impact on the people who use them if they are trusted by their readers, viewers or listeners and can influence their opinions' (2018a: 32). Prompts such as 'offers a range of opinions', 'helps me make up my mind' and 'is of high quality' are used in their consumer surveys.

The ACMA model also includes impact as part of its 'news engagement' indicator, with the ACMA stating that it will draw on the Ofcom approach, for example by using surveys on which sources consumers consider high quality, for example, as well as seeking additional data on aspects such as sharing news online (ACMA 2020a: 52).

Figure 3.4, from the 2018 consumption survey, provides a useful indication of some of these points for selected digital news sources (Ofcom 2018b: Slide 98).

In the Trinity Mirror matter, Ofcom (2018a) noted that affected titles rated relatively low on these measures. However, in the Sky/21C Fox matter, Ofcom (2017: 70) used its data to conclude:

> the evidence suggests that Sky News is held in similar regard to the public service broadcasters in terms of importance, trustworthiness and impartiality. We may therefore be more concerned about a transaction involving Sky News than we would be were a less trusted news provider involved.

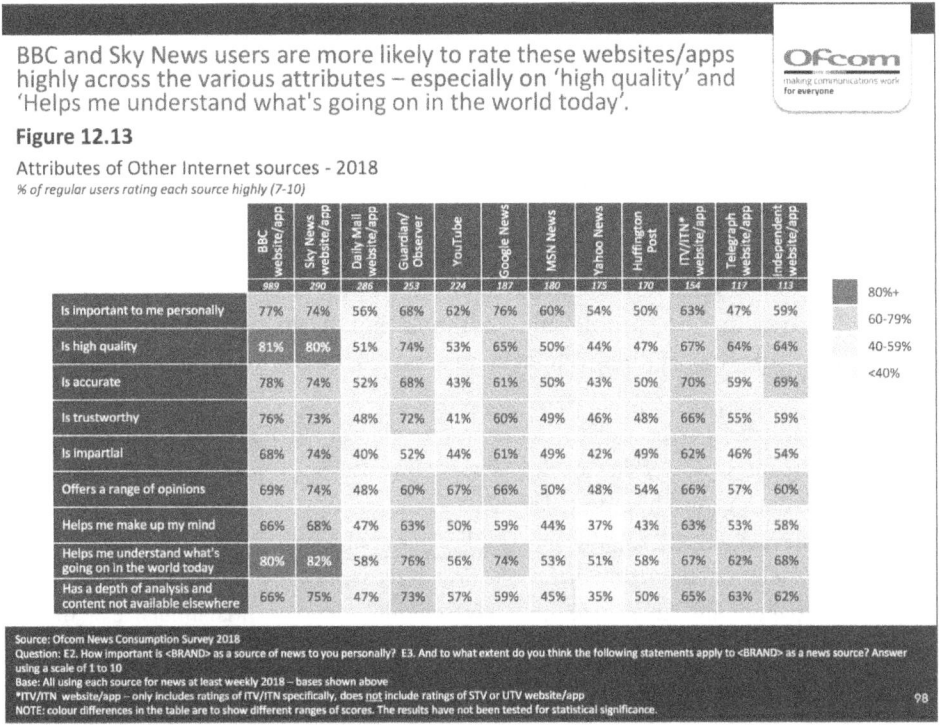

FIGURE 3.4: Ofcom consumption survey.

Contextual factors

Ofcom argues that, 'The importance of contextual factors arises from the fact that the operating environment can differ between news sources and news organisations' (2015: 13). To this end, while quantitative metrics such as those considered above are an important part of assessing plurality, 'a purely mechanistic approach' may fail to appreciate these differences between news organizations.

In its framework document, Ofcom gave the following (non-exhaustive) list of examples of contextual factors:

i. governance models – such as trusts, publicly limited companies with shareholders, private companies, and statutory corporations;
ii. funding models – such as advertising revenues, circulation revenues, subscription fees, and public funding;
iii. the potential power or editorial control exercised by owners, proprietors or senior executives within news organizations;

iv. internal plurality – i.e., how far an organization enables, supports or promotes a range of internal voices and opinions;
v. market trends and potential future developments;
vi. regulation and oversight, in some cases based on statutory obligations – e.g., Ofcom's Broadcasting Code or the BBC's own editorial or regulatory processes and compliance.

Ofcom has noted that news standards on a matter such as impartiality differ across platforms and applicable rules, commenting on the importance of the 'due impartiality' rule that applies to television services under the Broadcasting Code:

> From a regulatory perspective, broadcasters are subject to impartiality requirements, while newspapers and websites are not. Ofcom's Broadcasting Code requires that 'news in whatever form, must be reported with due accuracy and presented with due impartiality'. The requirement for 'due impartiality' is not absolute and broadcasters have a degree of editorial discretion in the selection of the news agenda. We recognise that the impartiality rules may contribute as a safeguard against potential influence on the news agenda by media owners, but they cannot themselves necessarily ensure against it.
> (2015: 13)

All of the contextual matters nominated by Ofcom are matters that could apply equally in Australia and like jurisdictions. While aspects such as governance models and internal plurality have received scant attention from Australian policymakers, the problems of sustaining traditional business models have been the focus of recent consideration, especially since the Australian Competition and Consumer Commission (ACCC) pointed to the threats to traditional revenue sources and the risks posed to independent critique of government actions, including at a local level. In addition, as is evident from the report of the Senate Media Diversity inquiry, noted above, news standards is increasingly being seen as an important related aspect of a diverse media environment. Recent work by the ACMA could also be seen as supporting an argument for an overhaul of content rules relating to impartiality (ACMA 2020b). We will return to the question of the relationship between media standards and plurality shortly but for now, it is worth noting a difference in the contribution of contextual matters seen in Ofcom's application of the framework in two recent matters.

In the Trinity Mirror decision, Ofcom did not identify any internal plurality concerns. It noted a study (Cushion et al. 2016, later published as Cushion et al. 2018) of coverage of the 2015 UK election which indicated the newspapers that were the subject of the review were cited far less frequently in broadcast coverage, indicating a lower level of influence.

In the Sky/21C Fox matter, after conducting its assessment of the availability, consumption and impact elements, and before considering contextual factors, Ofcom examined the aspect of 'preventing any one media owner or voice having too much influence over public opinion and the political agenda' (2017: 78). It considered the potential for influence by individuals within the media group following the proposed transaction, taking account of its findings on reach, etc.; comments made in submissions to it; the observations of Lord Justice Leveson in the 2012 inquiry; and the results of the study by Cushion et al. Ofcom concluded that there was a risk that the editorial stance of Sky News could be made to align with other news sources in the combined group 'through the selection and omission of stories or through the choice of commentators invited on to Sky News' (2017: 87). In its view, there were aspects of internal plurality that could mitigate this level of influence. These included the impartiality rules in the Broadcasting Code, the likely adverse reaction of audiences to any interference, and a culture of editorial independence at Sky. Yet, overall, Ofcom argued that these were not sufficient to address its concerns about the potential for influence.

In the section below explaining how the ACMA proposal builds on some aspects of the Ofcom model, we note some reservations among researchers about the design and effectiveness of the Ofcom measurement framework, as well as the important critique of the legislative trigger that restricts the circumstances in which the regulator comes to apply its framework to a specific scenario. However, the impression we gain from the distance of another jurisdiction leads us to observe that the UK regulatory framework does at least provide Ofcom with the scope to consider a range of factors that might assist it to make a decision in the public interest. Recent policy work by the ACMA – explored in the section below – shows that there may be additional considerations that need to be taken into account in other contexts but, in principle at least, most of the UK factors should be able to be replicated in like jurisdictions, such as Australia.

ACMA's news measurement framework

Although the ACMA has no direct regulatory responsibility to routinely monitor and report on media diversity, one of its broadcasting functions is 'to report to, and advise, the Minister in relation to the broadcasting industry, internet industry and datacasting industry' (s 10(1)(q) of the Australian Communications and Media Authority Act 2005). Read together with the objects of the Broadcasting Services Act 1992 mentioned earlier and the powers in Part 13 of that Act to conduct investigations and inquiries, ACMA can be seen to have a general remit, though not an obligation, to monitor diversity. As the media ownership rules provide it with no discretion or requirement to exercise a judgement on a question such as 'sufficient plurality', the ACMA's monitoring functions must necessarily compete for resources with its other work. This has resulted in decades of inattention to the issue; the regulator has actively considered issues of media diversity only on the few occasions of alleged breaches of the ownership and control rules. It is worth making the contrast here with the ACMA's highly activist approach, beginning in 2020, in relation to disinformation. This included both an initial Position Paper (ACMA 2020c) and a report to the Minister assessing a self-regulatory code developed by industry (ACMA 2021). While its reporting and advisory function under the Australian Communications and Media Authority Act 2005 extends to 'the internet industry', it has no power to act in relation to disinformation nor even the equivalent of the narrow but definite obligations concerning compliance with the remaining media ownership rules.

We argue that such inattention calls for revitalized thinking for a media policy agenda – and one that connects with other developments in the contemporary media ecosystem. As Jolly and Pickard suggest, a multi-pronged anti-concentration reform strategy capable of dealing with the rise of platforms, including through robust anti-trust (or competition policy) interventions, and responses to the decline of public interest journalism should form the basis for an integrated approach (Jolly and Pickard 2021: 4). This kind of approach assumes the intractable structural problem in neoliberal capitalist societies: market failure arises with concentrations in corporate media power to the detriment of citizens who increasingly depend on communications media infrastructure in their everyday lives.

Against this background, the publication in late 2020 by the ACMA of a series of reports on diversity and localism, including a proposal for a 'news measurement framework' was a significant event, even if it had no immediate regulatory implications. Its objectives are located in the significant shifts in news markets and in the consumption of news over the last few decades. The ACMA made it clear at the time of publishing the report – in an environment where a Senate inquiry had been launched into 'media diversity in Australia' – that, 'We are not proposing to implement the measurement framework outlined in this paper at this stage' (ACMA 2020a: 2). Nevertheless, its future focus and its attempt to link diversity and localism made it a policy paper deserving of serious consideration. Since it was released, there has been a change in the federal government, and a rekindled interest expressed by the new government in 2022 was followed in early 2023 by a short consultation paper (ACMA 2023) seeking comments on aspects of the measurement framework presented in the earlier paper.

Importantly, the report recognizes that the availability of different forms and sources of news, including from international sources and via digital platforms, means that a new approach to measuring diversity is needed (ACMA 2020a: 3). These market changes have in turn affected local news and public interest journalism, with the broader financial challenges having flow-on effects for the production of local news. However, in an environment where regional newspapers and also regional television bulletins have been closed, suspended or moved online, the ACMA suggests that there is only limited work undertaken to identify specific geographic areas of concern or to try to map all the sources of news: 'Data about local news availability is highly fragmented, with most studies to date looking at specific platforms or types of news content, without seeking to map or identify all participants in the market' (ACMA 2020a: 4).

Although the ACMA does not explicitly say so – and instead prefers to speak in more general terms of the impact of internationalization, the internet and digital platforms on these two components that have long been a part of distinct public policy initiatives – it is clear from the report that levels of local content need to be considered alongside structural aspects such as who provides that content and whether the provider is part of a larger media group, hence the connection between localism and diversity. Group editorial positions, though not explicitly mentioned by the ACMA, also need to be considered in this context. Furthermore, the ACMA points to the well-established approach to charactering the dual functions of local media: building community identity and cohesion; and providing civic or public interest journalism that helps to inform public debate and democratic decision-making (ACMA 2020a: 14).

There are echoes here of what Napoli (2007: xvi) describes as the work of the Federal Communications Commission in the United States in the early 2000s and the 'disappointing paucity' of previous research addressing the link between the two issues of diversity and localism, and 'their relationship to the foundations of our democratic process'.

In the following part of this section we provide a description of the elements of the ACMA's proposed framework, before considering what might be missing from it.

Elements of the measurement framework

In designing its framework, the ACMA started with the twin topics of diversity and localism and then identified three aspects of each that were taken as core sub-categories. The three aspects of diversity are: source diversity ('Australians have access to news from a range of sources and media voices'); content diversity ('Australians have access to news sources containing a diversity of information and viewpoints'); and diversity in consumption ('Australians consume a diverse range of views from a variety of sources'). The three aspects of localism are: civic journalism ('Australians have access to news of public significance aimed [at] informing democratic processes'); originality ('Australians have access to unique news stories'); and connection ('Australians have access to news relating to their town or locality') (ACMA 2020a).

Some of the sub-categories of diversity and localism are seen as being interconnected with one another: within diversity, consumption and source are related measures; within localism, connection and civic journalism are related measures; while across the two categories, content diversity is related to civic journalism and source diversity is related to originality, as well as content diversity and originality being related to one another. These relationships are represented in Figure 3.5.

Given the interconnectedness of several of the sub-categories, the ACMA devised a series of indicators and framing questions that would assist in measuring the sub-categories and, by extension, the two overarching categories of diversity and localism. For example, it was thought that an indicator of 'availability of sources' with a framing question such as, 'What sources of news and opinion are available to Australians?', could provide insight into both source diversity (one of the sub-categories of diversity) and connection (one of the sub-categories of localism).

Eight such indicators and framing questions were devised in order to measure the six sub-categories, with these eight metric sets then allocated to one of

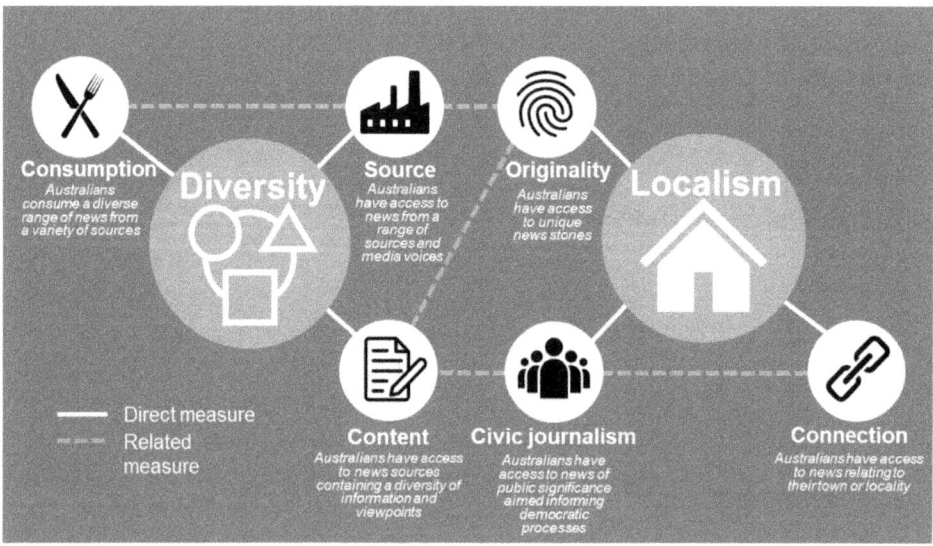

FIGURE 3.5: ACMA's 'Key Measures of Diversity and Localism' (ACMA 2020a: 39, Figure 3.9).

three groups, according to whether they could be seen as being largely about 'news infrastructure', 'news output' (also called 'news content') or 'news engagement'. News infrastructure indicators would assess 'supply-side factors of news production' and provide 'a more detailed examination of cross-platform news media markets') the output indicators would assess 'journalistic output, including the type and qualities of the stories or articles produced in news markets across Australia'; and the engagement indicators would examine 'demand-side factors' and provide information on 'the actual reach and influence of news sources' as well as 'what drives news consumption habits' (ACMA 2020a: 39–40).

The eight metric sets in their three categories are shown in table in Figure 3.6 developed by ACMA.

The ACMA's news framework is part of an exploratory research paper it published at the end of 2020; although comments on it were invited in January 2023, the framework has not been implemented and there are no decisions on the specific tools that would be used to obtain the data set out in the table in Figure 3.6, should the framework be adopted. As a result, although the ACMA's thinking moves beyond Ofcom's on the place of localism within a news measurement framework, the ACMA has none of Ofcom's experience in developing and applying consumption metrics such as 'reach' and 'share of references'. That said, its paper does outline some important and innovative aspects such as the benefits of changing the geographic unit used to assess local media from radio licence areas to local government areas (ACMA 2020a: 27, 33). Combining geographic sample from all local news sources in twenty localities would enable it to compare 'geotypes' (52).

On consumption, the ACMA proposes 'an assessment of the relative popularity of cross-platform news sources in Australia, by reach and frequency of use (nationally representative)' (40). It indicates that its approach could be to adopt Ofcom's share of references measure 'using a consistent methodology and definition of news' (52).

On content diversity, the ACMA suggests that 'a sample of news content could be assessed for both originality and the range and types of topics that are reported on' (2020a: 30). It suggests the geographic sample from twenty localities could be classified and analysed according to criteria such as hard or soft news, originality, referenced or quoted sources, and whether it relates to the local area (2020a: 48). A limitation in its proposed approach, however, is that 'viewpoint' diversity is represented by the number of quoted sources, without any further analysis of the content (e.g., political coverage). It recognizes that there may be some possible stakeholder concerns with the regulator assessing news content, although it also makes the point that it could commission work, citing Ofcom's commissioning of research from Cardiff University as an example (48–49).

Category	Indicator	Framing question	Measure
News infrastructure	1. Availability of sources	What sources of news and opinion are available to Australians?	> Source diversity > Connection
	2. Availability of journalists	How many journalists contribute to the production of local news?	> Source diversity > Originality > Connection
	3. Number of owners	How many people exercise control over Australia's most influential sources of news?	> Source diversity
News content	4. Range of topics	How much variety is present in Australia's news media market?	> Content diversity > Originality
	5. Range of viewpoints	How many viewpoints are presented in Australia's news media market?	> Content diversity > Civic journalism
	6. Local relevance	To what extent does local news cover matters of local significance?	> Content diversity > Connection > Civic journalism
News engagement	7. Consumption	What are the most consumed sources of news in Australia?	> Consumption diversity > Civic journalism
	8. Impact	What are the most impactful sources of news in Australia?	> Consumption diversity > Civic journalism > Connection

FIGURE 3.6: ACMA's 'Indicators of Diversity and Localism' (ACMA 2020a: 7, Table 1).

Building on Ofcom's measurement framework

The ACMA's work in developing a measurement framework is an important step in developing an approach to media diversity that recognizes both the dangers of a concentrated contemporary media market and the need to connect aspects of public policy – diversity and localism – that will often be closely integrated. The Ofcom model is of course far more developed than the ACMA proposal and has been in operation for several years; not surprisingly, the critiques of it point to some areas where the ACMA framework could also be adapted and improved. Indeed, ACMA itself says that it could be possible to combine elements of the EU model in the Media Pluralism Monitor and the UK model and that 'a bundle of metrics assessment approach … could be adopted from the outset to enable a broad ranging assessment' (2020a: 41–42). Below, we consider three specific areas in which the experience in the United Kingdom can inform the improvement of the Australian model, before moving onto two other key issues: the treatment of digital platforms and automated curation, and new methods of classifying the content that would be considered as part of any measurement of media diversity.

Among the criticisms of the Ofcom approach are those made by Rachel Crauford Smith who has outlined problems with the three quantitative criteria used by Ofcom to measure plurality in local areas (2015: 316), arguing that the system offers little protection for local audiences (321). Stephen Barnett (2015: 51–56) forcefully criticizes Ofcom's 'share of references' methodology which he notes resulted in the conclusion in 2013 that in overall group of news sources the BBC had a 44 per cent share of references, while the News Corp newspapers had 4 per cent (53). Among other points raised, Barnett notes the campaigning nature of the newspapers and a tendency towards a more balanced and detached tone in BBC news reports. He concludes: 'the power to exercise [...] passion and thus to influence hearts and minds is missing from [Ofcom's] purely consumption-based and perception-based calculation based on responses to consumer surveys' (54).

This failure to capture the agenda setting role of media is noted by ACMA (2020a: 41), even though it ultimately opts for the share of references metric as an approach that could be adapted for Australia. We note that Ofcom itself has acknowledged some limitations in the design of its framework, including the possible privileging of broadcast over print and online media, but asserting that there is no widespread acceptance of an appropriate measure (2021b: 24; 2021c: 30) and hence the importance of relying on a basket of measures, as it does, rather than a single metric (Ofcom 2018b). In its latest report on the topic (Ofcom 2022: 41), Ofcom has proposed a 'share of attention' measure that would look at 'the attention which individual people give to a specific news source, relative to their wider news diet' and enable consideration of the influence of intermediaries on the market overall or over specific demographic groups.

Higher level criticisms of the UK system have been directed at the overarching benchmark of 'sufficient plurality'. Arnott (2010: 245) notes there is no definition or solid indication as to what constitutes 'sufficient plurality' while Gibbons (2015: 28) proposes an alternative to 'sufficient plurality' based on the question, 'Are media users exposed to all significant standpoints of opinion?' Schlosberg and Freedman (2020: 119) have argued that as a result of the absence of a definition for 'sufficient' plurality, along with the failure to conduct any baseline assessment of existing levels of plurality and instead to apply the test only in the case of specific transactions, 'the default benchmark of sufficiency is perennially the status quo', rendering the test unfit for purpose. In the previous chapter, we proposed a public interest test for media mergers based on the concept of a 'reduction in diversity', taking into account a series of interconnecting issues such as the sustainability of local businesses; the encouragement of original and local news content; quality of content, in terms of the promotion of professional news standards; and modes of delivery and consumption, including the 'automated curation' of digital platforms. This means that the measurement tool does not need to be used, in the absence of a merger proposal, for an assessment of whether there is sufficient diversity.

The questions remains, though, as to whether these interconnecting issues are just addressed in relation to a specific merger, or whether they are part of a baseline or periodic assessment of the overall state of diversity, either nationally or in a local area. With some modification of the ACMA model, the issue of sustainability of local businesses could be a part of the inquiry into news infrastructure, while quality could be considered as part of the news content category, and modes of consumption via digital platforms could be investigated as part of the news engagement inquiry. The obvious outstanding element, however, is some consideration of automated curation as part of the digital platform environment. This does not fit neatly into any of the three ACMA categories, and, in our view, it could be considered with another omission from the ACMA model: contextual factors.

'Contextual factors' is a crucial element in the design of the Ofcom framework. Even without considering the role of digital platforms and automated curation, adding the element of context would help to demonstrate the importance of a more far-reaching review of viewpoints as a part of the testing of content diversity. It would also allow, as an alternative or addition to considering quality as part of 'news content', some attention to the applications of industry standards concerning accuracy, fairness, transparency and protection of privacy. And it would also prompt consideration of economic aspects such as revenue and market position that, over twenty years ago, the Productivity Commission (2000, Chapter 10) suggested should be taken into account (along with number of licences and actual use of media) when measuring concentration in a cross-media environment. Most importantly, though, the contemporary equivalent of measures such as 'number of licences' is, of course, the effect of automated curation and the relationship of digital platforms to news producers and news consumers.

Accounting for automated curation and digital platforms

Assessing the impact of digital platforms remains a challenging issue for Ofcom and for the Media Pluralism Monitor. Helberger et al. (2020) note in their work for the Canadian Government that a dimension of exposure diversity has emerged to address the ways in which recommenders and algorithms structure the delivery of content in an environment featuring an overabundance of information. They suggest that the two most significant potential consequences of recommenders, and the filters bubbles they can promote, are that people are not as exposed to points of view that depart from their own, and therefore it is less likely that the democratic function of establishing a common news agenda – formerly the job of mainstream media – will be fulfilled. We explored this problem in the previous chapter. However, the challenges presented by automated curation go beyond aspects of exposure diversity as they call on and shape the dynamics of business-to-business relationships: recall the market power that Google and Facebook were said by the ACCC to have.

Ofcom has at least attempted to represent the role of digital platforms when assessing plurality in a merger scenario and in its research on news consumption. However, these attempts have not been without problems. In Ofcom's 2018 news consumption results, Facebook's share (for news, not all social media), when considered just as the total number of people reporting they use it for news, was 34 per cent. But when frequency of use was added and considered relative to all other news sources, Facebook's share dropped to 8 per cent. Applying the same approach, Google's share (which in this measure comprised Google search, Google News and YouTube) dropped from 21 per cent to 6 per cent (see Ofcom 2018b: slides 24 and 83). While these results are worth investigating, Scholsberg and Freedman (2020) argue that Ofcom's approach to platforms is deficient in that it disguises the actual sources of news content. They give the example of a user who obtains news from the BBC website and the BBC's Facebook page: in order to include Facebook as a distribution source, Ofcom's approach effectively double counts the BBC as a content source. The effect is that there appears to be more plurality than really exists. On the other hand, if the user obtains news from a variety of content sources via Facebook, Ofcom's approach will under represent the level of plurality because it will identify only one source – Facebook (Scholsberg and Freedman 2020: 121). Schlosberg and Freedman (121) note that this limitation in the Ofcom model became apparent during the assessment of the Sky/21C Fox transaction by the Competition and Markets Authority in 2018, with the result that the CMA reallocated some intermediary shares (in the share of references measure) to conventional news sources. The authors argue that while platforms such as Facebook and Google are important gateways to news, they should not be counted as news sources in their own right. Instead,

> the role of intermediaries can and should be properly assessed by reference to the news sources that are actually consumed through their networks. This would help to ensure that market shares are more appropriately attributed to those who produce and provide the news whilst also enabling regulators to develop, monitor and enforce standards of algorithm governance in support of plurality objectives.
>
> (127)

In our view, the consideration of digital platforms and their relationship with news needs to go beyond the (necessary) tracking and attribution of news sources. Just as localism needs to be considered as a twin issue alongside – perhaps even as part of – media pluralism, plurality needs to be considered alongside the algorithmic delivery of news content. As we note above, in the Preliminary Report of the Digital Platforms Inquiry, the ACCC recommended an algorithms regulator but then backed away from this in its final recommendations and settled for the establishment of a Digital Platforms Branch within its own structure and the inclusion in the News Media Bargaining Code of a requirement for platforms to give advance notice to news businesses of certain algorithmic changes that would have a significant effect on referral traffic. More recently, the proposed European Media Freedom Act has embraced a similar concern for actions that affect the services of news businesses: Article 17 would require very large online platforms to notify media services of changes and to 'engage in a meaningful and effective dialogue with the media service provider' to resolve the problem and avoid future problems.

While it is not yet clear whether the EU Parliament will support Article 17, in our view both it and the notice provision in the News Media Bargaining Code (s 52S) are minimal and insufficient mechanisms for addressing the algorithmic power of digital platforms with respect to news and journalism. We think it was a mistake by the Australian Government to back away from the establishment of a more wide-ranging regulatory function in relation to algorithms. This decision failed to take account of the social dimensions or consequences of algorithmic activity – beyond their effects on competitive markets – that we are most concerned about in this volume. In our view, a more formal regulatory mechanism for the oversight of algorithms is inevitable, preferably within a media regulator as a complement to the market-focussed role of a competition regulator. Importantly for the present discussion, one function of this new regulatory activity could be that ACMA has data on the significance of automated curation and digital platform delivery for use in its assessment of media diversity. ACMA could then conduct the kind of analysis proposed by Helberger (2021) and noted in Chapter 1, such as whether the effect of specific recommender systems is to expose users only to information within their existing expectations or whether they achieve a greater level of exposure. While 'delivery' or 'distribution' could be its own category in the ACMA model, as we also think there is a pressing need for the addition of 'contextual factors', we are agnostic as to the consideration of this element in its own right or a part of contextual factors.

We note that Ofcom, in its most recent consideration of plurality in relation to online news (Ofcom 2022), has not only proposed a new measure – 'share of attention' – that could take account of the use of intermediaries, but it has also begun to consider tools that might be adopted to promote media plurality in a digital platform environment. It uses four categories of tools to characterize these approaches: increasing transparency, empowering user choice, direct interventions, and sustainability of news providers (Ofcom 2022: 47). Algorithmic auditing is one aspect of increasing transparency, aiming to reveal biases in algorithms or manipulation of rankings. This could involve assessment of whether the content seen by users reflects their expectations ('empirical auditing') as well as considering 'whether due diligence and algorithmic testing protocols are being applied and acted upon' ('governance testing') (49). This tool contrasts to approaches that can be characterized as 'direct plurality interventions' which could involve statutory obligations for intermediaries to actively support visibility and discoverability of high quality journalism, or to actively deter content such as misinformation which might be harmful to media plurality (52). While at this stage Ofcom has only sought feedback on these ideas, it does not appear to favour direct intervention, citing concerns over the difficulties in promoting or deterring some forms of content and the possible distortion of competition. In Australia, however, there has already been statutory recognition of the desirability of encouraging original news content, and this was secured through competition law when the News Media Bargaining Code was introduced. Furthermore, after approximately two years' experimentation with industry self-regulation of mis- and disinformation, the Australian Government has announced an intention to introduce a co-regulatory regime in which the ACMA will have information-gathering and enforcement powers (Rowland 2023). Accordingly, action is already being taken in other contexts on matters which could also promote media pluralism in a digital platform environment. Finally, the absence of any initial baseline assessment of plurality (whether by way of a 'sufficiency' test or otherwise) was a key failing in the UK approach, and in Australia, there is the opportunity to correct this by conducting such an assessment. Indeed, it is encouraging to see

ACMA propose a 'news diversity baseline' as a part of its approach (ACMA 2020a: 42). In fact, in the two or more years since ACMA conducted its research, and in the absence of any action by the ACMA itself, the not-for profit group Public Interest Journalism Initiative (PIJI) commenced a large-scale newsroom mapping project, charting closures and expansions of news producers around Australia and mapping the sources of news content in selected locations (PIJI 2022). The importance of this work by PIJI was acknowledged by ACMA in its later paper (ACMA 2023) inviting comments on the framework. The scope of this task – potentially, all newsrooms in Australia – is admirable, and in our view, it is an exercise that should be supported by government, not left to the vagaries of philanthropic funding. Importantly, resource limitations mean that to date PIJI's work has been manual, imposing a necessary limit on its scale. In this respect, the Media Pluralism and Online News project has attempted to offer a way forward.

New approaches to classifying online news: The media pluralism and online news project

The broader purpose of the 'Media Pluralism and Online News' project was to track the dynamic developments in the way news is produced and consumed online, examining whether and the extent to which it is a part of public policy designed to promote pluralism.

One of the key aims of the project is to discover methods of computationally evaluating media pluralism that are relevant for assessments of multi-platform news ecosystems. As we explained above, the concept of 'public affairs' allows us to separate out and identify the categories of content that contributes to media pluralism.

The main dataset was the scrape of the homepages of the top twenty Australian news sources as identified by Roy Morgan Single Source News data (Roy Morgan 2018). The timeframe was across three months in 2019, and the Australian Federal election was underway. That election returned the ruling conservative government led by Scott Morrison for a period of three years (until 2022, when a Labor government came into power). We used four cross sections of the data: six-hourly, daily, weekly and monthly. The tool we developed classifies the content into public affairs and non-public affairs, and provides the proportion of the total number of articles that are considered public affairs for each publication. To analyze the data the Sydney Informatic Hub (SIH) data scientists in consultation with project investigators built a basic text classifier for Public Affairs (PA) vs. Non-Public Affairs (NPA) classification of media articles. The project made iterative 'machine learnt' improvements on previous project classifiers in terms of robustness of a PA/NPA classifier to changes in time of publication.

The Media Pluralism Project Dashboard represents those top twenty online media outlets, and then groups them together to highlight the media ownership of these outlets, for example 'Nine Entertainment' or 'Born Digitals' (MPP 2020). This enables the analyst to select a particular aspect of the media market based on the purpose of the research. For the purposes of this chapter, it is useful to compare Australia's two largest media groups discussed in the previous chapter (News Corp and Nine Entertainment) according to their relative market share, content output and managerial perspectives. The MPP dashboard allows us to interrogate at least some aspects of the second of these elements – news content. The data group for News Corp included data from adelaidenow.com.au, couriermail.com.au, dailytelegraph.com.au, heraldsun.com.au, news.com.au and theaustralian.com.au. These comprise the websites of the News Corp mastheads located in four of the five mainland state capital cities (the exception being Perth where Seven West Media owns the only newspaper) and the national daily, *The Australian* as well as News Corp's online-only site, news.com.au which publishes its own content and acts as an aggregator of articles from other sites in its group. The data group for Nine Entertainment included data from 9news.com.au, afr.com, smh.com.au and theage.com.au. The first of these is the website of Nine's free-to-air television service, while the second is the online version of its national daily, *The Australian Financial Review*, and the final two are the online outlets of its metropolitan daily newspapers in Sydney and Melbourne. The timeframe selected was across the three months of data capture, which was the entire PA/NPA dataset.

The first parse of these data enabled us to determine the PA/NPA distribution of the two media groups, as represented by Figure 3.7, where Group A is News Corp and Group B is Nine Entertainment, noting that the former includes six 'mastheads' while the latter only includes four.

From Figure 3.7, we can determine that most of the media publication occurred within April and May, which was a critical moment in the Australian Federal election. Despite different publication rates ($n \cong 2600$ article per month), we noted that News Corp publishes just as much NPA, if not more, than it does PA. In contrast, Nine Entertainment publishes significantly more PA content than NPA content. (We should note here that different results would be returned if, within these groups, the more 'tabloid' mastheads in each were compared to the more 'broadsheet' mastheads.)

In terms of the topic analysis comparison between these two media groups, it is possible to then drill into the PA/NPA content to understand the sort of content that these two media organizations publish. Figure 3.8 is the topic distribution graph of the two media groups.

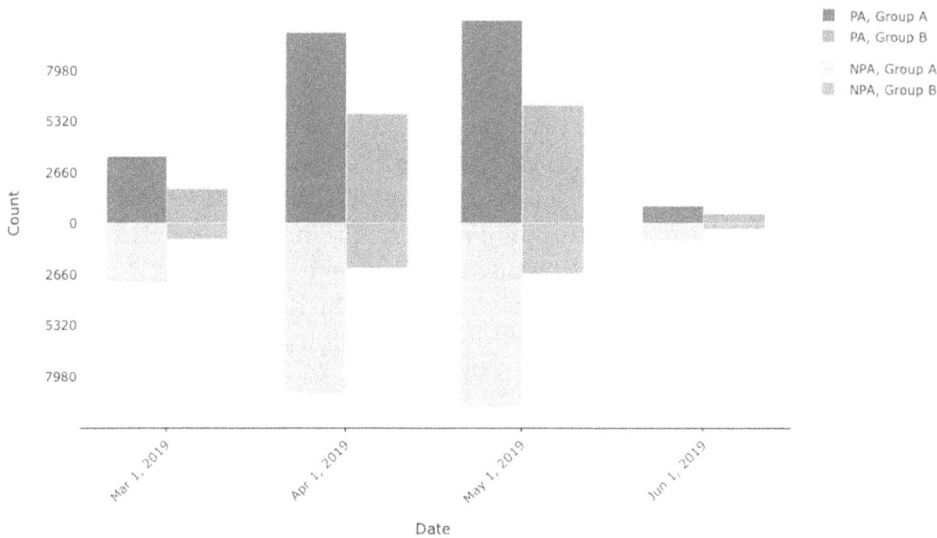

FIGURE 3.7: PA distribution by groups of publishers. News Corp is Green, Nine is light green.

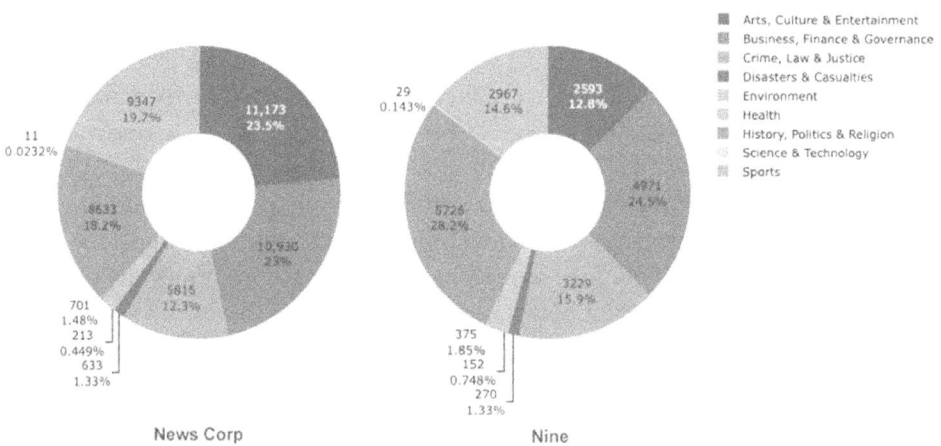

FIGURE 3.8: Topic distribution by groups of publishers.

The top topics News Corp was concerned with during this period are Arts, Culture & Entertainment; Business, Finance & Governance; Sports; and History, Politics & Religion. Nine Entertainment was similarly interested in these areas, however, it had a greater interest in History, Politics & Religion and less of an interest in Arts, Culture & Entertainment.

Conclusion

This chapter has taken a comparative approach to the measurement framework applied by Ofcom in the United Kingdom and the model recently proposed by ACMA in Australia. It has identified some known flaws in the UK approach and used these to critique the Australian proposal, identifying aspects in which the new model could be improved. It has shown how a computational approach to the classification of online news content will, in time, bring a step change in the ways in which content can be considered as part of an overall assessment of media diversity or plurality. And, perhaps most importantly, it has argued for the significance of automated curation and the role of digital platforms to be embedded as an element of any measurement tool.

It is critical to remember, however, that the diversity measurement framework is only one side of the overall media diversity regulatory regime. The other, which we explored in the previous chapter, is the tests that are applied at a time when a transaction is proposed that might affect that level of diversity. The relationship between these two sides of regulation is highlighted by Rachael Craufurd Smith (2015) who notes the move away from fixed ownership limits (or 'bright-line regulation') towards a 'flexible, multi-faceted approach' for assessing media plurality (310) but concludes that after about ten years of this system, the United Kingdom should consider moving back to 'bright-line' regulation (320–22).

The United Kingdom is far ahead of Australia in terms of having both a measurement framework and a public interest test to apply to media mergers; its failing is in not taking the step to connect the two by conducting a baseline assessment of diversity at national and local levels. In Australia, the ACMA has at least arrived at the point of giving serious consideration to the measurement framework but there has not yet been any renewed interest in the rules that apply to mergers in a contemporary media environment. Instead, the 'bright lines' of sector-specific regulation are being gradually erased, with what appears to be a growing confidence in the role of competition law to serve all legitimate public policy purposes, including news media. This was the aspect we ended on in the previous chapter, finding that competition law is not fit for this purpose, and that Australia, like the United Kingdom, is in need of a public interest test.

In the meantime, the Australian Senate's media diversity committee has published a report calling for a multi-stranded response to media reform, recognizing the consequences of no longer 'fit-for-purpose', ineffective regulation (Senate 2021: x). The Committee argued that 'the growing concentration of media ownership, where too much influence is in the hands of too few organisations', together with the dominance of large technology firms, could 'compromise news delivery for all Australians' (108, para. 6.95). The Committee's principal recommendation is that a judicial inquiry with the powers of a royal commission into media ownership concentration be established, as called for by half a million signatories to the petition to Parliament instigated by the former Prime Minister, Kevin Rudd. Although its proposed judicial inquiry is not something likely to directly assist with the development of an effective measurement tool, its concluding remarks align to some extent with our own diagnosis of pluralism and media concentration. It argues:

> Reform should be based in the recognition that reliable news is essential for our future as a nation. It should take into account that misinformation and disinformation have serious and real consequences for our national and local communities, our democratic institutions and the health of our society.
>
> (Senate: 109, para. 6.105)

Other components of a multi-stranded reform package recommended by the Committee include: better targeted funding for the national broadcasters (the ABC and SBS), for the news agency AAP, and for public interest journalism; consideration of 'a single, independent media regulator to harmonise news media standards and oversee an effective process for remedying complaints'; amendments to existing laws including measures around taxation, defamation and press freedom; and improvements to the National Broadband Network (Senate: xv).

Although the rejection of some of the Committee's key recommendations by both major political parties means they are unlikely to ever be adopted and enacted in any systematic way, the inquiry served to rally support from members of the community as well as lobby groups, political activists and researchers across the country. The real policy challenge lies in convincing parliament to act on the sophisticated and forward-thinking work of its own media regulator and to recognize the need to look beyond competition law as the sole instrument for securing the public interest in a vibrant and diverse local media environment.

REFERENCES

ACMA (2020a), *News in Australia: Diversity and Localism – News Measurement Framework*, Melbourne: ACMA, https://www.acma.gov.au/publications/2020-12/report/news-australia-diversity-and-localism. Accessed 4 February 2021.

ACMA (2020b), *Attitudes to News Today: Impartiality and Commercial Influence – Quantitative Research*, Melbourne: ACMA, https://www.acma.gov.au/publications/2020-01/report/australians-and-news-impartiality-and-commercial-influence. Accessed 16 February 2021.

ACMA (2020c), *Misinformation and News Quality on Digital Platforms in Australia: A Position Paper to Guide Code Development*, Melbourne: ACMA, https://www.acma.gov.au/online-misinformation-and-news-quality-australia-position-paper-guide-code-development. Accessed 26 June 2020.

ACMA (2021), *A Report to Government on the Adequacy of Digital Platforms' Disinformation and News Quality Measures*, Melbourne: ACMA, https://www.acma.gov.au/report-government-adequacy-digital-platforms-disinformation-and-news-quality-measures. Accessed 10 April 2022.

ACMA (2023), *A New Framework for Measuring Media Diversity in Australia: Consultation Paper*, Melbourne: ACMA, https://www.acma.gov.au/consultations/2023-01/new-framework-measuring-media-diversity-australia. Accessed 19 January 2023.

Arnott, Craig (2010), 'Media mergers and the meaning of sufficient plurality: A tale of two acts', *Journal of Media Law*, 2:2, pp. 245–75.

Barnett, Steven (2015), 'Plurality and public service broadcasting: Why and how PSBs deserve protection', in S. Barnett and J. Townend (eds), *Media Power and Plurality: From Hyperlocal to High-Level Policy*, London: Palgrave Macmillan, p. 45.

Berry, Mark and George Spittle (2019), 'Media mergers and the critical impact of non-price considerations: A New Zealand case study', *Journal of European Competition Law and Practice*, 10:2, pp. 101–08.

Bleyer-Simon, Konrad, Brogi, Elda, Carlini, Roberta, Nenadic, Iva, Palmer, Marie, Parcu, Pier Luigi, Verza, Sofia, Viola de Azevedo Cunha, Mario and Žuffová, Mária (2021), *Monitoring Media Pluralism in the Digital Era: Application of the Media Pluralism Monitor in the European Union, Albania, Montenegro, Republic of North Macedonia, Serbia & Turkey in the Year 2020*, Centre for Media Pluralism and Media Freedom, Florence: European University Institute.

Brevini, Benedetta and Ward, Michael (2021), *Who Controls Our Media? Exposing the Impact of Media Concentration on Our Democracy*, Surry Hills: GetUp!

Bucher, Tania (2018), *If … Then: Algorithmic Power and Politics*, New York: Oxford University Press.

Cairncross, Frances (2019), *Cairncross Review: A Sustainable Future for Journalism*, London: Department for Digital, Culture, Media & Sport, https://www.gov.uk/government/publications/the-cairncross-review-a-sustainable-future-for-journalism. Accessed 4 March 2023.

Centre for Media Pluralism and Media Freedom (2022), *Monitoring Media Pluralism in the Digital Era: Application of the Media Pluralism Monitor in the European Union, Albania, Montenegro, the Republic of North Macedonia, Serbia and Turkey in the Year 2021*, Florence: European University Institute, https://cadmus.eui.eu/handle/1814/74712. Accessed 19 July 2023.

Chadwick, Paul (1989), *Media Mates: Carving up Australia's Media*, South Melbourne: Macmillan.

Collins, Richard and Cave, Martin (2013), 'Media pluralism and the overlapping instruments needed to achieve it', *Telecommunications Policy*, 37:4&5, pp. 311–20.

Commerce Commission (NZ) (2017), *Determination: NZME Limited and Fairfax New Zealand Limited*. Wellington: Commerce Commission.

Competition and Markets Authority (2018), *21st Century Fox, Inc and Sky Plc: A report on the anticipated acquisition by 21st Century Fox, Inc of Sky Plc*, London: CMA, https://www.gov.uk/government/publications/cma-phase-2-report. Accessed 30 January 2023.

Convergence Review (2012), *Convergence Review Final Report*, Australia: Department of Broadband, Communications and the Digital Economy.

Craufurd Smith, Rachel (2015), 'Bright-line versus responsive regulation: Some thoughts from the United Kingdom', in P. Valcke, M. Sukosd and R. G. Picard (eds), *Media Pluralism and Diversity: Concepts, Risks and Global Trends*, London: Palgrave Macmillan, pp. 310–24.

Cushion, Stephen, Kilby, Allaina, Thomas, Richard, Morani, Marina and Sambrook, Richard (2016), 'Newspapers, impartiality and television news: Intermedia agenda-setting during the 2015 UK general election campaign', *Journalism Studies*, 19:2, pp. 162–81. https://doi.org/10.1080/1461670X.2016.1171163.

Cushion, Stephen, Kilby, Allaina, Thomas, Richard, Morani, Marina and Sambrook, Richard (2018), 'Newspapers, impartiality and television news: intermedia agenda-setting during the 2015 UK General Election campaign', *Journalism Studies*, 19:2, pp. 162–81.

Gibbons, Thomas (2015), 'What is "Sufficient" plurality?', in S. Barnett and J. Townend (eds), *Media Power and Plurality: From Hyperlocal to High-Level Policy*, Houndmills: Palgrave, pp. 15–30.

Given, Jock (2003), *Turning off the Television: Broadcasting's Uncertain Future*, UNSW Press: Kensington.

Given, Jock (2007), 'Cross-media ownership laws: Refinement or rejection?', *University of New South Wales Law Journal*, 30:1, pp. 258–68.

Helberger, Nalati (2021), 'On the democratic role of news recommenders', in N. Thurman, S. C. Lewis and J. Kunert (eds), *Algorithms, Automation and News: New Directions in the Study of Computation and News*, London: Routledge, pp. 14–33.

Helberger, Natali, Moeller, Judith and Vrijenhoek, Sanne (2020), 'Diversity by design: Diversity of content in the digital age', *Discussion Paper for the Government of Canada*, February, https://www.canada.ca/en/canadian-heritage/services/diversity-content-digital-age/diversity-design.html. Accessed 30 January 2023.

Jolly, Sanjay and Pickard, Victor (2021), *Towards a Media Democracy Agenda: The Lessons of C. Edwin Baker. LPE Project*, https://lpeproject.org/blog/towards-a-media-democracy-agenda-the-lessons-of-c-edwin-baker/. Accessed 30 January 2023.

Media Pluralism Project Website (2019), 'The role of a pluralistic media in Australia's democracy', 13 May, https://mediapluralism.org.au/2019/05/the-role-of-a-pluralistic-media-in-australias-democracy/. Accessed 30 January 2023.

Media Pluralism Project Dashboard (2020), Computational tool available at https://mediapluralism.sydney.edu.au. Accessed 19 July 2023.

Napoli, Philip M. (ed) (2007), *Media Diversity and Localism: Meaning and Metrics*, New York: Routledge.

Napoli, Philip M. (2015), 'Media ownership and the political economy of research in US media policymaking', in S. Barnett and J. Townend (eds), *Media Power and Plurality: From Hyperlocal to High-Level Policy*, Houndmills: Palgrave, pp. 101–15.

Nielsen, Rasmus Kleis (2015), 'Local newspapers as keystone media: The increased importance of diminished newspapers for local political information environments', in R. K. Nielsen (ed.), *Local Journalism: The Decline of Newspapers and the Rise of Digital Media*, London: I.B.Tauris & Co. Ltd., pp. 51–72.

Ofcom (2012), 'Measuring media plurality Ofcom's advice to the Secretary of State for Culture, Olympics, Media and Sport', 19 June, https://www.ofcom.org.uk/consultations-and-statements/category-1/measuring-plurality. Accessed 30 January 2023.

Ofcom (2015), 'Measurement framework for media plurality: Ofcom's advice to the Secretary of State for Culture, Media and Sport', 5 November, https://www.ofcom.org.uk/consultations-and-statements/category-1/media-plurality-framework. Accessed 30 January 2023.

Ofcom (2017), 'Public interest test for the proposed acquisition of Sky plc by 21st Century Fox, Inc: Ofcom's Report to the Secretary of State', 20 June, London: Ofcom. https://www.ofcom.org.uk/consultations-and-statements/category-3/public-interest-test-sky-fox. Accessed 28 November 2021.

Ofcom (2018a), 'Public interest test for the acquisition by Trinity Mirror Plc of the publishing assets of Northern and Shell Media Group Limited: Ofcom's advice to the Secretary of State', 31 May, https://www.gov.uk/government/news/statement-merger-between-trinity-mirror-plc-and-northern-shells-publishing-assets. Accessed 30 January 2023.

Ofcom (2018b), 'News consumption in the UK: 2018', https://www.ofcom.org.uk/research-and-data/tv-radio-and-on-demand/news-media/news-consumption. Accessed 30 January 2023.

Ofcom (2020), 'Public interest test on the completed acquisition by *Daily Mail* and General Trust pie of JPI Media Publications Limited and thus the "I" Newspaper: Ofcom's Advice to the Secretary of State', 10 March, https://www.gov.uk/government/collections/daily-mail-and-general-trust-plc-dmgt-acquisition-of-jpi-media-publications-limited. Accessed 24 August 2021.

Ofcom (2021a), 'The future of media plurality in the UK including Ofcom's consultation on the media ownership rules review', 15 June, https://www.ofcom.org.uk/consultations-and-statements/category-2/future-media-plurality-uk. Accessed 14 November 2021.

Ofcom (2021b), 'The future of media plurality in the UK: Ofcom's report to the Secretary of State on the media ownership rules and our next steps on media plurality', 17 November, https://www.ofcom.org.uk/consultations-and-statements/category-2/future-media-plurality-uk. Accessed 14 November 2021.

Ofcom (2021c), 'News consumption in the UK: 2021', 27 July, https://www.ofcom.org.uk/research-and-data/tv-radio-and-on-demand/news-media/news-consumption. Accessed 30 January 2023.

Ofcom (2022), 'Media plurality and online news', 16 November, https://www.ofcom.org.uk/research-and-data/multi-sector-research/media-plurality. Accessed 30 January 2023.

Park, Sora, Fisher, Caroline, McGuinness, Kieran, Lee, Jee Young and McCallum, Kerry (2021), *Digital News Report: Australia 2021*, 23 June, Canberra: News & Media Research Centre, University of Canberra, https://apo.org.au/node/312650. Accessed 30 January 2023.

Park, Sora, McGuinness, Kieran, Fisher, Caroline, Lee, Jee Young, McCallum, Kerry and Nolan, David (2022), *Digital News Report: Australia 2022*, 15 June, Canberra: News & Media Research Centre, University of Canberra, https://www.canberra.edu.au/research/faculty-research-centres/nmrc/digital-news-report-australia-2022. Accessed 30 January 2023.

Public Interest Journalism Initiative (PIJI) Website (2022), 'The Australian newsroom mapping project', https://anmp.piji.com.au/. Accessed 23 September 2022.

Roy Morgan (2018), 'It's official: Most Australians now visit news or newspaper websites', Press Release, 24 May, http://www.roymorgan.com/findings/7595-top-20-news-websites-march-2018-201805240521. Accessed 30 January 2023.

Roy Morgan (2021), 'New Roy Morgan cross-platform audience results show 2020 was a year of growth for Australia's Leading Mastheads', 12 February, http://www.roymorgan.com/findings/8624-roy-morgan-cross-platform-audiences-december-2020-202102120412. Accessed 30 January 2023.

Rowland MP, The Hon Michelle (2023), 'New ACMA powers to combat harmful online misinformation and disinformation', 20 January, https://minister.infrastructure.gov.au/rowland/media-release/new-acma-powers-combat-harmful-online-misinformation-and-disinformation. Accessed 30 January 2023.

Schlosberg, Justin and Freedman, Des (2020), 'Opening the gates: Plurality regulation and the public interest', *Journal of Digital Media & Policy*, 11:2, pp. 115–32.

Select Committee on Communications (2014), *Media Plurality – 1st Report of Session 2013–14*, London: House of Lords, The Stationary Office Ltd.

Senate, Environment and Communications References Committee (2021), *Media Diversity in Australia*, December, Canberra: Parliament of Australia, https://www.aph.gov.au/Parliamentary_Business/Committees/Senate/Environment_and_Communications/Mediadiversity/Report. Accessed 10 December 2021.

Sims, Rod (2018), *Address to the 2018 Annual RBB Economics Conference*, RBB Economics Conference, Sydney, 29 November, https://www.accc.gov.au/speech/address-to-the-2018-annual-rbb-economics-conference. Accessed 30 January 2023.

Trappel, Josef and Tomaz, Tales (eds) (2021), *The Media for Democracy Monitor 2021: How Leading News Media Survive Digital Transformation*, Gothenberg: Nordicom, University of Gothenberg.

4

Problem Definitions in European Policy Debates on Media Pluralism and Online Platforms

Kari Karppinen

Introduction

Policymakers and experts around the world are currently debating regulatory solutions to the challenges of digital platforms and their implications for media policy goals, such as freedom of expression and media pluralism. But what are the actual problems that these proposals seek to solve, and what can different ways of framing the policy problems tell us about the underlying assumptions and political rationalities related to media pluralism as a policy goal?

This chapter analyzes these problem definitions with a focus on recent European media policy, where the notion of media pluralism has long been considered a fundamental yet contested policy aim. In the past decades, media pluralism has usually been invoked in European policy debates around the issues of media ownership concentration, the role of public service media, and media subsidies. Often these debates have been marked by conflicts between market-oriented and cultural or democratic political rationalities and their conflicting conceptions of media pluralism (Karppinen 2013).

In recent years, debates on media pluralism have shifted to involve questions around the power of digital platforms, algorithms, filter bubbles, disinformation and related risks and problems. These debates now add a new layer of ambiguity to the debates on media pluralism, including new problem definitions, stakeholders, policy interests, potential solutions, and potentially new political rationalities for defining media pluralism as a policy aim.

The chapter reviews recent European media policy debates, including academic commentary, policy documents produced by the Council of Europe and the European

Union, and monitoring reports, such as the Media Pluralism Monitor (MPM), which has recently been redesigned to account for the impact of digital developments. Based on these, the chapter identifies four prominent problem definitions related to: the crisis of legacy media, algorithmic manipulation, lack of transparency and the concentration of power. I will then critically assess each of these problem definitions and their limitations from the perspective of media pluralism.

The role of problem definitions in platform politics

Instead of offering a detailed policy analysis of regulatory responses to the problems of platforms, the aim of this chapter is to examine the political rationalities and problem definitions that underlie current expert and policy debates on digital platforms and their impact on media pluralism. The premise of the approach is that emerging policy problems, such as those raised by digital platforms, are not merely a reflection of objective realities that exist independently of politics.

Drawing on post-positivist or discursive approaches to policy studies, it can be argued that public and policy debates and other governmental practices also produce and construct the problems that require political attention (e.g., Fischer 2003: 4–5; Bacchi 2009, Bacchi and Goodwin 2016). Others strands of public policy studies have also emphasized that policymaking is not a linear process of rational problem solving. Policy action requires that social issues are first conceptualized as policy problems, to which political initiatives and available solutions can be presented as answers (e.g., Kingdon 2003). Therefore, the framing of issues as problems that require political attention is part of politics as much as the debate over alternative solutions. This makes the definition of policy problems a site of definitional struggle and political contestation, with different stakeholders having an interest in framing the problems in particular ways. Problem definitions and framings also have political consequences in shaping the terms of debate, the choice of policy arenas and the range of alternative options available to policymakers. For example, if problems associated with platforms are framed as a competition policy issue, they will be assigned to different domains of policymaking, with their own competencies, criteria and tools, than if they are framed as media or cultural policy problems.

This raises a need to critically examine the problem representations related to platforms in public, policy and expert debates. The focus on problem definitions and the construction of the policy agenda can be regarded as particularly important in the context of policy change and emerging policy areas. Several scholars have noted that recent political concerns over platforms are often driven by 'public shocks', or scandals related to issues, such as election manipulation, disinformation or privacy and data breaches (Ananny and Gillespie 2017). However, not all scandals lead to policy action. Instead, the success of some problem representations over others also depends on their ability to become institutionalized and normalized in the routines of policymaking (Hay 2004). Subsequent questions then arise on what considerations are missing from the policy agenda, and what kinds of 'policy silences' they produce (Freedman 2010).

In this chapter, I assume that there are a range of factors that influence the problem definitions and the agenda of digital platform politics. These involve media and public debates, stakeholder interests and lobbying, institutional and governmental logics, and expert discourses.

Problem representations can also be linked to broader 'political rationalities' that underlie policy discourses (Bacchi and Goodwin 2016: 43). Political rationalities involve different conceptual logics, justifications for regulatory intervention, conceptions of appropriate forms of intervention and notions of who is responsible for addressing policy problems. In media policy debates, for example, a neoliberal political rationality can be associated with problematizations where media is conceptualized purely in economic or market terms, whereas political rationalities of welfare, citizenship and democracy often underlie more interventionist policy discourses. While current digital policy debates can at least partly build on the rationalities and problem definitions of established media policy debates, the digital platforms also create new problems, mobilize new stakeholders with vested interests and raise new public interest concerns. Potentially these amount to new political rationalities for conceptualizing media pluralism as a policy issue.

The chapter focuses empirically on policy discourses within the European Union (EU) and the Council of Europe, both of which have recently issued several initiatives related to digital platforms and their impact on media freedom and pluralism. The EU initiatives, such as the new Digital Services Act package, Media and Audiovisual Action Plan, and the European Democracy Action Plan, include proposals for binding regulations as well as recommendations and discussion papers. The Council of Europe recommendations, on the other hand, are non-binding but still influential as a reflection of policy argumentation, discourses and values beyond the EU. The expert committees of the Council of Europe also have a long history of keeping the issues of media pluralism and concentration on the policy agenda in Europe. Finally, I will also refer to the academic reports such as the MPM, which aims to identify risks to media pluralism in EU member states, also including risks related particularly to online platforms. These documents also communicate with broader academic commentary, which arguably also shapes the problem definitions adopted in policy discourse.

I will draw on examples from these different policy contexts to illustrate different problem definitions, their limitations and underlying assumptions. However, the analysis does not constitute a comprehensive review of policy debates at the European level to cover differences between institutions or changes over time. Instead, the four sets of problem definitions that I have identified function more as examples of how different ways of problematizing the role of platforms produces different political rationalities for promoting media pluralism. Before discussing the problem definitions, I first briefly review the background of media pluralism as a policy aim in European media policy debates and discuss how digital platforms have challenged existing policy paradigms.

Media pluralism as an aim in European policy debates

The notion of media pluralism has received significant attention in European media policy debates for several decades. Media pluralism is also enshrined in Article 11 of the Charter of Fundamental Rights of the European Union as a fundamental principle alongside freedom of expression and media freedom. Similarly, the Council of Europe and the European Court of Human Rights have long emphasized the link between media pluralism and the freedom of expression.

As an abstract principle, the notion of media pluralism has been subject to multiple definitions and aspects. At a general level, however, the debate often converges around the core aims of promoting citizens' access to a wide range of viewpoints and preventing undue concentration of media power in the hands of few dominant actors (e.g., Council of Europe 2018a). The overriding logic here links media pluralism with freedom of expression and the aim of creating a favourable environment for participation in public debate by all people (e.g., Nenadic and Milosavlevic 2021: 92). In these debates, media pluralism has been viewed not only as a consequence of free expression but also its precondition, which creates obligations for media policy to take positive measures to safeguard and promote media pluralism (see Kenyon 2021).

The fact that media pluralism has emerged as a common aim, shared by almost all sides in media policy debates, however, does not mean that there are no conflicting values and interests. As Robert Picard (2017: 256) puts it, agreeing on common European policy and finding evidence to support it has been 'a Sisyphean task with numerous starts, stops, retreats and restarts'. Understood to include both national and European-level initiatives, Picard argues that European media pluralism policies 'have not yet produced any clear objectives or policy agreement about how to pursue media pluralism despite far greater policy attention to the issue than in other parts of the world' (Picard 2017: 256).

There are differing opinions on the meaning and nature of media pluralism as a theoretical, political or empirical concept, and the concept can easily be adjusted to different political purposes (see Karppinen 2013). The aim of promoting media pluralism can be seen as a meeting point for different demands rooted in different social values, interests and normative conceptions of the role of media in society. Roughly speaking, there have been two competing paradigms, or political rationalities of media pluralism competing for a hegemonic position in European media policy, which also reflect wider controversies in European media policy.

First, much of the policy debates on media pluralism have focused primarily on economic concerns related to competition, free markets and consumer choice. This focus in partly explained by the founding rationale of the EU to promote internal European markets. The market-driven discourse often approaches media pluralism quantitatively in terms of consumer choice, available outlets or content options. Although most would acknowledge that media pluralism also relates to cultural and political concerns, these are often either marginalized or elided with the quantitative and consumer-led conception of pluralism as consumer choice in this discourse.

On the other hand, there is a democracy-driven discourse, which has challenged the market-driven conceptions of pluralism and diversity. Its proponents have tried to link pluralism with broader public interest values, and more multifaceted ideals of democracy, the public sphere and culture. These ideals are often used to justify, for example, the role of public service media, community media and minority media. If the former rationality has been dominant within the European Commission, the latter has received more attention within the European Parliament, the Council of Europe and some member states (Karppinen 2013).

These two logics can be paralleled with Edwin Baker's distinction between commodified and non-commodified logics in American debates on media concentration and pluralism. The commodified logic's ultimate concern is with fair competition and the provision of commodities to consumers, whereas non-commodified rationale derives essentially from democratic theory and the egalitarian commitment to the democratic distribution of communicative power in the public sphere and 'wide and fair dispersal of power and ubiquitous opportunities to present preferences, views, visions' (Baker 2007: 7).

These competing rationalities have involved different understandings of media pluralism, its measurement, the appropriate means to promote it and the policy issues it covers. In terms of concrete policy issues, media pluralism has historically been associated above all with the problem of media ownership concentration and its implications for political pluralism. In the last couple of decades, however, the definitions of media pluralism as a policy issue have constantly expanded beyond media ownership to also include issues related to cultural, geographic and minority issues. Other prominent issues raised in European debates on pluralism include the role of public service media, risks of political interference or abuse of power by media owners, lack of transparency in media ownership, shortcomings in inclusiveness and gender balance, and deficiencies in ensuring safety of journalists (e.g., CMPF 2021; Nenadic 2019).

Most of these concerns belong to the competence of EU member states, as the EU itself has little direct competence in the fields of media or cultural policy, apart from general competition policy. Within the EU, one response to this has been to focus on the ostensibly uncontroversial aim of developing better tools for monitoring and measuring media pluralism, instead of harmonizing regulation. The tool developed within the EU for this purpose, the MPM, has stated an aim to bring 'a stronger evidentiary basis to define priorities and actions for improving media pluralism' and to 'ensure a uniform basis for dealing with pluralism issues and provide a more objective basis for the often heated political and economic arguments' (KU Leuven–ICRI 2009, 3).

The MPM, implemented by the Centre for Media Pluralism and Media Freedom at the European University Institute, does not aim to directly measure the state of media pluralism but instead seeks to identify risks related to various aspects of media pluralism to bring those questions to the policy agenda. This makes it a particularly interesting tool from the perspective of constructing policy problems.

The approach of the MPM thus recognizes the multi-faceted and normative character of media pluralism as a policy objective as well as the political sensitivities surrounding its regulation. With reference to the reports and resolutions of the Council of Europe and the European Parliament and incorporating dimensions of media pluralism defined in academic and policy debates, the MPM defines media pluralism broadly. This involves 'all measures that ensure citizens' access to a variety of information sources and voices, allowing them to form opinions without the undue influence of one dominant opinion forming power' (KU Leuven–ICRI 2009: 2) and 'the scope for a wide range of social, political and cultural values, opinions, information and interests to find expression through the media' (KU Leuven–ICRI 2009: 5).

Both the Council of Europe and the current EU approaches have thus explicitly defined media pluralism as an issue that goes beyond media ownership. The MPM, for example, encompasses four major areas (basic protection, market plurality, political independence and social inclusiveness), with each broken down into several sub-areas and indicators (KU Leuven–ICRI 2009). From the beginning, the European Commission also instructed that the monitoring should take into account the implications of recent technological changes for the pluralism and diversity debate, noting that 'concern expressed regarding media pluralism and diversity may inter alia also be concern regarding structural changes that are taking place as a result of new technology, and the impact these may be having on media output' (European Commission 2007: 2).

From media to information pluralism

The original idea of the MPM was to consider not only media supply but also distribution mechanisms and potential access to media as relevant aspects (KU Leuven–ICRI 2009: 73). However, it was only in the last decade that debates on media pluralism have in earnest shifted to account for the structural power of digital platforms in shaping the information environment. These changes have gradually also become more prominent in the European media policy and in the subsequent revisions of the MPM methodology (see e.g., Council of Europe 2018b; CMPF 2021).

In contrast to earlier debates on cultural and media policy, these new issues also involve a significant shift in the role of the European and national policymaking. Media and cultural policies have traditionally belonged to the competence of individual member states but the regulation of global digital platforms is an issue where especially the smaller member states have little leverage compared to the EU. Consequently, the European Union and larger member states like Germany and France have adopted an increasingly interventionist stance towards the digital platform companies, trying to position themselves as global forerunners in the effort to regulate digital platforms (e.g., Helberger 2020; van Dijk 2021). Many of the recent initiatives of the EU are not only recommendations but also binding regulation, which shapes the policies of member states, and in some cases, policy trajectories in the rest of the world. Consequently, it is relevant also from the broader global perspective of media pluralism to examine the underlying political rationalities of these debates.

The recent EU initiatives that address the power of social media platforms and media pluralism include recommendations and codes of conduct, such as the Action Plan Against Disinformation, binding regulation, including the Digital Services Act package, and support and innovation schemes, such as the EU Media and Audiovisual Action Plan. Furthermore, the role of digital media is also central in more general strategy documents, such as the European Democracy Action Plan and the European Digital Strategy.

While the notion of media pluralism itself has not necessarily been at the core of the debate on digital platforms, it is becoming evident that the problems and solutions offered in these initiatives are also shaping the debates on media pluralism. As Nenadic (2019: 131) argues, when social media platforms have challenged the position of media organizations as privileged information gatekeepers, the established approaches and concepts have proven inadequate for evaluating media pluralism and the different entities that compete in media markets. New approaches to media pluralism require a more nuanced consideration of actors and the production of 'news' and information. Consequently, Milosavjevic and Nenadic (2021) argue that there is a shift from media to 'information pluralism'. Instead of focusing only on particular actors defined as media companies, pluralism policies should be 'media and platform agnostic' and focus on the outcome that needs protection.

Similarly, the Council of Europe (2018b: 2) highlights the role of intermediaries as a range of actors who perform curatorial and editorial roles through moderation and ranking of content, and 'exert forms of control which influence users' access to information online in ways comparable to media, or they may perform other functions that resemble those of publishers'.

Reflecting these changes, the EU MPM has also been revised to include issues and potential risks to pluralism with regard to online platforms in particular (Brogi 2020). New indicators cover, for example, issues related to the net neutrality rules, protections against hate speech, online platforms concentration and competition, sustainability and viability of legacy media, and other measures taken by member states, such as 'digital service tax' to help pluralism or other measures to support alternative media business models.

The range of initiatives that deal with digital platforms and media hardly constitute a coherent new framework or paradigm of thinking about media pluralism. Instead, they are marked by conflicting political rationalities and interests. Much like previous media policies, the approaches to digital platforms combine the rationalities of promoting European markets and competitiveness with ideas of fundamental rights and democracy.

Like previous debates on media pluralism, policy initiatives indicate different understandings of what pluralism is and what role can regulation and media policy play in promoting it. There is an emerging consensus that digital platforms increasingly influence media pluralism and perhaps even that new regulation and oversight is necessary. However, it is often unclear what precisely are the problems that regulation should address and with what objectives. As Nenadic (2019: 137) notes, there seems to be a lack of benchmarks against which to evaluate the impact of the activities of intermediaries on media pluralism.

If the traditional debates were marked by a conflict between the rationalities of market-driven and democracy-driven conceptions of media pluralism, the emerging discussions on platforms seem to retain these tensions, while adding a new layer of contestation involving new stakeholders, different understandings of pluralism as a policy aim, diverging conceptions of the nature of platforms as media actors.

Problem definitions and conceptions of pluralism in recent platform policies

In the following, I will turn to analyze some of the prominent problem definitions in recent European platform and media policy debates and discuss their implications for media pluralism. I outline four prominent problematizations that recur in European policy debates on digital platforms, with examples from policy documents. I have focused on problem definitions that reflect concerns for media pluralism, democracy and the public sphere – although they are not always discussed under the label of media pluralism – and have not included problem definitions that focus on other harms associated with platforms, such as national security risks, privacy or public health.

The following four categories of problem definitions are a reconstruction of themes found across policy documents and academic debate. They do not mirror the positions of specific stakeholders or institutions, although I do also discuss the possible origins and interests behind the problem definitions. The problem definitions are not comprehensive of all policy debates and the categorization is naturally open to both conceptual and empirical challenge and questioning. Instead of systematically mapping of all policy discourses, the aim here is to illustrate the role of problem definitions by critically examining how some prominent problem definitions shape policy debates.

Platforms as a threat to legacy media and 'responsible journalism'

One prominent problem definition in European policy debates centres around concerns for the sustainability of domestic media industries and 'quality journalism' in competition with mostly US-based digital platforms and new patterns of media use. In these discussions, media pluralism is typically understood in terms of availability of different journalistic outlets and content options. This is perceived to be under threat when traditional media, as largest investors in news content, face declining resources and fewer journalists to produce news and other public interest content.

As an example of this problem definition, the European Commission has recently launched a 'Media and Audiovisual Action Plan' (2020a), with aims to 'boost European media and help maintain European cultural and technological autonomy in the Digital Decade' and help Europe's media 'not only to be resilient but also to remain competitive at European and global levels'. Similar concerns over the production of reliable media content can also be found in other Commission initiatives, such as the EU's Digital Strategy and the European Democracy Action Plan (European Commission 2020b).

The crisis of journalism narrative, which has become familiar in both academic and policy debates on journalism, is also present in the Council of Europe documents. The 'declaration on the financial sustainability of quality journalism in the digital age', for example, underlines the importance of pluralistic media and quality journalism for democracy, and how digital transformation has compromised the 'traditional business models' that have supported this role (Council of Europe 2019).

It is widely accepted that platforms have impacted the business of traditional media and journalism, so the concern is not surprising. The terminology and framing of the problem, however, are interesting. The notion of quality journalism is here strongly associated with traditional media, which is described as offering 'diverse, credible, interesting and timely information available to the public' and juxtaposed with 'propaganda, misinformation and disinformation proliferating on social media' (Council of Europe 2019).

The concerns for democracy and media pluralism are here almost elided with the competitiveness of the legacy media industry. Besides the language of democracy and the societal role of quality journalism, the same concerns are often framed in terms of fair competition or 'a level playing field'. Embedded in the discourse is the idea that European domestic media face unfair competition or asymmetrical relationship from the dominant digital platforms, which distorts 'normal' media market competition. In line with the policy debates, the revised MPM framework now also includes indicators for 'media viability' and the sustainability of quality journalism as potential risks to media pluralism. As Brogi (2020) notes, the assumption here is that 'the journalistic profession is facing a deep crisis' – mainly because of online platforms disrupting the traditional business models of news media.

The logic of problematization that places existing, national media institutions against dominant digital platforms is, of course, not unique to European debates. In analyzing Australia's digital platforms inquiry, Flew and Wilding (2021: 54), for example, identify 'a newfound, or perhaps rediscovered, recognition of the 'public good' status of news and journalism' among policymakers. This problem definition has gained even more prominence around the world after the coronavirus pandemic, which has accelerated the economic crisis of journalism and generated new calls for public support to media organizations (CMFP 2021b).

The notion of 'crisis' is not anything new in academic and policy debates on journalism and several scholars have critically examined the uses of crisis narrative in these debates (e.g., Brüggeman et al. 2016; Zelizer 2015). From the perspective of media pluralism, the assumptions of the crisis narrative can also be critically questioned. On the one hand, it is obvious that the digital transformation and the decline in the number of professional journalists and news outlets have implications for media pluralism, in the form of both structural diversity of news sources as well as the production of journalistic content. On the other hand, as Brüggeman et al. (2016) argue, the crisis framing is not simply a neutral description of the situation but often also a means by which strategic actors frame the situation and try to influence media policy making to align with their motives. The crisis of journalism discourse is thus an example of a problem definition that is driven by stakeholder interests and lobbying.

In media policy debates, abstract principles such as media pluralism often function as much as rhetorical devices used by self-interested agents than as analytical tools for policymakers (e.g., Karppinen 2013). For example, notions of pluralism and diversity have long served as convenient keywords for justifying measures to support domestic media and cultural production, even when the measures are originally driven more by the interests of the industry than social, cultural or democratic policy rationales.

In this sense, the association of media pluralism with the protection of domestic or European media industry is not anything new as it resembles the problematization of 'Americanization' that was prominent in European media policy in the past decades. Regarding discourses on digital technology, however, the emphasis on terms like quality journalism and responsible media represents a notable discursive shift from debates of only a decade ago, when it was commonplace in both academic and policy discourse to view new digital media technologies as tools that will lead towards pluralization of the public sphere, precisely because of their ability to challenge the concentrated power of traditional or mainstream media (e.g., Castells 2007). For many, the disruption of legacy media was then above all a positive development that would widen the spectrum of voices that have access to the public sphere.

In contrast, the new digital media are now increasingly seen as threatening media pluralism by compromising the sustainability of the previously maligned traditional media. From the perspective of media pluralism, the discursive shift also raises uncomfortable questions of whether the emergence of new dominant platforms has been different from what was anticipated, providing too much or wrong kinds of pluralism, or if these discourses employed different conceptions of media pluralism as a media policy aim to begin with.

Algorithmic manipulation as a threat to democracy

Another problem representation that is prominent in current European policy debates relates even more directly to digital technology itself as a threat to media pluralism and the proper functioning of democracy more broadly.

As Barrett et al. (2021) put it, the relations between digital technologies and democracy in public policy discourses are often capricious. In line with academic debates, where debates on digital technology have shifted emphasis from empowerment to threats to democracy, public and policy discourses now increasingly focus on malicious uses of technology, including mis- and disinformation, polarization, media manipulation and propaganda – a constellation of issues that Freelon and Wells (2020: 145) call 'the defining political communication topic of our time'.

Problem definitions around this constellation of issues are certainly not difficult to find in recent European policy debates on media pluralism. The High Level Group on Media Freedom and Pluralism nominated by the European Commission articulated already in 2013 many of the current concerns related to filter bubbles, recommendation systems and the personalization of news and the negative impact on media pluralism, and ultimately on democracy, if 'citizens only get news on subjects they are interested in, and with the perspective they identify with' (Vīķe-Freiberga et al. 2013: 27).

Since then, the European Commission has made issues of algorithmic online manipulation a focus point of several initiatives and expert reports. The reasons and objectives of the new EU Digital Services Act, for instance, discusses 'manipulative techniques' and 'systemic risks' associated with digital services, seen as a 'source of new risks and challenges, both for society as a whole and individuals using such services', including citizens' 'limitations to express themselves and other societal harms' (European Commission 2020c. n.pag.).

Similarly, the Council of Europe (2018c) report on the human rights implications of automated data processing and algorithms identifies a number of human rights concerns triggered by the increasing role of algorithms in decision-making, including 'their potential for harming the freedom of information and freedom of expression of individuals, groups and whole segments of societies' through the 'fragmentation of the public sphere and to the creation of "echo chambers" that favour only certain types of news outlets, thereby enhancing levels of polarisation in society' (17). Another Council of Europe (2018b) recommendation on the roles and responsibilities of internet intermediaries explicitly frames algorithms as a media pluralism problem, arguing that states should develop 'co-regulatory policies addressing the algorithmic systems that govern the distribution of online content and specifically political advertising and political communication, with the aim of enhancing exposure diversity'.

From the perspective of media pluralism, these concerns differ from the focus on European media discussed above. Whereas the concerns over media industries and journalistic production clearly focus on the traditional aspects of content and source diversity, the problematization of algorithmic manipulation explicitly focus on media use and exposure diversity, understood as the range of viewpoints individuals consume, as opposed to the range of content available across the media system in principle (see, e.g., Helberger 2018; Napoli 2011).

In contrast to concerns for traditional media, this problem definition is not as easily identified with any specific stakeholders or interest groups. Instead, policy discourses and problem definitions around algorithmic manipulation seem to be influenced by popularized terms, such as disinformation, echo chambers and filter bubbles, which either implicitly or explicitly appear in most of the policy and expert papers on media pluralism.

Despite routine references to these terms in policy debates, many scholars have noted that there is a gap between policy uses of these terms and the actual research on the mechanisms and prevalence of filter bubbles, echo chambers and polarization (e.g., Bruns 2021; Zuiderveen Borgesius et al. 2016). Consequently, these terms are often poorly defined and used loosely as a general justification for policy attention, rather than explaining how these problems, or measures to address them, would specifically impact media pluralism. Conceptualization of media pluralism, beyond the assumption of narrowing exposure caused by social media, is thus often lacking in the discourses that problematize the new algorithmic affordances and their impact on democracy.

This vagueness has led many scholars to criticize these popularized notions and lament that the focus on technology itself may even direct attention away from more pressing problems that require political attention. As Bruns (2021: 33–34) puts it, as 'highly evocative but ill-defined metaphors', filter bubbles and echo chambers 'constitute an unfounded moral panic that presents a convenient technological scapegoat (search and social platforms and their affordances and algorithms)'.

Similarly, Barrett et al. (2021) argue that policy debates are often overly focused on technology's effects on democracy, and although policymakers often refer to their desire to strengthen democracy and mitigate technological threats, the ideas of 'proper' or 'healthy' functioning of democracy in these debates are often poorly defined.

Again, this is not to say that algorithmic manipulation or technological affordances are not worth problematizing from the perspective of media pluralism. However, it is worth noting that problem definitions that emphasize the agency of technology or algorithms have implications for the policy debate. The focus on technology may, for example, invite 'technological solutionism' that aims to solve problems by tweaking the algorithms, instead of addressing broader problems related to the media infrastructure, economic incentives, and the distribution of communicative power (see Morozov 2013).

Lack of transparency and accountability as a policy problem

A third common theme in problematizations of digital platforms' role in society, and their impact on media pluralism, is transparency and lack of accountability. This is a problem definition also driven by academic researchers who often rely on data provided by platforms to study their impact on society.

The idea of transparency has long been central in European debates on media pluralism. Measures and monitoring to promote transparency of media ownership and control have been seen as important both as a basis for regulation but also in itself. Transparency and monitoring measures have been the focus of the EU approach to media pluralism since the launch of the MPM, which itself is an attempt to enhance the 'auditability' of media pluralism and create publicly available information about risks to pluralism.

The Council of Europe has also underlined in numerous instances underlined the importance of media ownership transparency for safeguarding public debate in democratic societies, arguing that transparency of media ownership makes 'media pluralism effective by bringing ownership structures behind the media – which can influence editorial policies – to the awareness of the public and regulatory authorities' (Council of Europe 2018a: n.pag.).

This logic of emphasizing transparency is also extended to questions beyond media ownership, including other control arrangements, journalistic practices and especially in the context of digital intermediaries, information on how media content is algorithmically managed, edited, curated and created (Council of Europe 2018a).

There is a widespread perception in public, policy and academic discourses that digital platforms present a particular problem from the perspective of transparency, as citizens have limited access to the techniques and processes that determine what they see online (Barrett 2021: 9). This is reflected, for example, in the metaphor of the 'black box' and the emergence of a whole field of studies on algorithmic accountability and transparency (e.g., Diakopoulos 2016; Pasquale 2016).

The lack of transparency is a central focus of the EU's Digital Services Act package and its justifications, which refer to the idea that platforms increasingly deploy recommendation systems that shape our information environment without necessary transparency obligations about these systems. The measures proposed to address this problem include, for example, new reporting obligations for platforms, requirements regarding transparency of moderation and recommendation systems, and special access for vetted researchers to the data necessary to understand the systemic risks that very large online platforms pose to media freedom (European Commission 2020c).

What makes transparency interesting as a problem definition is that it is a notion that almost anyone can embrace, perhaps apart from those with proprietary interests related to algorithms. Yet the emphasis on transparency can also have contradictory and unintended implications for the shaping of public and policy debates. Critics have noted that policymakers tend to offer transparency as a universal solution to a variety of problems, particularly in contexts characterized by a high degree of uncertainty (August and Osrecki 2019). As such, it can also function as a substitute for more concrete and meaningful measures to regulate the platforms or promote pluralism.

Transparency can refer to information available both 'downwards' to the public and 'upwards' to the regulators or other monitoring bodies, each with their own rationales (Craufurd Smith et al. 2021). Downwards transparency links with the ideas of media literacy and the assumption that more information will lead to more competent media use. Upwards transparency, on the other hand, presumes that platforms will act more responsibly when monitored. However, both assumptions can be questioned. Transparency alone does not necessarily lead to more informed users or more institutional accountability, and in some cases demands for more information and visibility may even have paradoxical consequences of producing more opacity or only an illusion of accountability (e.g., Ananny and Crawford 2018; August and Osrecki 2019; Stohl et al. 2016). This can make the focus on transparency somewhat evasive: assessing the impact of digital platforms obviously requires transparency but information alone will not solve the problems associated with concentrated media structures and lack of media pluralism.

Concentration of power as a problem in itself

Finally, I discuss a problem definition that relates to all of the themes discussed above but points to a more general, systemic style of problematization. A common theme here is to emphasize the mere size of the platforms, the unprecedented scale of power concentration and the problems this creates for regulation. As Brogi (2020: 6) argues,

> while in the traditional media landscape risks stemmed mainly from the dominance of media outlets at national level, which was easier to regulate (e.g., by media ownership limitations), in today's digital world such dominance by global platforms is much more challenging and difficult to deal with, not only in terms of market dominance.

Similarly, the Council of Europe (2018b) notes how the concentration of power and network effects have led to the existence of dominant entities that are 'in positions of influence or even control of principal modes of public communication'. This power can also be conceptualized in market terms, as in the EU Digital Services Act package that aims to address the 'systemic risks' arising from the role of digital platforms as gatekeepers with 'the power to act as private rule-makers' that control important ecosystems in the digital economy (European Commission 2020c). These initiatives thus recognize that platforms have 'structural power' to shape and determine the structures within which other actors in society must operate (Horten 2016: 5).

Although the Digital Services Act does not further discuss media pluralism as a distinct risk, it clearly assumes that there is a relationship between the size of a service and the potential for harm (Broughton Micova 2021). The nature of the harms associated with size can be conceptualized in different ways. However, the concentration of power can also be viewed as problematic in itself beyond the identification of specific harms. In fact, there is also a potential tension between current initiatives that seek to address specific concerns arising from the role of platforms as facilitators of speech and the problematization of concentration of power itself. As Helberger (2020: 848) argues, 'by formalizing and reinforcing the role of platforms as governors of online speech, […] the current initiatives also further reinforce the opinion power of these platforms and thereby their political power'.

From the perspective of media policy, this discourse relates to some of the basic controversies in policy debates on media pluralism, and the question of whether concentration of power is a problem itself or only when concrete abuses or negative consequences of that power, such as risks to the diversity of views, can be demonstrated. It can be argued that simply allowing dominant actors to emerge in the media system is already problematic. As Baker (2007: 16, original emphasis) argues, concentration of media ownership creates the possibility of enormous, unchecked power, and 'even if this power were seldom if ever exercised, the democratic safeguard value amounts to an assertion that *no democracy should risk the danger*'. Instead, the media should be structurally egalitarian to allow a wide and fair dispersal of power and equal opportunities to exercise influence for different actors in society.

In line with this, it can be argued that media pluralism policies in the digital environment should be primarily about dispersing the communicative power of the dominant actors and the creation of counter powers, instead of only alleviating some of the harms associated with that power (see Helberger 2020). This is perhaps the most fundamental problem with digital platforms, which also underlies many of the other problems. However, it is not necessarily the one emphasized in policy discourses because it is much more difficult to solve than the other problem definitions discussed above. Potential solutions offered to the concentration of platform power can include breaking up dominant platform companies, preventing certain anti-competitive practices, or creating alternative, countervailing powers. As Helberger (2020: 849) notes, however, competition law is suited to deal with opinion power only to a limited degree. Instead, linking this problem definition to effective solutions would require reconceptualizing media concentration policy in ways that go beyond current measures of audience reach or ownership limitations.

Discussion

Media pluralism and diversity are notoriously contested concepts that have different meanings in different contexts, so much that they have traditionally been used to argue for a range of policies that can be mutually contradictory. Attempts to promote one form of pluralism through policy measures may well undermine other forms of pluralism. If addressing media pluralism with common European policy and finding evidence to support it has been 'a Sisyphean task' before (Picard 2017), there is no reason to think that platformization makes the task easier.

Problem definitions guide policy discourses and shape the options available to policymakers. There is a need, therefore, to critically examine the political rationalities of current policy debates and the assumptions about media pluralism that underlie those debates. Currently, those assumptions are rarely expounded in policy discourse. Problematization of the crisis of legacy media, algorithmic manipulation, lack of transparency and the concentration of power, each implies different political rationalities, and therefore shapes the policy discourses and expectations placed on policymakers.

These four problem categories are not comprehensive, and they also overlap to a significant degree. Yet there are also potential tensions and contradictions between them and their assumptions regarding media pluralism as a media policy goal. These tensions are reflected, for example, in the fear that measures that focus on the relationship between digital platforms and traditional media or technological solutions to the governance of algorithms may end up reinforcing the role of already dominant actors rather than dispersing communicative power.

It can also be argued that focus on these problem definitions may divert attention away from other major problems or contribute to lack of a more coherent overall framework for regulating the digital platforms and media pluralism. Van Dijck (2021), for example, has argued that the EU approach to platforms has failed to 'see the forest for the trees', because it has focused on individual issues, instead of a more holistic, principle-based approach. Similarly, other scholars have called for a more coherent overall approach to platform policy, driven by clearly defined normative principles and policy goals (Helberger 2020).

However, the point here is not to argue for one problem definition over the others, or to judge any of them as unfounded. The broader aim of the chapter is to illustrate that problem definitions do not emerge naturally, as neutral reflections of empirical reality, but they are social constructions, shaped by public debates, available metaphors and concepts, media coverage and individual events, and often different stakeholders' strategic attempts to frame policy debates in a particular way. These problem definitions also have influence on policy outcomes by guiding policy-makers considerations, available options, and legitimating policy approaches or evaluation criteria.

It has been noted before that policy discourses on technology tend to suffer from a more general problem of inconsistent or poorly defined policy aims and values, which can lead to regulatory complexities (Barrett et al. 2021). The public shock-driven nature of policy discourses, the influence of interest groups, reliance on metaphors, and the general uncertainty about future development of the digital media environment can all contribute to the problem of inconsistent problem definitions and objectives. Further discussion on the relationship between media pluralism and the digital platforms thus requires conceptual clarity as well as empirical research on the actual impact of proposed regulations.

REFERENCES

Ananny, Mike and Crawford, Kate (2018), 'Seeing without knowing: Limitations of the transparency ideal and its application to algorithmic accountability', *New Media & Society*, 20:3, pp. 973–89, https://doi.org/10.1177/1461444816676645.

Ananny, Mike and Gillespie, Tarleton (2017), *Public Platforms: Beyond the Cycle of Shocks and Exceptions*, Oxford: Oxford Internet Institute, http://blogs.oii.oxac.uk/ipp-conference/sites/ipp/files/documents/ananyGillespie-publicPlatforms-oii-submittedSept8.pdf. Accessed 19 January 2023.

August, Vincent and Osrecki, Fran (2019), 'Transparency imperatives: Results and frontiers of social science research', in V. August and F. Osrecki (eds), *Der Transparenz-Imperativ*, Wiesbaden: Springer VS, https://doi.org/10.1007/978-3-658-22294-9_1.

Bacchi, Carol (2009), *Analysing Policy: What's the Problem Represented to Be? Frenchs Forest*, Australia: Pearson.

Bacchi, Carol and Goodwin, Susan (2016), *Poststructural Policy Analysis: A Guide to Practice*, New York: Palgrave Macmillan.

Baker, C. Edwin (2007), *Media Concentration and Democracy: Why Ownership Matters*, New York: Cambridge University Press.

Barrett, Bridget, Dommett, Katharine and Kreiss, Daniel (2021), 'The capricious relationship between technology and democracy: Analyzing public policy discussions in the UK and US', *Policy and Internet*, 13:4, pp. 522–543, https://doi.org/10.1002/poi3.266.

Brogi, Elda (2020), 'The media pluralism monitor: Conceptualizing media pluralism for the online environment', *Profesional de la Información*, 29:5, p. e290529, https://doi.org/10.3145/epi.2020.sep.29.

Broughton Micova, Sally (2021), 'What is the harm in size', *CRRE Issue paper*, https://cerre.eu/publications/what-is-the-harm-in-size/. Accessed 19 January 2023.

Bruns, Axel (2021), 'Echo chambers? Filter bubbles? The misleading metaphors that obscure the real problem', in M. Pérez-Escolar and J. M. Noguera-Vivo (eds), *Hate Speech and Polarization in Participatory Society*, London: Routledge, n.pag.

Brüggeman, Michael, Humprech, Edda., Nielsen, Rasmus Kleis, Karppinen, Kari, Cornia, Alessio and Esser, Frank (2016), 'Framing the crisis of newspapers: How debates on the state of the press are shaped in Finland, France, Germany, Italy, United Kingdom and United States', *Journalism Studies,* 17:5, pp. 533–51, https://doi.org/10.1080/1461670X.2015.1006871.

Castells, Manuel (2007), 'Communication, power and counter-power in the network society', *International Journal of Communication,* 1:2007, pp. 238–66, https://ijoc.org/index.php/ijoc/article/view/46. Accessed 19 January 2023.

CMPF – Centre for Media Pluralism and Media Freedom (2021), *Monitoring media pluralism in the digital era. Application of the Media Pluralism Monitor in the European Union, Albania, Montenegro, Republic of North Macedonia, Serbia & Turkey in the year 2020,* Fiesole FI: European University Institute, https://cadmus.eui.eu/bitstream/handle/1814/71970/CMPF_MPM2021_final-report_QM-09-21-298-EN-N.pdf?sequence=1&isAllowed=y. Accessed 19 January 2023.

Council of Europe (2018a), *Recommendation CM/Rec (2018)1 of the Committee of Ministers on media pluralism and transparency of media ownership.* Adopted by the Committee of Ministers on 7 March 2018, Strasbourg. https://rm.coe.int/0900001680790e13. Accessed 19 January 2023.

Council of Europe (2018b), *Recommendation CM/Rec(2018)2 of the Committee of Ministers to member States on the roles and responsibilities of internet intermediaries.* Adopted by the Committee of Ministers on 7 March 2018. https://rm.coe.int/1680790e14. Accessed 19 January 2023.

Council of Europe (2018c), *Algorithms and Human Rights. Study on the Human Rights Dimensions of Automated Data Processing Techniques (in Particular Algorithms) And Possible Regulatory Implications.* Prepared by the Committee of Experts on Internet Intermediaries (Msi-Net), Strasbourg. https://rm.coe.int/algorithms-and-human-rights-en-rev/16807956b5. Accessed 19 January 2023.

Council of Europe (2019), *Declaration by the Committee of Ministers on the financial sustainability of quality journalism in the digital age.* Adopted by the Committee of Ministers on 13 February 2019, Strasbourg, https://rm.coe.int/090000168092dd4d. Accessed 19 January 2023.

Craufurd Smith, Rachael, Klimkiewicz, Beata and Ostling, Alina (2021), 'Media ownership transparency in Europe: Closing the gap between European aspiration and domestic reality', *European Journal of Communication,* 36:6, pp. 547–62, https://doi.org/10.1177/0267323121999523.

Diakopoulos, Nicholas (2016), 'Accountability in algorithmic decision making', *Communications of the ACM (CACM),* 59:2, pp. 56–62, https://doi.org/10.1145/2844110.

European Commission (2007), *Indicators for Media Pluralism in the Member States – Towards a Risk-Based Approach.* Tender Specifications. SMART 007A2007/0002. Brussels, March 2007.

European Commission (2020a), *Europe's Media in the Digital Decade: An Action Plan to Support Recovery and Transformation,* Communication from the Commission to the European Parliament, the Council, the European Economic and Social Committee and the Committee of the Regions, COM(2020) 784 final, Brussels, 3 December.

European Commission (2020b), *On the European Democracy Action Plan. Communication from the Commission to the European Parliament, the Council, the European Economic and Social Committee and the Committee of the Regions*, COM/2020/790 final, Brussels, 3 December.

European Commission (2020c), *Proposal for a Regulation of the European Parliament and of the Council on a Single Market For Digital Services (Digital Services Act) and Amending Directive 2000/31/EC*, COM(2020) 825 final, Brussels, 15 December.

Fischer, Frank (2003), *Reframing Public Policy: Discursive Politics and Deliberative Practices*, Oxford: Oxford University Press.

Flew, Terry, Martin, Fiona and Suzor, Nicolas (2019), 'Internet regulation as media policy: Rethinking the question of digital communication platform governance', *Journal of Digital Media & Policy*, 10:1, pp. 33–50.

Flew, Terry and Wilding, Derek (2021), 'The turn to regulation in digital communication: The ACCC's digital platforms inquiry and Australian media policy', *Media, Culture & Society*, 43:1, pp. 48–65.

Freedman, Des (2010), 'Media policy silences: The hidden face of communications decision making', *International Journal of Press/Politics*, 15:3, pp. 344–61, https://doi.org/10.1177/1940161210368292.

Freelon, Deen and Wells, Chris (2020), 'Disinformation as political communication', *Political Communication*, 37:2, pp. 145–56.

Helberger, Natali (2018), 'Challenging diversity – Social media platforms and a new conception of media diversity', in Martin Moore and Damian Tambini (eds), *Digital Dominance: The Power of Google, Amazon, Facebook and Amazon*, New York: Oxford University Press, pp. 153–75.

Helberger, Natali (2020), 'The political power of platforms. How current attempts to regulate misinformation amplify opinion power', *Digital Journalism*, 8:6, pp. 842–54.

Horten, Monica (2016), *The Closing of the Net*, Cambridge: Polity Press.

Karppinen, Kari (2013), *Rethinking Media Pluralism*, New York: Fordham University Press.

Kenyon, Andrew (2021), *Democracy of Expression: Positive Free Speech and Law*, Cambridge: Cambridge University Press.

Kingdon, John W. (2003), *Agendas, Alternatives, and Public Policies*, 2nd ed., New York: Longman.

Klimkiewicz, Beata (2019), *Pluralism in a Hybrid Media Environment from the User Perspective*, Fiesole FI: European University Institute, https://cadmus.eui.eu/bitstream/handle/1814/65604/CMPF_2019_02.pdf?sequence=4&isAllowed=y. Accessed 19 January 2023.

KU Leuven–ICRI (2009), *Independent Study on Indicators for Media Pluralism – Towards a Risk-Based Approach*, Belgium: European Commission, https://ec.europa.eu/information_society/media_taskforce/doc/pluralism/pfr_report.pdf. Accessed 19 January 2023.

Morozov, Evgeny (2013), *To Save Everything, Click Here: The Folly of Technological Solutionism*, New York: Public Affairs.

Napoli, Philip M. (2011), 'Exposure diversity reconsidered', *Journal of Information Policy*, 1, pp. 246–59.

Nenadic, Iva (2019), 'To understand media pluralism is to understand changes in news media and journalism advanced by digital technologies', in A. Giannakopoulos (ed.), *Media, Freedom of Speech, andDemocracy in the EU and Beyond*, Research Paper No. 10, The S. Daniel Abraham Center for International and Regional Studies, Tel Aviv: Tel Aviv University.

Nenadic, Iva and Milosavljevic, Marko (2021), 'Regulating beyond media to protect media pluralism: The EU media policies as seen through the lens of the media pluralism monitor', in S. Adam Matei, F. Rebillard and F. Rochelandet (eds), *Digital and Social Media Regulation*, London: Palgrave, pp. 89–116.

Pasquale, Frank (2016), *The Black Box Society: The Secret Algorithms That Control Money and Information*, Cambridge and London: Harvard University Press.

Picard, Robert (2017), 'The Sisyphean Pursuit of media pluralism: European efforts to establish policy and measurable evidence', *Communication Law and Policy*, 22:3, pp. 255–73.

Stohl, Cynthia, Stohl, Michael and Leonardi, Paul M. (2016), 'Managing opacity: Information visibility and the paradox of transparency in the digital age', *International Journal of Communication*, 10:2016, pp. 123–37.

Valcke, Peggy, Sukosd, Robert and Picard, Robert (eds) (2015), *Media Pluralism and Diversity: Concepts, Risks and Global Trends*, London: Palgrave Macmillan.

Van Dijk, José (2021), 'Seeing the forest for the trees: Visualizing platformization and its governance', *New Media & Society*, 23:9, pp. 2801–19.

Vīķe-Freiberga, Vaira, Däubler-Gmelin, Herta, Hammersley, Ben and Poiares Pessoa Maduro, Luis Miguel (2013), *A Free and Pluralistic Media to Sustain European Democracy: The Report of the High Level Group on Media Freedom and Pluralism*, Brussels: European Commission, https://ec.europa.eu/information_society/media_taskforce/doc/pluralism/hlg/hlg_final_report.pdf. Accessed 19 January 2023.

Zelizer, Barbie (2015), 'Terms of choice: Uncertainty, journalism, and crisis', *Journal of Communication*, 65:5, pp. 888–908.

Zuiderveen Borgesius, Frederik J., Trilling, Damian, Möller, Judith, Bodó, Balázs, de Vreese, Clas H. and Helberger, Natali (2016), 'Should we worry about filter bubbles?', *Internet Policy Review*, 5:1, https://doi.org/10.14763/2016.1.401.

5

Automation, News and Social Media Pluralism

Jonathon Hutchinson, Tim Dwyer and Derek Wilding

Introduction

In this chapter, we assess the impact of automation on the production, distribution and consumption of news media, with particular attention placed on how this is undertaken within non-commercial contexts alongside increasingly visible commercial, platformized versions. We contend that over the past decade, social media platforms have created their own publishing environment within the broader digital media environment in which information is created and shared. This rapidly changing context brings with it important implications for voice plurality and wider assessments of news diversity. The impact of this ecosystem's evolution has resulted in not only a shift in how news is produced but also how it is produced for new platform-specific affordances such as visibility, shareability and what we frame here as algorithmic suitability. Algorithmic suitability is the process that online content producers engage in to ensure their work is not only published across a variety of platforms but it also aligns with the ever-changing visibility dynamics of these platforms: news production for an 'algorithm imaginary' as Bucher (2016) would argue.

In commercial media spaces, algorithmic suitability has become common place for online content producers to ensure their efforts are seen by as many individuals as possible. There are a number of techniques that are employed by online content producers to ensure their work lines up with the unseen aspects of platform infrastructures such as the algorithms that drive the numerous versions of user 'feeds'. These include the 'up next', 'recommended for you' or 'others are watching' types of content suggesting mechanisms that attract the majority of views across platforms. While this practice has been successfully implemented within the broader cultural production sphere (Hutchinson 2019, 2021), it also extends across news production in a more contemporary sense.

In this chapter, we therefore locate social media diversity within the operations and practices in the contemporary digital media ecosystem. As we will reveal in detail, the availability of social media diversity lies not with one single entity alone – the producer, the consumer or the platform. Rather, it is a combination of all three agents working together that allows specific media diversity diets to be offered. While a number of current debates suggest an important role of platforms is to shape content visibility for continued plurality (van de Bulck and Moe 2017; Sørensen and Schmidt 2016), there are other aspects to this discussion indicating that users take a more active role in curating their own experiences (Lingel 2021; Stepnik 2019). We argue that it is a combination of platforms, together with users, directing to what extent a diverse media experience is contextually attainable. In those situations where there is media diversity failure, we argue that public service media can make available news curation processes to educate and inform citizens on public affairs issues.

In the chapter, we identify examples of content production and consumption practices that have emerged as platforms continue to dominate the digital media space (Moore and Tambini 2018). We first highlight how audiences have changed and been shaped by platforms and their affordances, to create new forms of audiences, communities and ad-hoc-publics (Bruns and Burgess 2015; Bruns 2019). These digital media uses and their consumption have arisen in concert with the technological. In the next section, we investigate how media production itself has shifted to accomodate the digital consumption practices across social media platforms. It is through the exploration of audiences and producers that we can begin to understand how producers, users and platforms are in a continual dance with each other to negotiate, interpret, renegotiate and develop new understandings and knowledge. Finally, we connect these practices with news production processes and focus on YouTubers who have integrated their journalistic practices within contemporary digital media production and consumption.

A changing automated news environment

The news media environment is continually evolving as new technologies emerge, adapt and become enmeshed with the news cycle. We have seen an expansion in the forms of automation (Thurman et al. 2018), the integration of bots as news creators and distributors (Guzman 2019; Ford and Hutchinson 2021), and increasing use of metrics that drive compounding kinds of automation practices (Peterson-Salahuddin and Diakopolous 2020). What had previously been described as a turn to a holistic user-focused media environment during the mid

2000s (Jenkins 2006; Bruns 2008) has evolved beyond that demotic moment (Turner 2010) to a realization of how everyday users are now creating content in innovative ways that incorporates these automation practices.

What has been described as the platformization of cultural production (Nieborg and Poell 2018; Neiborg et al. 2021) encapsulates how these practices have been influenced, and continue to influence, the technological environment in which they operate. At the core of this argument is the emerging field of algorithmic visibility, which provides an account of how users are implementing techniques to increase their visibility across social media platforms (Bishop 2019; Petre et al. 2019). YouTube has the lure of increased socio-cultural and economic capital for its content producers as many monetize their content through increased views. Instagram provides users the option to 'swipe up' on a user's Reels which is only available to those users who attract large audiences. Twitter has even experimented with 'Super Followers' as a means of attracting monetization to the platform and its users, especially its content producers (Kim 2021). While platforms continue to shift and change how they attract producers and users to their content, the commonality is that they are all providing some kind of variation that integrates a technological affordance to connect users around the content. Often, these affordances are built on automated systems and processes.

Frequently these infrastructures are unseen and operate in the background of a user's purview. The infrastructures that determine how content is produced, published, distributed and ultimately consumed are all captured by the digital intermediation process. Digital intermediation is the combination of:

1. *Technologies* – the physical devices such as smart phones but also, and more importantly, the databases, sensors, interoperability systems and processing units that parse the data through our communication systems;
2. *Institutions* – digital agencies that promote the visibility of content but also the regulatory systems and cultural institutions that are part of the social media ecosystem; and
3. *Automation* – the processes and technologies that are intangible, such as algorithms, machine learning and artificial intelligence that drive the physical intermediation devices within cultural production (Hutchinson 2021).

The automation aspect of digital intermediation is of particular interest here in that it directs how the technologies will be presented to their users. These kinds of mechanisms, that were highlighted above, are often based on a user's past activities, the network of the users' friends, and may also include the enterprise characteristics of the facilitating platform (Gillespie 2010). In other words, the content that I am exposed to as a suggested video is based on what I have previously watched, what my friends are watching (based on my Google contacts) and also whichever channels and online content producers YouTube is highlighting at that moment. It is this temporal mechanism that suggests popularity has become a significant measure for visibility across platforms.

Virality is a useful measure here, which is also the backbone for how social media platforms operate. Dwyer and Martin (2019) argue, 'Social media platforms need content to go viral – it's an important element of their business models to encourage people to boost content, and especially content which might signal widespread, commonly held tastes and interests' (260). Yet the paradox of this moment is that virality is dependent on visibility, which is the communication processes associated with platformization. The social media logics (van Dijck et al. 2018) are embedded within the content which in turn makes that content valuable, shareable and visible. Dwyer and Martin go further to argue:

> News media visibility then accelerates and extends a story's spread, and gives it further legitimacy, ensuring further circulation beyond the original social networks. A loop like this ensures that there is a steady stream of virtual news media events making its way into the news feeds of any platform that uses algorithmic curation. So our choice of which events to share becomes a kind of 'best of' selection, influencing the velocity at which stories diffuse, and the overall reach into the myriad of internet-worked distribution platforms.
>
> (260)

In the scenario outlined above, the concept of platformization underpins how content is not only shared but also how it is created by the online content producers who make the works. Platformization, according to Nieborg and Poell (2018: 4275) is, 'the penetration of economic and infrastructural extensions of online platforms into the web, affecting the production, distribution, and circulation of cultural content'. It is fair to argue, then, that online content producers are exposed to a range of changes and adjustments that platform providers make to their digital offering. It promotes an environment that is constantly in a state of flux; where online content producers, and the audiences for that matter, are similarly adjusting to these changes. Arriagada and Ibáñez (2020: 1) note that these platform disruptions for content creators can be defined in three ways: 'in the form of communicative styles, as a sense of temporal acceleration, and as a constant negotiation with other actors in the social network through which commercial activities are configured.' As such, these three driving disruptions ensure online content creators are continually evolving to align with the platforms that host and make visible their content.

With this as a backdrop, content creators need to adopt and then adjust how they undertake their weekly, or daily, practices and align these with the affordances of social media platforms. In this engagement process around the content creation, there are three distinct stakeholder groups engaging in cultural production: the online content creators, the audience and the platform. Under the guise of platformization, as one of the actors adjust, correspondingly, so too do the others. For example, should those who work at the platform provider discern that the audience is becoming more interested in certain videos then the platform will tweak the visibility of that category. Online content producers will then create content with relevant elements to accomodate that aspect of visibility; and audiences will then be exposed to increased levels of that preferred content. It is clear there is a dynamic relationship between these three actors, and this scenario can play out across a variety of genres and sub-genres on social media. Importantly, it raises further issues around the extent to which diversity of content is available on social media platforms, and how that might take shape.

It is instructive if we take a detour and focus on YouTube as a key platform that embodies the actor relationships highlighted above. The role of the algorithm has an increased ability to shape and determine what becomes visible to users; and thereby potentially influencing what users are interested in and continue to view. If we examine the top video categories on YouTube to demonstrate how the relationship operates, we can highlight why popular content creators create the content that they do, within the context of increased visibility. The top five content categories of 2021 on YouTube were Gaming, Make-up & Beauty, Reviews & Unboxing, ASMR (or so-called 'Autonomous Sensory Meridian Response') and Vlogging. At the time of writing, these are the YouTube categories that attract the most video contributions by content creators, and they are also the same categories that receive the highest amounts of engagement (YouTube, 2021) – in other words, there is a direct correlation between production and consumption. If a content producer is aspiring to reach new audiences, it makes sense that they align with these already well-established categories and create content that provides them with the best opportunity to increase their viewership and therefore, their visibility.

This is the exact scenario the YouTuber Derek Muller highlights in the video 'My video went viral. Here's why' (5.2 million views) posted to his channel, *Veritasium*. In this video, the creator talks about an earlier video that went viral and why that video was pushed in front of more viewers by the YouTube platform over the many other videos he has produced for the platform. In the video, it is explained that because of the high level of content that is published to the platform, approximately 500 hours every minute (YouTube 2021), users are essentially 'ignorant' to most of the content on the platform as there is too much content available on the platform for any single person to consume. Yet it is precisely as a result of this level of saturation of media content that the

YouTube algorithm is in place to help users navigate the catalogue of extensive content by tailoring their interests to all of the available content that is published on YouTube. Muller further explains the presence of three stakeholders (albeit not conceived as in the digital intermediation framework but nonetheless the same actors) – the audience, the content creators and the algorithm – and describes how they are consistently chasing each other to discern what the other two stakeholders are interested in. Finally, in McLuhanesque-like overtones, Muller suggests that in fact the algorithm becomes the point of interest that both creators and audiences are watching. Both the process of digital intermediation and Muller's personal experience demonstrate how platformization and popularization play an integral role in how content is made visible, consumed by audiences, and then shared amongst their networks.

News too is subject to elements of this dynamic platform environment, especially on YouTube, which can potentially be a significant issue for this particular form of content creation. While there has been a parallel broader industrial shift from journalism to other forms of entertainment types of roles (Sherwood and O'Donnell 2018), there remains a systemic underlying 'winner-takes-all' issue for online content creators seeking increased visibility. In these scenarios, the intervention of specific cultural institutions is required to engage publics around diverse and public affairs content selection, beyond what is simply deemed algorithmically popular by the judgement of a social media platform. In economic terms, this is a market failure space where public service media is well positioned to interpolate audiences. From a media diversity and pluralism perspective, it represents a crucial opportunity for public media to be proactive. It thus ensures that users of these services have access to, and are able to engage with, media from a variety of perspectives and voices. But, as we have argued in this section, it is not as simple as just starting a channel on YouTube and growing an audience: it calls for a strategic and considered process to address these inherent risks of operating on commercial social media platforms such as YouTube.

When should PSM engage this environment? The case for algorithmic PSM

Before examining specific news case studies on YouTube, it is useful to reflect on how *public media organizations* can play a role in media diversity across increasingly automated systems of our platformed societies. Public media organizations are a very particular style of organization in that they are not designed to generate profits, but rather, they perform a specific public service purpose. In a Reithian sense, this is to *inform, educate and entertain*, but this approach has been required to evolve in the constantly changing environment of public media. Coupled with consistent attacks from conservative governments (Barnett 2021), public service media has had to dramatically shift beyond the market failure model (Tracey 1998) and toward one of increased digital presence (Debrett 2010) and indeed innovative practices (Hutchinson 2017). Now, the need for public service media to address and respond to an algorithmic media era is very clear.

As outlined in the section above, content is called to be created in an 'algorithm-ready' capacity – something that Bucher (2017) argues is an imagined algorithm: an action where we might expect how an algorithm behaves and treats certain media production accordingly. But what does that mean when it is something that is not as tangible as media, but rather resembles the characteristics of a culture? Ted Striphas (2015) signposts the terrain of 'algorithmic culture' as inevitable, and yet potentially problematic for digital societies if incorrectly managed by the institutions who facilitate media and culture. Public media are increasing their use of algorithms to produce content, and, more importantly, to publish and distribute its content. Sorensen and Hutchinson (2018) have explored some of the European public media's adoption of automated media recommender systems while also highlighting a number of issues that require addressing to avoid media populism and maintain its core public service remit. In their research they found that algorithms do not necessarily solve curatorial problems, but rather can be effective *alongside* or as a complement to human judgement. What remains key though, is transparency in how decisions are being made through PSM recommender systems.

Ford and Hutchinson (2021) focused on the efforts of the Australian Broadcasting Corporation (ABC) and its 'ChatBot' News Messenger Service. In this work, they argued that the chatbot is not only a form of algorithmic journalism, but an innovative method for public service media to educate its audience on effective information retrieval within an increasingly automated media environment. For the most part, the automated chatbot is now operated by ABC journalists but it does draw on a database of automated responses when communicating with its users.

In both of these examples (which are also available to private media of course), we can see public service media using strategic approaches to address, and to some extent mitigate, the negative effects of an algorithmic culture. Digital intermediation is a key aspect of an 'algorithmic PSM': it is an approach to embody the core principles of public media, while positioning it within the new large-scale algorithmic processes in our platformed societies. It has the potential to level out what Striphas calls out as 'elite culture' in lieu of public culture. Algorithmic PSM, with a digital intermediation process, enables PSM organizations to remain visible across a number of social media platforms, especially visually based platforms dominated by social influencers such as Instagram and YouTube – and thus, strengthens its universal reach and appeal. Instead of publishing and distributing content that is simply commercially motivated on these platforms, algorithmic PSM embodies the processes and dynamics of cultural and digital intermediation to distribute socially relevant content for the maintenance of a more democratized public sphere.

The contemporary media ecology no-longer addresses a single capital 'P' public but rather a number of fragmented and niche audiences across multiple platforms with specialist interests. At its best, this is the strength of algorithmic media – to connect specific media content with interested audiences. But we have also seen the ugly side of unchecked and inappropriate algorithmic media through oppression and bias, politics, disinformation and discrimination through design. Critical algorithmic studies have highlighted that there is immense political power in how information infrastructure shapes our social and cultural lives: algorithms have become brokers in our social and connective lives as Tania Bucher notes (2018). Similarly, Safiya Umoja Noble (2018: 1) lays out a strong human rights critique of artificial intelligence use and how it can be the basis for social inequality through 'technological redlining'. She argues algorithmic use, particularly through automated decision making systems creates and deepens 'inequalities by race... just because [users] are Black or Latino'.

The 2018 report released by the AI Now Institute highlighted that the technology industries, especially those creating and developing algorithms and automated decision-making systems, are predominantly filled by white males, inherently limiting the diversity and application of these technologies (Whittaker et al. 2018). This environment, which presents itself often through recommender systems, is in stark contrast to the approach of public media that creates media to celebrate diversity and encourage a cohesive society, among other purposes. However, recently we have seen social cohesion movements in the platform space with the collective de-platforming of users such as former US President, Donald Trump, 'due to the risk of further incitement of violence' as Twitter notes on its blog (Twitter Inc. 2021: n.pag.). Through these sorts of actions, there is a glimmer of hope that platforms may begin to exercise more care in the media they host and consider its implications, especially when under immense public pressure.

Sørensen and Schmidt (2016) have documented the emergence of algorithms within PSM, particularly in Europe, as one of the key areas where PSM can address a universality problem. But how can we move beyond PSM simply *using* algorithms and towards a more nuanced algorithmic PSM? The most important opportunity of algorithmic PSM is demonstrated through its increased reach (availability) and applicability (appeal) of content with high public value. Public service broadcasting has its own specific remit that promotes social cohesion, along with a history of creating media that is built on the foundations of its value system. PSM values include characteristics such as distance from vested interests, program maker independence, cultural and public sphere development, providing voices for minority groups, and provision for innovative digital programs and services (Tracey 1998).

In all of this discussion, the idea of personal media becomes critical to revisit. That is not to argue that we are all existing in so-called filter bubbles or echo chambers (Pariser 2011), and more nuanced scholarly literature has suggested a problematized relation to networks (Bruns 2019; Margetts et al. 2021). Rather, we are experiencing a moment that has highly personalized media experiences that hone our preferences and likes to present media in a personalized approach. van de Bulck and Moe (2017) draw on the work of Thurman and Schifferes (2012) to draw out the kinds of personalization that can be both explicit and implicit in media:

> Explicit personalisation involves a user making deliberate choices before receiving content, for example, asking news aggregator Google News to focus only on sports. Implicit personalisation is done by algorithms that process traces of previous choices to build a base for future personalisation, for example, through contextual recommendations, geo-tagging or filtering.
>
> (879)

What is important in this assessment of personalization is the lack of ability for users to be able to choose their own way through the automation process. It is a lack of transparency that inhibits a user's agency to direct the explicit kinds of personalization that they need. Within an automated media experience more broadly, users are denied any kind of 'lever' to adjust their automated lives; instead, they are presented with an interface that incorporates the three actors' perspectives that were outlined earlier (online content creators, the audience and the platform) into one general content feed. This may well be the space for public media to intersect with the overall automated media environment, continuing to provide that a broad and diverse media experience is maintained for users of these platforms.

There is work underway that is attempting to understand how recommenders can present a variety of content through randomization, serendipity and diversity. For example, Hellberger and Burri have worked on diversity as a media policy tool where they integrate a public media perspective noting it could, 'be a means for the public service media to gently nudge the audience toward making more diverse choices, based on their personal preferences and viewing habits' (2015: 1321). The challenge, not only for public media but for online content producers broadly, which includes journalists, is to balance the interests of media personalization by way of pluralistic diets.

Cultural intermediaries, influence and visibility

In the original Bourdieu (1984) sense, cultural intermediaries are those individuals located within the cultural production space, as agents to transfer knowledge and calibrate cultural understandings. Cultural intermediaries translate cultural media texts for broader audiences; for example, they might highlight the significance of the opera to a folk music fan or describe a pop culture phenomenon to someone unfamiliar with such a form. They operate at the boundaries of cultural production, increasing the significance of the creative industries. They contribute to the overall market effectiveness of those industries and champion the individual roles that emerge within these spaces. In this context, we can argue that in addition to traditional ideas around the democratic contribution to knowledge, news or public affairs creators have much to offer the society in which they operate. In this sense, cultural intermediaries enable multiple stakeholders to participate in societies by acknowledging, understanding and speaking through specific media texts.

Cultural intermediaries have also been articulated in a number of other ways within the creative industries. In each instance, they have taken on translation roles within advertising and marketing (Kelly 2014), fashion (Skov 2014), journalism (Smith Maguire and Mathews 2012) and hospitality (Ocejo 2014). Other scholars have argued that the role of the cultural intermediary has moved beyond the market-based operator (Negus 2010) and towards a socially engaged agent as a 'third wave cultural intermediary' (Perry et al. 2015: 724). In the latest iteration of the concept of cultural intermediaries, Hutchinson (2017) focuses on the networked communication arena to suggest that they can operate as influential agents amongst both large and niche audiences, across a number of social media platforms.

Into this networked media context, and in distinction to debates around internet-worked platforms or applications as digital intermediaries, the concept of cultural intermediaries' work as agential communication within emerging media ecosystems can add additional nuance. For example, a social influencer will produce content for a number of platforms for specific purposes because their audiences are present across several of them: TikTok for short videos, Twitter for text-based conversations and Facebook for commerce are but a few examples of why content is presented differently for each platform, from the same content creator. This suggests that a cultural intermediary as a social influencer will create material for the same moment to suit Instagram, YouTube, Snapchat, the podcast, the magazine, the Netflix series and so on and so forth. The cultural intermediary can be labelled as a digital first personality (Hutchinson 2019), suggesting they build their status as a social influencer first and then develop their celebrity status second. In building a paratext persona, social media enables users to create a public identity to increase their exposure for increased social and economic capital. This has been previously analyzed through the lens of persona studies, which 'describes the wider practice of constructing and constituting forms of public identity, with celebrities providing some of the most visible, performative and pedagogic examples of the practice' (Marshall et al. 2019: 289). In the persona studies context, we begin to understand how digital content creation can be organized and monetized.

Abidin (2016), for instance, highlights the platform-specific practice through the lens of influencer studies, arguing that:

> Influencers are everyday, ordinary Internet users who accumulate a relatively large following on blogs and social media through the textual and visual narration of their personal lives and lifestyles, engage with their following in digital and physical spaces, and monetise their following by integrating 'advertorials' into their blog or social media posts.
>
> (Abidin 2016: 1)

Abidin invokes the work of Senft (2013) and Marwick (2013) and their usage of the concepts of microcelebrity, digital traces and visibility. For Senft, microcelebrity is 'a new style of online performance in which people employ webcams, video, audio, blogs, and social networking sites to "amp up" their popularity among readers, viewers and those to whom they are linked online' (Senft 2008: 25). In this sense, influencers are using the affordances of social media to produce a specific style of media and address niche audiences to grow their popularity, while increasing their remuneration potential. Marwick locates this type of activity in the attention economy, which she notes, 'treats visibility as status, [and] makes it important for anyone who hopes to succeed in the technology industry to live at least somewhat in the public eye' (2013: 143).

In her evidence as a witness before the UK's House of Commons' Digital, Culture, Sport and Media Committee reference on 'Influencer Culture', Abidin responded to questions by providing the Committee with an argument linking platforms, influencer culture, scale and visibility, noting,

> We also need to remember that many influencers these days are not very visible to us. We need to think about the under-the-radar platforms, TikTok algorithms that do not show you exactly what is out there [...] subscription-only models where you need to pay to access this content [...] messaging groups that can fit between 1,000 and 4,000 people and have lots of influential people that the major news outlets don't even know about because they are all gated communities. To respond to the question, in terms of scalability, we need to consider what platform we are looking at. For a small-scale subscription platform, someone with 1,000 influencers may be

a mega-influencer because everyone in that space listens and responds to them. If you are on a more public platform like YouTube, surely you need to be somewhere 1 million and above to be considered one of the mega-influencers.

Abidin's evidence also provided the Committee members with a useful take on the term 'influencer':

> What is really packed into the word 'influencer'? We are implying that it is not just a person creating content but they are relying on their personal selves as a brand. They are showing their lives and having to put their lifestyles out there in order to gain a following, which is so different from a content creator who is only working on games and focused on something external to them.

Our previous research in South Korea has revealed a similar cultural intermediary framework in terms of *personal selves as brand* within the South Korean Mukbang phenomena; they are an example of online content creators who have pioneered online content creation techniques for other creators, comparable to the news creators we consider in this chapter. The South Korean BJs (Broadcast Jockeys) embody the cultural intermediary role and explain the joy and satisfaction they experience through broadcasting their eating experiences (Anon. 2017). They engage social networks to amplify their popularity, collaborate with other Mukbang influencers to increase their visibility, and ultimately influence their increasingly large audiences. Their hyper-visibility amongst their peers is evidence of successful media careers, where they perform their digital first personalities, moving easily between platforms to engage their temporal and transient audiences.

Online content creators, visibility and media diversity

In discussing news creators as a specific genre of online content creators, it is important to more fully describe the digital and networked environment in which online cultural intermediaries operate. As we have outlined, online content creators often work across multiple platforms and engage as cultural intermediaries to add value to the content they create, and to also demonstrate how cultural production inscribes particular values for broader audiences. However, this activity is to some extent blurred if the content creators do not 'mark out' audiences to have their content seen. To understand this from a content creator perspective, it is useful to briefly explore relevant algorithmic visibility and digital intermediation literature.

Sophie Bishop, in her 2019 *New Media & Society* article, argues that online content creators are playing 'the visibility game'; they adopt a series of navigation strategies to ensure that their content is seen across commercial social media platforms. Through this research, Bishop is highlighting the broader observation that online content creators are hedging their careers, and therefore livelihoods, on commercial platforms that tend to be opaque, and can change how content appears to audiences with little to no advanced warning notifications. It would be fair to observe that intermediation is occurring via both the platform and the content creator. In that sense, online content creators are consistently monitoring, negotiating and adjusting their work (Petre et al. 2019) to ensure their content remains relevant to the platform algorithm and does not become buried in the unconsumable quantity of content on the YouTube platform especially (Bódo et al. 2018).

As outlined above, platform media environments are saturated with media content – one recent calculation of YouTube has 720,000 hours of content uploaded every day; 83 per cent of TikTok's 1 billion monthly users regularly post videos; over 1000 photos are posted to Instagram every second; and Facebook remains constant as it generates 4 petabytes of data per day (SocialBlade 2021). While these are only a handful of examples of social media platforms, the content creation and publishing numbers are staggering and reinforce that no human will ever be able to watch, read, listen and engage with all the content that is created and published. This is the point where visibility becomes a critical moment that digital intermediation attempts to address. Digital intermediation's automation aspect especially assists users in finding content that is relevant to their interests and that they, and the connections in their networks, are likely to find of interest. Digital intermediation presents multiple challenges, especially in terms of media plurality.

News YouTubers and digital intermediation

To understand how news producers have positioned themselves alongside the platform affordances outlined above, we begin our analysis not by using the YouTube channels of established news providers but instead we focus on three specific case studies; we argue that they demonstrate important elements of the algorithmic visibility and digital intermediation affordances we have already outlined. While they have a focus on more culturally specific items that are consistent with social media platforms more broadly, they are very much addressing the news cycle, engaging in journalistic-like practices, but not necessarily following conventions that are typically associated with 'capital J' journalism.

The first of these news YouTubers is based on the West Coast of the United States. Philip DeFranco blends Hollywood-style entertainment alongside journalism to bring contemporary news items to his audiences, drawing on his team of researchers to produce a daily news channel, *The Philip DeFranco Show* (see Figure 5.1). The second case study shifts geographically to the United Kingdom to explore the endeavours of another celebrity news commentator – Russell Brand. While it might be argued that Brand is purely a celebrity phenomenon, his interest in sharing news and information with his audience on YouTube supported by his podcast, demonstrates that he brings journalistic techniques to report on the critical and newsworthy items of the day. The third case study examines Australian YouTuber, Jordan Shanks who operates the YouTube channel, friendlyjordies, not only because he occupies similar terrain to the other two YouTuber news creators but also because the creator has himself become a controversial and partisan figure in national politics. In each case study, it will become clear how these news online content creators are deftly using available platform affordances, while also engaging with public affairs journalism.

Philip DeFranco is 'an American news commentator and YouTube personality' (Crunchbase 2021), and this definition demonstrates the role of a journalist in this YouTube space is augmenting a traditional journalistic role with that of a digital first personality. DeFranco's catch cry is 'Sup ya beautiful bastards' followed by 'smash that like button to feed the algorithm gods' every time he starts a video in a trademark rhetorical flourish to welcome his fans back. The tag line is itself an acknowledgment of the impact of the YouTube algorithm overtly on his channel,

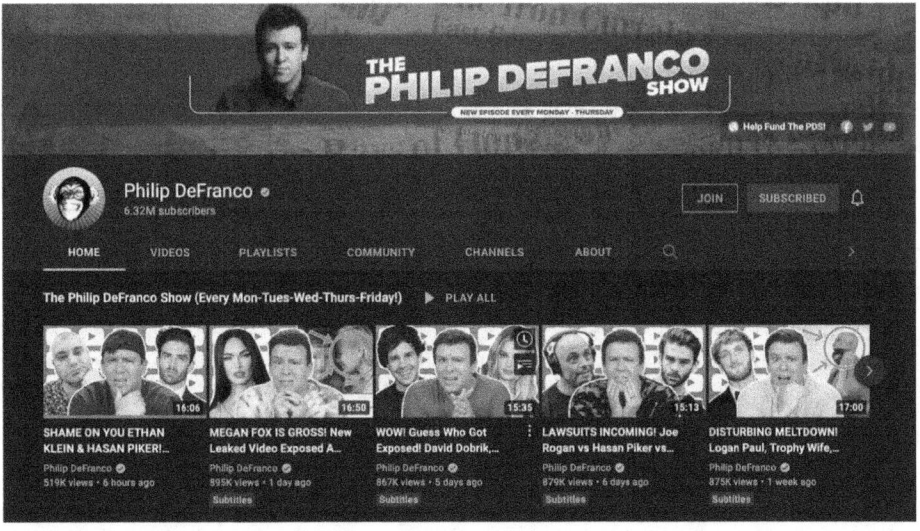

FIGURE 5.1: The Philip DeFranco show's YouTube page.

The Philip DeFranco Show. He appears hyper-aware of the algorithm to the extent that he often creates two videos for the day: the first is an algorithm-friendly video (safe poster image, clean video title, non-contentious material), and the second is the same video only with the more contentious material added. In this DeFranco acknowledges that the YouTube algorithm will bury contentious material, while alerting his audience to the inevitable impact from automated curation. He typically will direct his audience to the second video in his first, leveraging his own visibility to increase the views of the content that does not align so well with the YouTube algorithm. For DeFranco, his knowledge of the YouTube algorithm drives his approach towards content creation and news commentary.

While there are many takes on how to drive engagement to a YouTube channel, including from YouTube's own Creator blog, the social media management platform Hootsuite offers very useful insights into how to drive engagement on YouTube. It provides five steps:

1. Use effective thumbnail images for your video, with text.
2. Don't make the video about the creator, but about the interests of the audience.
3. React to trends, or be newsworthy.
4. Collaborate with other creators.
5. Track the performance through metrics and analytics (Hootsuite 2021).

While these strategies are mainly aimed at public relations and marketing campaigns, the key strategies can be seen throughout DeFranco's work. His thumbnail is consistently familiar and indicates who he will be talking about or with, complete with informative text and video titles. He covers content that can be described as contemporary public affairs, and he often engages with other collaborators to increase his audience size and engagement. Each of his videos is typically around the 15-minute mark, which is broadly consistent with the recommendations from YouTube for a suitable length for a video. According to SocialBlade, DeFranco is a B+ ranked YouTuber, with 6.32 million subscribers, 1.6 billion video views, 61st in their News Rank and earns approximately between $90,000 and $1.4 million USD per year (Social Blade 2021).

DeFranco can blend contemporary internet news items with an entertaining edge in a way that takes breaking news and then adds more detail and background. To do this, he will often use a controversial news item from the preceding 24 hours – that could be a major political moment in the United States, a key moment in internet culture such as influencer events, or perhaps a story that fits into the broader news cycle such as COVID-19, or some other coverage of public interest issues. DeFranco and his team will take a journalistic approach towards the news coverage by employing standard elements of journalism reportage – newsworthiness, neutral fact explanation, inverted pyramid story construction and a translation role of public issues for his broader audience. DeFranco as a news YouTuber brings his interpretative perspective to the journalism, adding context and background to these issues for his younger and entirely digital audience of news consumers.

Now we turn our attention to the United Kingdom and consider the journalistic practices of Russell Brand. In his 'Welcome to my YouTube Channel' video, Brand asks, 'What's this channel about? Well it's basically me breaking down the news, providing you with information you won't get on mainstream media analysed from a perspective of a man who's been on the inside'. In many ways, Brand is embodying the role of the typical news translator for his audiences, but which is then heavily doused with his opinion to add commentary or an explanatory layer for those who seek a 'Brand-esque' take on news events of the day. The channel has 6.39 million subscribers, over 993 million video views and has estimated yearly earnings of between $120,000 and $1.9 million USD (Social Blade 2023).

How can we describe Brand's influencer news style? Well significantly, his 'news update' commentaries can also frequently incorporate mainstream media breaking news items. For instance, in the lead up to Christmas 2021, *Russell Brand* released a video titled 'Is this a Joke: Boris' Christmas COVID corruption' #BorisJohnston #christmas #Politican. The video critiques UK Prime Minister Boris Johnston's apology where he claimed that an alleged staff party at

FIGURE 5.2: *Russell Brand* YouTube page.

the Prime Minister's official residence and office, Number 10 Downing Street, did not actually take place. This news item subsequently resurfaced and attracted a great deal of attention in the mainstream media, indicative of Johnson's capacity as Prime Minister. In his video, Brand begins his typical diatribe style with the hook observation that the government had secret parties where 'they' ignore their own rules'. He even shows several excerpts from ITV news including an item that informs the audience how, 'the week before Christmas as millions were cancelling plans a party may have taken place in the very building that had just proclaimed them banned last year' (Brand 2021: n.pag).

Brand excoriates the glaring double standards from a government that often referred to the importance of adherence to COVID-19 rules for the great majority.

> Isn't this what a lot of us secretly suspect, that it's rules for us but no rules for them? Okay, look we're all pretending we're a nation, we're all pretending that we're having one common experience, we're all pretending we're bonded by land, and law and flag, so let's make sure we're all obeying the same rules. But what are the rules [...] oh it depends on who you are.

Brand riffs animatedly on the leaked video from Number 10 and how this was the real concern that 'infuriated' Johnston, prompting his strategic communications management of the scandal. Brand's news commentary video is an ideal running time for YouTube and delivers the kind of news entertainment that exploits the platform's affordances. It's a sophisticated, if overly drawn-out, analysis that refers to the 'inability to sustain an allusion' that the Government staffers 'legitimately obey their own rules'. No doubt Brand taps into a cynical citizenry that searches for meaningful influencer insights into the corrosion or corruption of political power. In short, Brand's oeuvre blends news, satire and entertainment that is in sync with both audience and platform demands.

Again, the production crew behind the Russell Brand YouTube channel are very sensitive to the impact of the YouTube algorithm, as are most YouTubers who base their income on the monetization of their channels. Like DeFranco, they negotiate the digital affordances that are part of the platform to ensure that their videos remain relevant, searchable and indeed visible. Building on the affordances of the YouTube platform, the YouTube creator blog advises:

> We recommend videos based on things such as: what your audience watches and doesn't watch, how much time they spend watching, what they like and dislike, if they mark a video as 'not interested', and on satisfaction surveys. So, rather than

trying to find a secret code to these systems, focus instead on making videos that you think will resonate with your audience.

(YouTube 2021)

To that end, Russell Brand regularly creates and posts videos that are around 12–15 minutes in length, consistent with the channel metrics of this audience who are likely to watch videos of that duration. His most recent video at the time of writing had received over 195,000 views, suggesting the production approach for YouTube is more sophisticated than simply 'making videos [they] think will resonate with [their] audience'. Russell Brand is a useful example of a news YouTube Channel that has incorporated the technological *and* cultural affordances of the platform to produce a product that is of high value with a large audience. The community building aspect of news YouTubers is clear, as the channel incorporates the input from their fan community into the content that is created for their audience – Brand often prompts his audience in his videos to 'tell us what you think in the comments below'. This affective labour then feeds into the automated aspect of the algorithm by increasing 'what their audience

FIGURE 5.3: The YouTube page of the friendlyjordies.

likes' and 'how much time they spend on the video', as per the YouTube creator recommendations.

To move away from Northern Hemisphere YouTubers, we now turn our focus to an Australian-based YouTuber, Jordan Shanks, who is the face of the friendlyjordies channel. This is a channel of particular interest to us not only because of its skill in pirouetting around the technological and cultural affordances of the YouTube platform but also due to its encounters with the Australian legal system. To highlight the legal issues at play, it is important to first understand the channel and its approach towards content creation and publication, before we highlight the legal tensions surrounding Shanks and his production team of the friendlyjordies YouTube channel.

Like the DeFranco and Russell Brand channels, the friendlyjordies channel also demonstrates the kind of traits that satisfy the algorithmic requirements around the visibility conundrum all YouTubers face. It has effective poster images, uses video titles strategically and creates videos in the most likely timeframes to appease its audiences. It also talks about content that interests its core audience and other less addicted visitors, and it incorporates metrics into content production to increase views. In other words, it has a carefully cultivated relationship with the YouTube algorithm. But unlike the other two channels, the friendlyjordies has built its following on comedy, satire and pop cultural references *together with* political commentary and public affairs journalism (see Hall 2022). This makes it difficult to pigeonhole its key identity, Shanks, as an entertainer, online content creator or journalist; each has its own set of content ruling systems.

The friendlyjordies is listed as a B+ level YouTube channel according to data analytics group SocialBlade (2023), with 1.03 million subscribers, over 207 million video views and yearly earnings of between $31,900 and $511,200 USD. In all three instances of these news YouTubers, they are operating for visibility to reach their existing audience and to attract new audiences. These content production strategies show scant regard for regulatory frameworks, prioritizing techniques that enable increased monetization of their content, given that their YouTube channels are the main source of income. In this light, we argue that an eclectic range of content, including fake and misleading content, is created with visibility in mind, where visibility has a direct relationship with monetization – as its core concern – with less interest in existing regulatory guard rails. In some ways, this is consistent with earlier media forms such as commercial radio, where pranks or stunts – such as the notorious 2DayFM pre-recorded Royal prank call over which a London nurse suicided (Wilding 2015) – were sometimes used to maximize audiences with little regard for regulation.

Shanks is 'an Australian political commentator, stand-up comedian and YouTuber' (Wikipedia 2021). He embodies the blurring around the professional categories he has adopted – a kind of hybrid political entertainer–news influencer. On his path to local celebrity status, he supported his career through live stand-up comedy shows, but probably his greatest claim to fame arrived when he started his response style videos for *The Bachelorette* and *Married at First Sight* television series. Beyond these initial steps into celebrity, he has found a local point of notoriety in becoming a vocal political critic-commentator, with a specific focus on the conservative Liberal National Coalition party which was in government in New South Wales until early 2023. As one of the key antagonists of the NSW government, he has spearheaded social media protest such as #koalakiller, which highlighted the lack of government support for forestry habitats for koalas, and more recently he has made allegations of corruption and misconduct on the part of former Deputy Premier of NSW, John Barilaro. This prompted Barilaro to launch defamation proceedings against him, before announcing that he was resigning from parliament.

Providing grist to Shanks' mill, the former Premier of the NSW, Gladys Berejiklian, while being investigated by the state's anti-corruption body for a possible breach of the public trust, also resigned from politics (McGowan and Davies 2021). In his own public announcement of his resignation from parliament, Barilaro referenced the ongoing defamation case between himself and Jordan Shanks. 'It's unbelievable that I have to defend myself from vile and racist attacks in a social media setting by individuals and a trillion dollar company like Google' (Seven News 2021). Barilaro later settled his defamation case with Shanks in return for an apology and a payment towards legal costs (but no award of damages) and an agreement to edit the videos to remove the offensive material; however, Barilaro continued his action against Google as publisher of the YouTube videos (McGowan 2021). In June 2022, Barilaro won this action against Google and was awarded AUD 715,000.

This is the kind of public affairs content that Shanks' YouTube work exists on. At one level gossip and political vitriol, it blurs the line between a more traditional news format and a highly opinionated influencer format. The public service broadcaster in Australia – the ABC – and its media watchdog program 'Media Watch' has taken a close interest in Shanks' work and defamation cases, noting that the friendlyjordies audience is often 'young, alienated and for politicians hard to reach' (MediaWatch 2021). In its coverage of the legal cases that emerged from the channel and the high-profile politician, it became clear the sort of news coverage that Shanks produces would never be undertaken by risk averse mainstream media houses. Yet this kind of newsy public affairs content is emblematic of how the oftentimes polarizing 'influencer' styled news that appears on YouTube may be significantly more powerful than that which is pushed out from traditional news outlets.

Conclusion

In this chapter, we have described how news production and consumption is changing within our current digital media lives, swept along with the broader shifts underway in digital media content. By locating news production within the platformization of our mediatized communication experiences, we are able to highlight how a new set of affordances have become key elements in how content is produced, and how this is tethered with algorithmic visibility practices. Ultimately, we are describing how users are exposed to these sorts of content production techniques, how content surfaces, and how it can be conceived in relation to traditional ideas of media pluralism. We have argued that through the description of digital intermediation processes, it is clear that unseen infrastructures of digital content production have shifted away from those of traditional processes and must now be understood to incorporate the impact of automation for content production. Content production no longer is merely based on a producer's focus, an audience's interest or a platform's agenda: it is the combination of these three actors that determines what content is created by the specific production techniques employed. Within the news and journalism space, we are seeing cultural shifts around these practices. In the examples of Russell Brand, Philip DeFranco and Jordan Shanks, these celebrity news influencers have successfully navigated the platformed affordances of YouTube to create their channels and grow sizeable audiences. In so doing, they have generated significant incomes that support the crews involved in producing content for these channels. In each scenario, these journalists have a specific take on public issues for their very specific and niche-like audiences. DeFranco dabbles in internet culture and public affairs, Brand fashions his take on politics and surveillance, while Shanks' preference is state politics and the environment. On the surface, some practices of these news influencers resemble those of contemporary journalists. But with the rise of these online content creators, there also emerges a media pluralism dilemma which focuses clearly on the tension between increased visibility on commercial platforms and the inability to call these online content creators to account in the public interest. While they do report on items of interest to their publics, beyond the commentary there is no official mechanism that their professional journalism colleagues have that ensures they correct mistakes or enable their audience to respond to their content.

In this context, public service media could be one strategy to help in securing media diversity within the affordances of a platformized society. With the knowledge of how such environments operate, based on the successes of those news YouTubers detailed in this chapter, public media could be continuing to develop its presence in this space. After all, it has the remit to innovate within the digital media space by continually experimenting with new ways to disseminate information to its audiences.

Building on the European experiences of public media and algorithms, and the knowledge of how human intervention needs to remain in content production and distribution processes, public media are well placed to continue to ensure media diversity and pluralism remain where market failure is obvious; and to provide valuable insights for other voices wishing to operate in this digital media space. In the following chapter, we explore news curation and major social media platforms in the East Asian region.

REFERENCES

Abidin, Crystal (2016), '"Aren't these just young, rich women doing vain things online?": Influencer selfies as subversive frivolity', *Social Media + Society*, 2:23, pp. 1–17.

Anon. (2017), in-person interview with the author and Mukbang eaters Mino and Yasikee, Republic of Korea, 28 November.

Arriagada, Arturo and Ibáñez, Francisco (2020), '"You need at least one picture daily, if not, you're dead": Content creators and platform evolution in the social media ecology', *Social Media + Society*, 6:3, https://doi.org/10.1177/2056305120944624.

Assenmacher, Dennis, Frischlich, Lena, Clever, Lena, Quandt, Thorsten, Trautmann, Heike and Grimme, Christian (2020), 'Demystifying social bots: On the intelligence of automated social media actors', *Social Media + Society*, 6:3, https://doi.org/10.1177/2056305120939264

Barnett, Stephen (2021), '100 years of the BBC: Britain's extraordinary gift to the world, but for how much longer?', Shirley Williams lecture, 3 December, https://camri.ac.uk/blog/2021/12/03/steven-barnett-delivers-shirley-williams-lecture/. Accessed 19 July 2023.

Bishop, Sophie (2019), 'Managing visibility on YouTube through algorithmic gossip', *New Media & Society*, 21:11, 2589–606.

Bodó, Balazs, Helberger, Natali, Eskens, Sarah and Möller, Judith (2018), 'Interested in diversity', *Digital Journalism*, 7:2, pp. 206–29.

Bourdieu, Pierre (1984), *A Social Critique of the Judgement of Taste*, 1st ed., London: Routledge.

Brand, Russell (2021), 'Russell Brand's YouTube channel', YouTube, 9 December, https://www.youtube.com/watch?v=TBKhyvchCOc. Accessed 19 July 2023.

Bruns, Axel (2008), *Blogs, Wikipedia, Second Life and Beyond: From Production to Produsage*, New York: Peter Lang.

Bruns, Axel (2019), *Are Filter Bubbles Real?* Cambridge: Polity.

Bruns, Axel and Burgess, Jean (2015), 'Twitter hashtags from ad hoc to calculated publics', in N. Rambukkana (ed.), *Hashtag Publics: The Power and Politics of Discursive Networks*, Peter Lang, pp. 13–27.

Bucher, Taina (2018), *If... Then: Algorithmic Power and Politics*, Oxford: Oxford University Press.

Van den Bulck, Hilde and Moe, Hallvard (2017), 'Public service media, universality and personalisation through algorithms: Mapping strategies and exploring dilemmas', *Media, Culture & Society*, 40:6, pp. 875–92.

Cotter, Kelley (2018), 'Playing the visibility game: How digital influencers and algorithms negotiate influence on Instagram', *New Media & Society*, 21:4, pp. 895–913.

Crunchbase (2021), 'Phillip DeFranco', https://www.crunchbase.com/person/phil-defranco. Accessed 27 June 2023.

Debrett, Mary (2010), *Reinventing Public Service Television for the Digital Future*, Bristol: Intellect Books.

Diakopolous, Nicholas (2020), 'Computational news discovery: Towards design considerations for editorial orientation algorithms in journalism', *Digital Journalism*, 8:7, pp. 945–67.

Van Dijck, Jose, Poell, Thomas and De Waal, Martijn (2018), *The Platform Society: Public Values in a Connective World*, New York: University of Oxford Press.

Dwyer, Tim and Martin, Fiona (2019), 'Understanding viral news sharing', in F. Martin and T. Dwyer, *Sharing News Online: Commentary Cultures and Social Media News Ecologies*, Cham: Palgrave Macmillan, pp. 257–83.

Ferdinands, B. (2016), *Drink this tea and look like me* (Honours), Sydney: University of Sydney.

Flew, Terry (2021), *Regulating Platforms*, Cambridge: Polity.

Ford, Heather and Hutchinson, Jonathon (2021), 'Newsbots that mediate journalist and audience relationships', in N. Thurman, S. C. Lewis and J. Kunert (eds), *Algorithms, Automation, and News: New Directions in the Study of Computation and Journalism*, New York: Routledge, pp. 34–52.

Gillespie, Tarleton (2010), 'The politics of platforms', *New Media and Society*, 12:3, pp. 347–64.

Guzman, Andrea L. (2019), 'Prioritizing the audience's view of automation in journalism', *Digital Journalism*, 7:8, pp. 1185–90.

Hall, Chris (2022), 'Friendlyjordies leading the way for new public interest journalism', *Independent Australia*, 7 September, https://independentaustralia.net/business/business-display/friendlyjordies-leading-the-way-for-public-interest-journalism,16743.

Hartley, John, Burgess, Jean and Bruns, Axel (2013), *A Companion to New Media Dynamics*, New York: Wiley.

Hootsuite (2021), 'How to create a social media calendar: Tips and templates', *Hootesuite*, https://blog.hootsuite.com/how-to-create-a-social-media-content-calendar/. Accessed 16 May 2021.

Hutchinson, Jonathon (2017), *Cultural Intermediation and Audience Participation in Media Organisations*, New York: Palgrave Macmillan.

Hutchinson, Jonathon (2019), 'Digital first personality: Automation and influence within evolving media ecologies', *Convergence: The International Journal of Research into New Media Technologies*, https://doi.org/10.1177/1354856519858921.

Hutchinson, Jonathon (2021), 'Digital intermediation: Unseen infrastructures for cultural production', *New Media & Society*, 26:5&6, pp. 1284–300, https://doi.org/10.1177/14614448211040247.

Jenkins, Henry (2006), *Convergence Culture: Where Old and New Media Collide*, 1st ed., New York: New York University Press.

Kelly, Aidan (2014), 'Advertising', in J. S. Maguire and J. Matthews (eds), *The Cultural Intermediaries Reader*, London: SAGE Publication Ltd., pp. 67–76.

Kim, Tae (2021), 'Dorsey's refresh of Twitter hasn't convinced anyone', *Australian Financial Review*, 24 September.

Lingel, Jessa (2021), *The Gentrification of the Internet: How to Reclaim Our Digital Freedom*, Los Angeles: University of California Press.

MacGowan, Michael (2021), 'Friendlyjordies defamation case: Jordan Shanks apologises to John Barilaro to settle claim', *The Guardian*, 5 November, https://www.theguardian.com/australia-news/2021/nov/05/friendlyjordies-defamation-case-jordan-shanks-apologises-to-john-barilaro-to-settle-claim. Accessed 24 February 2023.

Margetts, Helen, Lehdonvirta, Vili, González-Bailón, Sandra, Hutchinson, Jonathan, Bright, Jonathan, Nash, Vicki and Sutcliffe, David (2021), 'The Internet and public policy: Future directions', *Policy & Internet*, 13:2, pp. 1–23.

Marshall, P. David, Moore, Christopher and Barbour, Kim (2019), *Persona Studies: An Introduction*, Washington, DC: Wiley.

Marwick, Alice E. (2013), *Status Update: Celebrity, Publicity, and Branding in the Social Media Age*, New York: Yale University Press.

Manovich, Lev (2001), *The Language of New Media*, Cambridge: MIT Press.

MediaWatch (2021), 'FrendlyJordies Arrest', ABC TV MediaWatch Program, 21 June, https://www.abc.net.au/mediawatch/episodes/jordies/13404388. Accessed 24 February 2023.

Moore, Martin and Tambini, Damian (2018), *Digital Dominance: The Power of Google, Amazon, Facebook and Apple*, New York: Oxford University Press.

Negus, Keith (2010), 'The work of cultural intermediaries and the enduring distance between production and consumption', *Cultural Studies*, 16:4, pp. 501–15.

Nieborg, David B. and Poell, Thomas (2018), 'The platformization of cultural production: Theorizing the contingent cultural commodity', *New Media & Society*, 20:11, pp. 4275–92.

Noble, Safiya Umoja (2018), *Algorithms of Oppression: How Search Engines Reinforce Racism*, New York: NYU Press.

Pasquale, Frank (2015), *The Black Box Society: The Secret Algorithms That Control Money and Information*, Cambridge: MIT Press.

Perry, Beth, Smith, Karen and Warren, Saskia (2015), 'Revealing and revaluing cultural intermediaries in the "Real" creative city: Insights from a dairy keeping exercise', *European Journal of Cultural Studies*, 18:6, pp. 724–40.

Peterson-Salahuddin, Chelsea and Diakopolous, Nicholas (2020), 'Negotiated autonomy: The role of social media algorithms in editorial decision making', *Media and Communication*, 8:3, p. 27.

Petre, Caitlin, Duffy, Brooke, Erin and Hund, Emily (2019), '"Gaming the System": Platform paternalism and the politics of algorithmic visibility', *Social Media + Society*, 5, October–December, pp. 1–12.

Poell, Thomas, Nieborg, David B. and Duffy, Brooke Erin (2021), *Platforms and Cultural Production*, Bristol: Polity Press.

Senft, Theresa M. (2013), 'Microcelebrity and the branded self', in J. B. John Hartley and A. Bruns (eds), *A Companion to New Media Dynamics*, New York: Wiley-Blackwell, pp. 346–54.

Seven News (2021), 'Deputy Premier John Barilaro announces resignation after Gladys Berejiklian stands down', *Seven News*, 4 October, https://7news.com.au/news/nsw/deputy-premier-john-barilaro-announces-resignation-after-gladys-berejiklian-stands-down-c-4141926. Accessed 19 July 2023.

Sherwood, Merryn and O'Donnell, Penny (2018), 'Once a journalist, always a journalist? Industry restructure, job loss and professional identity', *Journalism Studies*, 19:7, pp. 1021–38.

Skov, Lise (2014), 'Cultural intermediaries and fashion', in J. S. Macguire and T. Miller (eds), *The Cultural Intermediaires Reader*, London: SAGE Publications Ltd, pp. 113–14.

Smith Maguire, Jennifer and Mathews, Julian (2012), 'Are we all cultural intermediaries now? An introduction to cultural intermediaires in context', *European Journal of Cultural Studies*, 15:5, pp. 551–62.

Social Blade (2023), 'Analytics Made Easy', https://socialblade.com.

Sørensen, Jannick Kirk and Schmidt, Jan-Hinrik (2016), 'An algorithmic diversity diet? Questioning assumptions behind a diversity recommendation system for PSM', *RIPE@2016*, Antwerp, Belgium, 23 September.

Sørensen, Jannick Kirk and Hutchinson, Jonathon (2018), 'Algorithms and public service media', in G. Lowe, H. V. d. Bulck and K. Donders (eds), *RIPE@2017: Public Service Media in the Networked Society*, Gothenburg: Nordicom.

Stepnik, Agata (2019), *Algorithms as Culture: Active curation of news media on social platforms*, Masters thesis, Sydney: University of Sydney.

Striphas, Ted (2015), 'Algorithmic culture', *European Journal of Cultural Studies*, 18:4&5, pp. 395–412.

Thurman, Neil J., Dörr, Konstantin and Kunert, Jessica (2018), 'Journalists on their robot pretenders', in *Algorithms, Automation and News: An International Conference*, Munich, Germany, 22–23 May.

Thurman, Neil J. and Schifferes, Steve (2012), 'The future of persoanlization at news websites', *Journalism Studies*, 13:5&6, pp. 775–90.

Tracey, Michael (1998), 'Principles of public service broadcasting', in *The Decline and Fall of Public Service Broadcasting*, Oxford: Oxford University Press, pp. 18–32.

Turner, Graeme (2010), *Ordinary People and the Media: The Demotic Turn*, London: SAGE Publications Ltd.

Twitter Inc. (2021), 'Permanent suspension of @realDonaldTrump', 8 January, https://blog.twitter.com/en_us/topics/company/2020/suspension. Accessed 12 January.

Whittaker, Meredith, Crawford, Kate, Dobbe, Roel, Fried, Genevieve, Kaziunas, Elizabeth, Mathur, Varoon, Myers West, Sarah, Richardson, Rashida, Schultz, Jason & Schwartz, Oscar (2018), AI Now Report 2018, New York: AI Now Institute, https://ainowinstitute.org/AI_Now_2018_Report.pdf. Accessed 19 July 2023.

Wikipedia (2021), 'Jordan Shanks (friendlyjordies)', https://en.wikipedia.org/wiki/Friendlyjordies.

Wilding, Derek (2015), 'The Summer 30 Royal Prank Call: Outcomes for Australian broadcasting regulation', *Journal of Media Law,* 7:1, pp. 92–107.

Yeung, Karen (2016), '"Hypernudge": Big Data as a mode of regulation by design', *Information Communication & Society*, 20:1, pp. 1–19.

YouTube Creator Academy (2021), 'Intro to making money on YouTube', YouTube, 21 November, https://creatoracademy.youtube.com/page/lesson/revenue-basics. Accessed 27 June 2023.

UK House of Commons (2021), Digital, Culture, Media and Sport Committee. Oral Evidence on 'Influencer Culture'. 13 July. Dr. Crystal Abidin. UK Parliament. Transcript available at https://committees.parliament.uk/oralevidence/2552/html/. Accessed 27 June 2023.

6

Researching Online News Media Diversities in China and South Korea

Tim Dwyer and Jonathon Hutchinson

Introduction

Transformations in digital media production, distribution and access to online news invite researchers to rethink the application of media policies in national media systems. Frameworks that were previously relied on for comparative national media system analysis now warrant reassessment. In this chapter, the argument is made that de-westernization of media studies should include media pluralism/diversity policies within the scope of that project, and this approach can advance our understanding of news media in China. Researching online news and diversity in Asian countries underscores the benefits of studying processes as well as systems, and the dynamic interactions between structure, agency and pathways of policymaking. In this chapter, we also discuss algorithmic aspects of news distributed on the Chinese WeChat social media platform in news media official accounts. Our analysis of online news surfacing in the Korean portal media ecology provides insights into automated news curation based on the manipulation for electoral purposes, already seen on a mass scale with the US presidential elections in 2016. The chapter is a contribution to developing our understanding of media pluralities across divergent media systems through theorized frameworks and empirical case studies.

De-westernizing media policy studies

In a talk given in 2017, Colin Sparks lamented the lack of progress in 'de-westernizing media studies' as seen over at least a fifteen-year period. Sparks' analysis was the theorization of new media and an attempt to better understand how superpower rivalry shapes the discipline. He identified the western origins of media studies in the propaganda studies work of Walter Lippmann, Edward L. Bernays and Harold Lasswell, noting that the legacy of cultural studies barely registered on the radar of the mainstream academy in Hong Kong. In his view, it would be larger epoch defining historical shifts, not technological change that will determine the possibility of de-westernizing media studies (Sparks 2017).

For us, a starting point in our research was the assumption that recognition of cultural and national differences is at the heart of any serious attempt to comparatively analyse issues in national media systems. In Hallin and Mancini's terms (from their 2004 book *Comparing Media Systems*), these western media ecologies could be accommodated within the North Atlantic or Liberal model (including nations such as the United Kingdom, United States and Canada), the Mediterranean or Polarized Pluralist (Italy, Greece, France, and Spain) and the Democratic Corporatist or North/Central European models (Belgium, The Netherlands, Norway, and Sweden) (Hallin and Mancini 2004).

Although these three models all assumed that political systems parallel media systems to various degrees, the researchers extended their widely used framework in *Comparing Media Systems Beyond the Western World (2012)*, which now presented an overtly non-western perspective (Hallin and Mancini 2012), while still risking a 'universalizing' western frame of reference.

In broad terms, their research efforts into comparative media systems had underscored the observation by some critics that both western and non-western media systems are *always* positioned within the host political cultures of the nation states in which they are embedded. The exercise, then, of comparatively analyzing media 'systems' beyond the West was productive for this research, as it served to construct a set of questions that highlight processes as well as systems and prompted reassessments of the dynamic interactions between structure, agency and pathways of policymaking.

In this chapter, we are less focused on these aspects of hegemonic power plays than we are in the specific merits of a de-westernized media policy studies (Park and Curran 2005) for reappraising the contribution of a key western policy concept such as media pluralism or its twin, diversity. We suggest that Park and Curran's proposition that 'media studies will benefit from developing a wider comparative perspective' is a truism and that media policy is a key component (Park and Curran 2005: 12).

We are specifically interested in exploring some twenty-first century attempts to recast ideas of media pluralism studies for researching diversity in news content. Recent critiques of western media studies analyses have currency for both theoretical and industry renewals. In his reassessment of the shifting normative values of western and eastern perspectives on media, Jin argues:

> The milieu surrounding media studies will be continuously changing, and it offers great opportunities for non-Western media studies to develop and advance their unique canons, but remain embedded in Western theories. With the emphasis of the perspectives of rich Asian history and culture, media scholars can develop new paradigms running through Asian domains. While it is not necessary for the perspectives and process to be radical, it should be convincing to grasp Asia as a formation of a changeable force to the West.
>
> (Jin 2021: 156)

Jin advances an East–West dialectical approach that considers trends in digital media technologies and argues such an approach will aid the advancement of new theories and norms in global media studies. Equally, though, the rise of platform studies has also shown itself to be a source of theoretical renewal. For example, Davis and Xiao in their recent article 'De-Westernizing Platform Studies: History and Logics of Chinese and U.S. Platforms', argue:

> we interrogate some of the assumptions that underpin Western platform studies through the lens of Chinese platforms. Our aim is to contribute to the project of de-Westernizing and reregionalizing Internet studies and at the same time to provide some new frameworks for understanding Chinese platforms on the basis that Chinese platforms presently provide the most prominent challenge to Western platform hegemony.
>
> (Davis and Xiao 2021: 105)

Our chapter seeks to engage with similar terrain against the backdrop of comparative media policy research. Media pluralism policies have been pursued as a priority in the West from at least the mid twentieth century (Dwyer 2019: 223–56). Arguably, the most developed exemplar of such policies in the twenty-first century finds the expression in the EU's Media Pluralism Monitor (MPM) which has evolved over a number of years to become a sophisticated tool for making assessments of risks to pluralism over a wide and insightful range of indicators. The MPM covers the areas of 'Basic protection, Market plurality, Political independence and Social inclusiveness' (MPM 2020). This means that indicators extend well beyond the usual media ownership concentration measures; aspects such as the conditions required for investigative journalism and access to internet infrastructure are all at play in the MPM-updated framework.

The updates to the MPM tool now cover new digital indicators for assessing member states' net neutrality, freedom of expression online, internet access, digital literacy, the role of media in democratic electoral processes and digital safety of journalists (MPM 2020). Researchers have noted that digital plurality, including broadband access, concentration of internet services and online content providers have been included in recent years (Nenadic and Milosavljevic 2019). Cross-platform distribution and the rise in the usage of social media platforms for accessing news content are also now considered (MPM 2020). It is worth noting that in one recent study of the cross-media usage repertoires among young Chinese adults and their political impacts, the researchers considered media consumption (not just 'news' repertoires) across twelve platforms, four traditional (TV, radio, magazine and newspapers) and eight social media platforms (WeChat, Qzone, Sina-Weibo, Baidu Tieba, Zhihu.com, Tianya Club, Douban.com and Guokr.com.). The researchers found in their sample that the most popular top four online social media platforms WeChat, Qzone, Sina-Weibo and Baidu Tieba are used significantly more than traditional media in this cohort, except for TV usage (Gong et al. 2020).

The development of algorithmic patterns in online news distribution and consumption through platformization dynamics has inevitably given rise to a renovated set of questions and re-framings for policymakers in nation states (Wilding et al. 2018; Flew and Wilding 2020: 6). In effect, these changed dynamics require new orthodoxies for expanding singular ownership focused conceptions of voice pluralism. Fenton et al. (2020) argue that in the context of increasing media concentration, there is a need for counter narratives and mechanisms 'to promote meaningful plurality' (2020: 104). These authors argue that the performance of news algorithms should be scrutinized so that they do not 'unduly favour particular types of news providers and voices over others' (2020: 105). We agree that online news distribution over intermediary platforms and their shaping algorithms should be seen to have a direct role in the selection of news articles surfacing on platforms, at both an aggregate and individual levels. As noted previously in Chapter 1, we would distinguish 'meaningful plurality' from the conceptualisation of 'sufficient plurality' found in UK law – and critiqued by (Gibbons 2015: 22–27), among others. The latter is concerned with the hard political decision limits or thresholds in law and regulation which impact on the number and 'sufficiency' of voices, while the former focuses on expanding formulations that apply in new media ecologies.

Earlier priorities, seen in the original versions of the MPM framework including the primary focus on issues of the risk of concentrated media ownership on media pluralism, have now been complemented by a broader range of indicators relating to the political economic and cultural context (MPM 2020). This shift to a more inclusive set of indicators is timely for a reassessment of media diversity in China, which has undergone a dramatic restructuring of its media and communications sectors in recent years (Hong 2017).

The Zouzhuanggai policy moment

It is not a straightforward matter to place an exact chronology on key moments in Chinese media policy in the internet era. As Zhao notes, the historic unfolding of media in China needs to be seen in terms of the post Mao economic reforms which are relevant to profit-making and propaganda priorities. This has involved the state both curtailing its role in subsidizing media operations and targeting 'the media and cultural sector as new sites of profit-making and capitalistic development [...] the state continues to restrict private capital, let alone the privatizing of existing media outlets' (Zhao 2008, 2012: 153). Her argument is therefore that the state has cultivated the media's entertainment function and accommodated private capital: 'it has developed a complex and differentiated policy regime' in relation to the participation of private capital in the media and cultural industries. Yet the guiding principle is that news and information is 'deemed sacred' and therefore ownership of news media outlets is monopolized by the state. The ideological field remains pivotal, and regulation of the media has expanded dramatically along with commercialization-marketization and rapid expansion in the media sector more broadly. Such structural management of the media is the job of a number of agencies under the direct aegis of the Communist Party of China (CPC) propaganda department (Zhao 2012: 153–54).

The complexity of unfolding media policy mechanisms can be seen in many initiatives. A noteworthy example emerging in the period 2010–12 was the policy of *'zouzhuanggai'* that was introduced by the CPC. Essentially a change in policy direction, its purpose was to, in a sense, liberalize or at least 'open up' Chinese media to more diverse forms of media. *Zouzhuanggai* 走转改 was an acronym that stood for three core ideas: to go to the grassroots; to transform work style; and to transform journalistic style (He 2012; Simons 2012). The new policy was concerned with a 'realist' news turn, an attempt to rein in less worthy commercialized journalism that had come to prominence in China and which the government felt it needed to intervene in for the sake of its citizens (He 2012).

The policy signalled serious changes to Chinese media that the Propaganda Department were seeking to implement. It can, therefore, be identified as a key moment of change when approaches to 'media governance' – another term which related to new policy directions – emerged. The *Zouzhuanggai* campaign was launched in 2011 with much fanfare by sending central-media organizations' journalists, who had mostly stayed indoors or in comfortable urban areas, to participate in and talk to their news sources more directly, in mostly underreported rural areas. Though criticized by some observers on the basis that, 'It's just another kind of formalism (形式主义) and movement (运动) to fake the Party's concern for the downtrodden', the campaign has turned out some quality journalism that brings audiences closer to the reality of China (Deng 2018). For example, CCTV journalists morphed into anthropologists in an outlying village in Xinjiang and followed young students with their cameras on their weekly 80-km mountainous trip to their school. The result is an insightful documentary series on the perseverance, sacrifices, sufferings of these young school children have to brave just in their pursuit for a school education (He 2012).

Arguably, the *Zouzhuanggai* policy was a response by the CPC to the transformation that was already well underway in Chinese media where traditional organizations now had to compete with dominant internet social media platforms of Weibo and WeChat, the Baidu search engine platform and hundreds of popular online news media outlets funded through advertising. As Simons has argued in the context of the devasting economic impact of platforms over traditional new media and how journalists were remunerated,

> long-form journalism, or journalism that took in-depth research, was not possible in most of the commercial outlets. Journalists regarded as high calibre generally worked for the state subsidised media […] Journalists were caught between commercialisation and control.
>
> (Simons 2012: n.pag.)

The *Zouzhuanggai* policy, then, sought to encourage more substantive investigative journalism based on interviews which excavated issues where truth mattered. Ironically, it isn't just privately owned media which have led the charge to commercialized news media in China. Party-controlled media commercialization directs urban mass appeal 'metro papers' (urban omnibus morning dailies) as subsidiaries of provincial and national party organs. Operating as semi-autonomous business units, these papers reach the rising affluence urban demographic and can have a critical voice at the municipal level and are thus often 'cash cows'; Zhao argues that through these papers (usually also online), the CPC is able to reach the urban middle class with whom it 'rearticulates the terms of its hegemony' (Zhao 2012: 158). The party-controlled papers target a range of readerships, including special interest groups (workers, women, youth) as well as intellectuals and financial and business elites 'with liberal and technocratic orientations'. While the print media (online and physical) remain central to the media and journalism in China, television, radio and the internet, and the mobile net have rapidly evolved from the beginning of the twenty-first century to offer a diverse range of formats (Zhao

2012: 159–60), and to which we must now add social media platforms such as Weibo and WeChat, search engines, news and video apps and live streaming video media within the broader social media environment.

Sukosd (2016) has identified several important structural factors at play for media diversity in China. In his 2016 chapter entitled 'How to Conceptualize Media Pluralization in China', he argues for modification and adaptation of the (western) MPM approach adopted in the EU/EC. He suggests that it needs to be substituted with his more nuanced approach that discusses the relevance of 'diversification' in various modes that 'fit with the realities of the Chinese media'. According to Sukosd, assessments of media pluralism in China assume 'the absence of official support' for the liberal democratic notion of pluralism. What is required, he suggests, is an analysis of the 'multiple forces and aspects of homogenization versus diversification of the Chinese media system' (Sukosd 2016: 153).

His adaptation of the MPM introduces a modified-for-China framework of party control (the 'basic domain' concerning legal and policy pillars in MPM terms) and economic reforms, diversification of ownership, control, media types and genres, geographic diversification, cultural and political pluralizations. Central to his analysis, he contrasts *diversification* with *pluralization*; this is a very important distinction for applying the model in a Chinese context. Diversification refers to top-down, state-controlled introduction of new platforms, channels and content whereas pluralization is concerned with more grassroots or bottom-up expansion of 'novel media spaces' created by party policies (Sukosd 2016: 153–54). This modified MPM framework is very useful for reassessing media diversity in contemporary China. It moves the analysis away from more inflexible assessments of political structures and culture seen in the ideas of political parallelism discussed earlier. The analysis in this chapter and in our broader Media Pluralism Project (discussed below) assumes, following Karppinen, that the ways in which media diversity and pluralism are mobilized in policy discourses is a definitional matter of political rationalities and that these concepts then become institutionalized and normalized in policy and expert discourses (Karppinen 2006: 54).

The greatest single force of media diversity in the post Mao era has been party endorsed measures for commercialization, market economy growth and competition. This has opened the way for the burgeoning expansion of media platforms, channels, genres, topics and content in general. The dramatic expansion of the Chinese internet, and in particular the mobile internet and social media platforms and applications, has underwritten new media diversities in general (Gong 2020: 3799–818).

In this context, the case of China requires an understanding of trends in dominant media-tech *platformization*, data surveillance flows, and broader system-wide innovation in connectivity and distribution, where these developments all portend radical implications for the news consumption. Algorithmic visibility of news has emerged as a key issue for those researching questions of media pluralism, and Chinese platforms are at the forefront of these trends (Zhang 2020). News content distribution is embedded in platform power debates in relation to how access is shaped by way of automated machine-learning processes. Research indicates that the way audiences become exposed to news content will increasingly be a matter of these automated, platform-based mechanisms (Wilding et al. 2018; Helberger 2018, 2021).

For example, Helberger's research points to the increasingly important role that recommender systems now play in news distribution. We noted above her argument that recommender systems can be theorized in terms of four varieties of algorithmic recommendation: liberal recommenders, participatory recommenders, deliberative recommenders and constructivist recommenders (Helberger 2021). While these varieties of priorities for algorithmic recommender systems are particularly relevant for public service media sites and platforms, they can be applied more broadly in relation to the role of commercialized personalized media delivery including non-western platforms. Public service media have a recent history of blending machine-determined automation alongside human-driven curation to effectively operate in increasingly automatic media content environments. We noted earlier that YLE, the Finnish public media broadcaster, has long given its journalists the ability to target their content via an insights dashboard that presents them with audience performance data (Hutchinson and Sørensen 2021).

The need to take new platform distributional processes into account in assessments of media pluralism has been recognized by EU Member states in EU Council deliberations. In their discussions in relation to findability and discoverability of pluralistic content, they have foreshadowed that future media policy needs to consider how algorithmic manipulation affects users' exposure to informational content and news sources as well as their overall consumption. Significantly, though, they have gone a step further by recommending that Member States' media policies should consider 'must show' rules and criteria for discoverability and findability to favour media pluralism and cultural diversity. The Council specifically invites the European Commission to:

> continue and further develop research to identify potential risks to media pluralism and further understand the changed position of editorial media outlets in relation to social media, search engines, video-sharing platforms and other media platforms; concepts of information science should explicitly be taken into account.
>
> (Council of the EU, paragraph 25, 2020)

Before we look in more detail at the various kinds of news content circulating on Tencent's WeChat official accounts, we will explore examples of emerging content diversities in the Chinese internet media ecology.

Identifying diversities in online news content in China

In contemporary Chinese media, there is a wide diversity in online news media formats which are produced for a range of audiences as a result of the interaction between the processes of *diversification* and *pluralisation* (Sukosd 2016: 154) mentioned above. While innovative new sites are created to address specific audience niches, it is the media workers in various roles, media managers, senior editors, journalists who will in practice enliven sustainable titles. Two notable examples in cosmopolitan Shanghai of these processes, and that display careful positioning of readerships, are *Pengpai (The Paper)* and *Sixth Tone*. These two publications share offices in Shanghai and are both part of the Shanghai United Media Group, which is a large state-owned corporation with editorial and funding links to the Municipal government in Shanghai. *Sixth Tone*, an English-language, outreach news website, was specifically established in 2016 with a remit to broaden the range of voices in China and Chinese journalism. Self-labelled as 'fresh voices from China', it aims to produce stories which cut through the daily news agenda with more incisive and thoughtful analyses of everyday China. In the publication's own words, 'Through fresh takes on trending topics, in depth features, and illuminating contributions, *Sixth Tone* covers issues from the perspectives of those most intimately involved to highlight the nuances and complexities of today's China' (sixthtone.com).

Aimed at younger and tertiary educated audiences, *Sixth Tone* is traversing new terrain in the Chinese news market with stories and topics that aim to satisfy the curiosity of foreign audiences, or domestic audiences, who will often have had exposure to western media forms. Janus-faced they produce sub-category themes ('tones') which consider 'daily', 'rising', 'deep', 'broad' and 'vivid' stories. For instance, the publisher suggests, 'Deep Tones' curates features 'that cut to the core of contemporary China. In depth, informed, and carefully crafted, every piece is carried by the voices of the story's participants'. Whereas 'Broad Tones' 'are contributions from individuals with unique perspectives to share [...] from experts and commentators to those whose voices are rarely heard'; 'Vivid Tones' are 'visual stories showing up-close and personal slices of contemporary China [...] fine-tuned to present diverse narratives through short videos, documentaries, photography, and data visualisation' (sixth.com). At the time of our data collection, *Sixth Tone* was publishing about five stories every day, either self-generated or translated from quality content sourced from within Chinese media.

Another interesting example of a diverse news source also produced by the Shanghai United Media Group, *The Paper*, specifically has its origins in the CPC seeking more influence in specific news outlets. In particular, the mobile app version of the newspaper was part of a pilot test for digital journalism undertaken by authorities in Shanghai. As Deng has explained (Deng, 2018), 'regaining lost influence' and 'winning public trust' are two principal objectives for wanting to grow *Pengpai (The Paper)*. Deng makes the argument that as a product of an alignment of the patron-clientelism model of the 'legitimacy-seeking' of the CPC, with 'confucian-minded' journalists and the quality information hungry public, *The Paper* has been guided to become a new voice capable of speaking both 'digitally and differently' (Deng 2018: 113). Deng's primary analysis is concerned with the operation of censorship, while also laying bare a key aspect of the new diversities within the Chinese news media ecology, at the intersection of marketization and CPC ideological renewal for more educated audiences (Deng 2018).

In parallel with the rise of *The Paper*, and clearly influenced by its success, other Chinese cities and provinces have launched similar news organizations spearheaded by news apps similar to *The Paper*, such as *Hongxing News* (上游新闻) in Chengdu and *Shangyou News* (红星新闻) in Chongqing, both key cities in southwestern China, and *Qiupai News* (九派新闻) in Wuhan in central China.

WeChat Official Accounts (WOA) news corpora

In our Media Pluralism and Online News project, we used a bespoke computational tool to analyze news articles scraped from 11 WeChat official accounts (WOA) over an eight-week period in 2019 (October–December 2019). The selection of news organizations includes more recent, 'born digital' publications such as *Sixth Tone* and *The Paper*, together with more mainstream titles such as the *Shanghai Daily*, Sohu, CCTV and Xinhua. They are a mix of Chinese and English language sites, whose audiences sometimes overlap.

The key purpose of this online news article collection was to assemble a range of official accounts available on the WeChat platform given that this feature has become an increasingly popular way of accessing platform-distributed news by different demographic groups. The Tencent owned platform has amassed over one billion users in China. News organizations in China tend to have a 24-hour news cycle approach for uploading batches of news articles to their WOA. These 'pushes' will vary between weekday and weekends and between the kind of news organization. As a 'party organ' journalist interviewed for this research explains:

We usually have three rounds of WeChat pushes on weekdays and two rounds of pushes on weekends because WOA has its limitation in pushing times per day. On weekdays, we prepare the morning news containing a list of news flashes with an audio news broadcast, between around 7.10 am to 8.10 am. Then we will start collecting the news and pitch them to our directors and finally select 3–4 pieces of news to make the second round WeChat push at 11.30 am. We prepare for the evening news push by selecting latest news from 3 pm to 8 pm, and we wait until 9 pm to 10 pm for the news app team's news column and then release the WeChat push.

(Interview, CPC Organ news journalist, March 2020)

TABLE 6.1: Sample of WeChat Official Accounts Publishers

Chinese	English	WeChat Acc
央视新闻	CCTV News	CCTVnewscenter
新华社	Xinhua News	xinhuashefabu1
人民日报	People's Daily	rmrbwx
中国日报	China Daily	CHINADAILYWX
上海日报SHINE	Shanghai Daily	SHDSHINE
Sixth Tone	Sixth Tone	Sixth Tone
搜狐新闻	Sohu News	News_Sohu
新浪新闻	Sina News	xinlang-xinwen
网易新闻	Netease News	wangyixinwen163
澎湃新闻	The Paper (Pengpai)	thepapernews
南方都市报	Southern Metropolis Daily by Southern Daily	nddaily

Our corpora of WeChat articles consists of approximately 7500 individual news stories across 11 WOA. The purpose of this analysis is to share some preliminary, and to some extent experimental, insights via a sample of 250 individual articles based on their titles and body text. In later analyses, we will examine the wider datasets from the total corpus of articles. Our intention here is to present the methodology, and then discuss a sample of news articles 'surfacing' on WOA, in order to focus on their diversity features in terms of sources and topics. Inter-annotator reliability was used on the WOA sample dataset to gauge how well the notion of PA/NPA converges amongst experts in the field (Figure 6.1).

Purpose
Accuracy: 90%, Cohen Kappa: 69%
Confusion matrix:

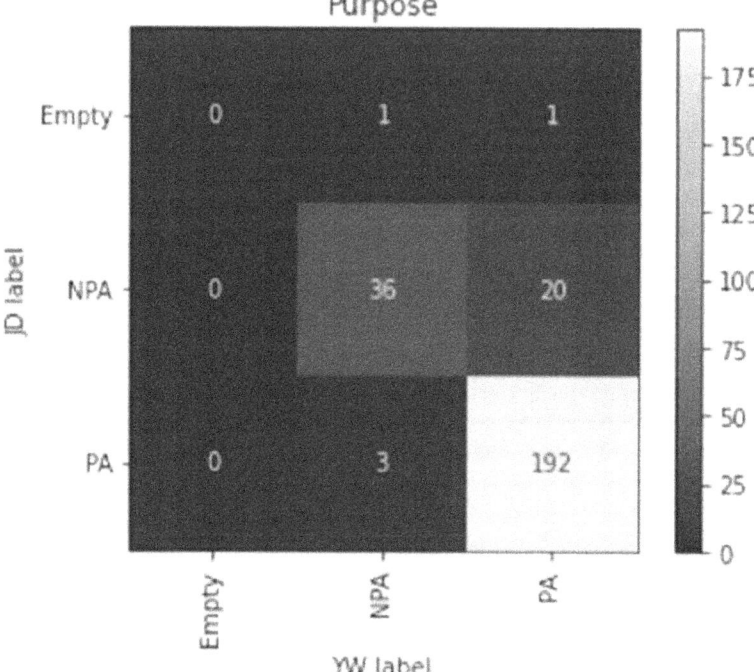

FIGURE 6.1: Intercoder reliability by purpose.

There was an overall agreement/accuracy rate of 90 per cent between our expert annotators (Figure 6.2).

Using the PA/NPA approach outlined in Chapter 3, we sought to identify broader trends and issues, as well as more fine-grained breakdowns of the story topics. The following examples of headlines from articles distributed by these news organizations on WOA can be interpreted as conveying a sense of such light and trivial content:

'The menu of the Japanese royal family.' *The Paper*
 'The most shameful 25 moments of all adults.' *Netease News*
 'Police announcement on "Shandong Baby Burying Case".' *The Paper*
 'Today, we value the peep and poop style of literary works.' *Sohu News*
 'A 7-year-old girl's eyes were rammed with paper slips, scholar master says he means no evil.' *The China Daily*

Primary topic
Accuracy: 52%, Cohen Kappa: 49%

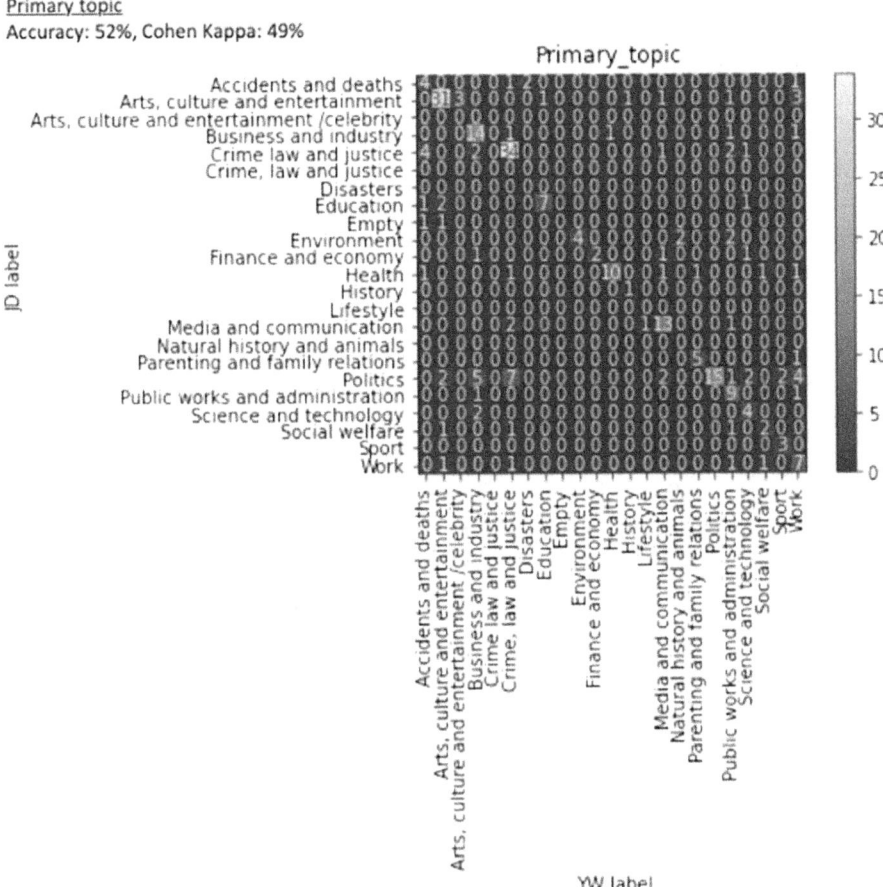

FIGURE 6.2: Intercoder reliability by topic.

'The Civil Affairs Bureau now permits concubine taking? Here is the latest.' *Southern Metropolis Daily by Southern Daily*

Based on this sample of WOA news stories, we argue that *serious and diverse* journalism topics have become quite rare. When the news does concern local or central politics, it tends to focus on a state leader's speech, personality cults, official policy and people being punished for various kinds of offences. Examples of these kinds of stories are evident in the following headlines:

'This is what you get for airing any anti-China opinions!' *CCTV News*
'Hong Kong residents now in action.' *The People's Daily*

'42 self-media video hosts have been prohibited from broadcasting for five years.'
The People's Daily

'Bravo! This is how PLA soldiers made their steel wills.' *CCTV News*

'Xi Jinping: People Construct the People's City.' *The China Daily*

'Now a criminal, this 16-year-old high scholar burst into tears.' *The China Daily*

'How do you feel to see Hainan Province from 600000 meters high in sky?'
Xinhua News

Reviewing these news articles has allowed us to make a number of observations regarding their most salient features and their overall high level trends. First, we observe that there is a chronic lack of serious (and therefore 'public affairs') content, including stories that discuss or analyze central government policy, or the national conferences. There is also a lack of international news in comparison to domestic news stories. Second, headline baiting is rampant. A part of this phenomenon is the preponderance of stories that deal with trivial matters, lifestyle, and generally infotainment stories. There is also an abundance of 'listicles' of various types. Again, this baiting and lighter content can be broadly seen as consistent with 'non-public affairs' content. The third clear trend in the sample articles is that English language media are more serious (or have more diverse public affairs content) than their Chinese language counterparts in terms of topic choices and news styles. This is to be expected given the educated, urban skew of these English language publications, and the broader tendency for these publications to have greater latitude in the range of topics that might otherwise attract censorship in Chinese language media outlets.

However, somewhat paradoxically, analysis of the data set indicates a quite complex answer to the question, 'Does the use of WeChat official accounts enhance news media diversity (and diversity of voices) in China?' We can say that, potentially, yes, even though a great deal of trivial and light content is published in these WOA. The principal reason for this relates to the inherent networked affordances arising from the use of WOA: the selection of a diverse range of accounts to follow, as in many social media settings, establishes the available menu of sources and therefore the news content. This approach can align with arguments around increased user agency when engaging with social media platforms, especially through algorithmic diversity within one's visible content (Lingel 2021). However, to lure readers, click bait headlines are rampant in the Chinese online news (and the WOA) ecology; news has become more focused on trivial quarrels amongst residents, traffic accidents, gossip, celebrity private life, criminal cases, medical misinformation, pop culture, nationalism, children education anxiety, kittens, pets, life lessons, all kinds of exaggerations, emotion pandering and base instincts.

News diversity, platformization, affordances

Beyond the high incidence of clickbait headlines, the platform affordances of publishers' news sites emerged as a focal point for us in analyzing WOA news stories. As a preliminary study before more detailed consideration which will use topic modelling of the dataset, we have used software tools to compare stories distributed on the WOAs. In our view higher levels of engagement with news articles points to a relationship between headlines, the news content and use of images. In the WeChat corpora, we have observed a correlation between posts that have high image counts and certain headlines. In particular, through an analysis of *Sixth Tone* and *Shine* data, we noted marked differences in the relationship between some headlines and higher image counts. In the sample of *Sixth Tone* news articles, certain headlines correlated with a high count of images. WeChat updates with high image counts include headlines such as 'School's out: China's Suddenly Disappearing English Academies' (seven images) or 'Yangtze Fishing Ban Leaves Communities High and Dry' (ten images). Figure 6.3 visualizes examples of articles from *Sixth Tone* with high image counts that also include higher level engagement headlines.

By contrast, the sample of WeChat news articles published by *Shine* (Figure 6.4) demonstrates high image counts for stories that are more closely grounded in public affairs content. For *Shine*, news articles with the highest image counts tended

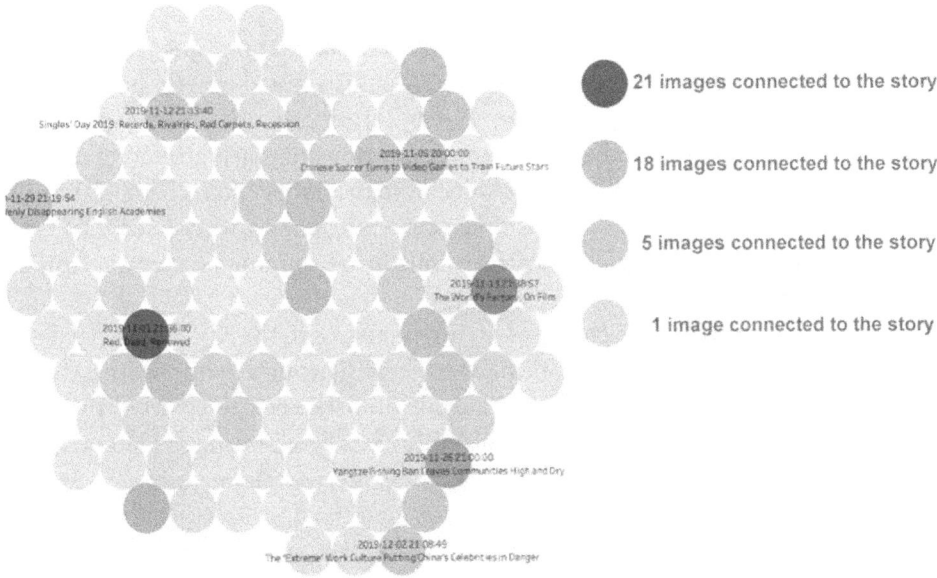

FIGURE 6.3: *Sixth Tone*: relationship between images and clickbait titles.

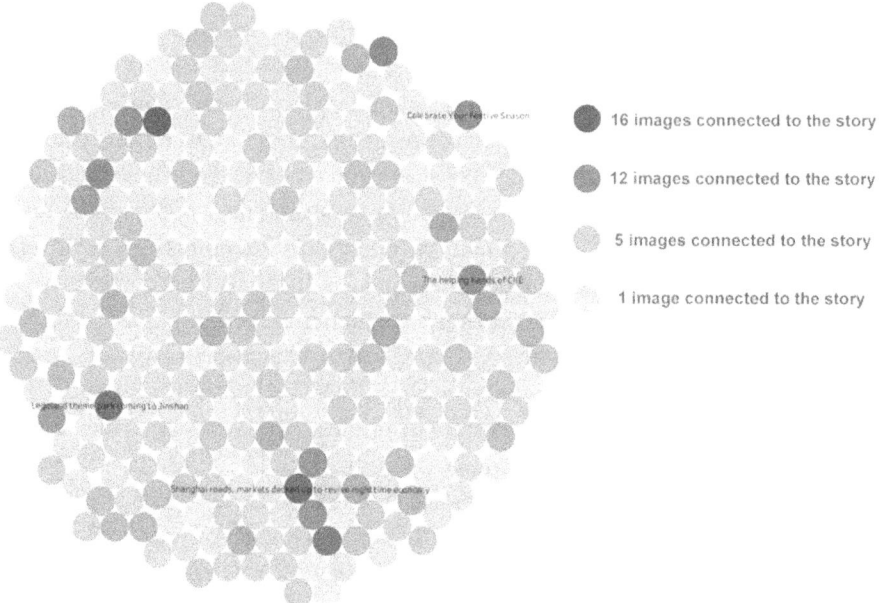

FIGURE 6.4: *Shine*: relationship between high image count and public affairs content.

to resonate with our classification using the public affairs content categories. For example, an article titled 'Shanghai Roads, Markets Decked Up to Revive Night-time Economy' has fourteen images.

These examples indicate patterns across the dataset, and that suggests engagement differences between publishers' news articles distributed on WeChat. Despite the lure of pure clickbait headlines, we note that there is a more specific platform affordance present on WOA that relates to the image availability: attracting readers both in terms of the construction of headlines and the public affairs perspectives in the news content (Taffel 2021). Algorithmic curation of news articles suggests that routines and logics of automated platformization are shaping how news content becomes visible for audiences

In the final sections of the chapter, we turn our focus to the Korean news media ecology to highlight the role of their news portals. Through policy synthesis and interviews with key Korean news media stakeholders, we sketch an outline for the shaping dynamics of their news media industry. By exploring the interactions between journalists, news production houses, the state, portals and users, we underscore the relations of news production and consumption locating the portals at the centre of the Korean media ecology. Our broader intention is to connect the Korean news media context to larger global news production and consumption scenarios across digital platforms, and to consider the implications for media pluralism.

Global platforms, news algorithms and media pluralism

The Reuters 2019 News Report notes that in Korea, 'home-grown portals have become the leading destination for news consumers ... and now online video and podcasts are beginning to disrupt the broadcast sector' (142). It notes, conservatively in our view, that Naver dominates online news consumption with 66 per cent and Daum (Kakao) with 34 per cent with an attractive mix of news, blogs, chat, shopping, games and e-mail. Another noteworthy trend is that 38 per cent of Korean audiences are using YouTube for news, well ahead of most other surveyed countries, and this resonates with comments provided to us by our in-country stakeholder interviewees. The webmetrics company, Koreanclick.com, recorded YouTube mobile app users spending on average 1094 minutes on the app in July 2018, while Naver App users spent about 700 minutes. It is interesting to note that the 2019 Reuters Korean country report found that

> concerns about fake news and misinformation (59%) are rising with concern focused on the distribution of politically extreme views on YouTube. Last year, the government examined ways to effectively regulate fake news online, but concluded that any governmental intervention might curtail freedom of expression.
>
> (Reuters 2019: 142)

Podcasts are increasingly popular as a source of information and, in addition, 9 per cent of those surveyed saying that they were using voice activated personal assistants for news.

Globally, our contemporary news diet is increasingly reliant on content that is sourced from social media platforms including Twitter, Meta, WeChat, TikTok (Douyin), YouTube and Instagram.

Access to news on smartphones has doubled in the past six years within countries such as Spain, the United States and the United Kingdom, while accessing news via Facebook has maintained at around 65 per cent of all users (Reuters 2018). However, according to Reuters, who surveyed more than 75,000 global users, we have witnessed the first recorded period where social media use for news has declined, largely it seems because of the rise of those same platforms championing their private messaging services (Reuters 2018). Users are moving towards private messaging services (the 'pivot to private') on platforms including on WhatsApp (54 per cent), Instagram (16 per cent) and less obvious platforms such as Snapchat (9 per cent). Reuters report that 'WhatsApp has become a primary network for discussing and sharing news in non-Western countries like Brazil (53%) Malaysia (50%), and South Africa (49%)' (Reuters 2019: 9).

These trends suggest that social media and messaging platforms remain significant intermediaries between publics and news journalism at the centre of the debates surrounding media pluralism. In their review of pluralism within the UK's news media ecosystem, the Media Reform Coalition (MRC) noted,

> The UK's media markets cannot be considered in isolation from the digital platforms and intermediaries that increasingly determine how audiences access and consume media content [...] these entities act as the gatekeepers determining how the public obtains information (through search); how people communicate (through social media) and how citizens access news and journalism.
>
> (MRC 2019: 14)

It seems to us that this kind of systemic overview, one that takes into account a range of interacting components and stakeholders that impact on the circulation and surfacing of news, is key to contemporary news ecology analysis.

However, as powerful and popular as they are, the US-centric social media platforms are but one source of contemporary news and journalism. Möller et al. (2019) note that there are usually three key pathways for accessing online news: visiting the news outlet homepage directly, through search engines and via social media. In their study, they found access through the news homepage directly equates to 33 per cent of users; encountering news through search is 32 per cent; 25 per cent of users access news through a combination of news websites and search; and 11 per cent access their news through social media. They also found that those users who are politically interested consume more content through social media, sending signals to the platform algorithms that they like the content, resulting in a tailored feed which then contains more of their sort of material. Their findings underpin three important areas for our research: first, the prevalence of accessing news online and questions of pluralism; second, the significance of platforms in accessing news; and third, the role of algorithms in news curation. The combination of these three significant changes in recent news consumption shifts the focus of journalism research towards the agency of platforms and portals, the relationship between humans and machines for accessing information, and the regulation that surrounds news availability and visibility.

Understanding the role of platforms relates to our broader project focus on news portals in general, and especially those in Korea. Platform studies have enabled researchers to identify a number of key aspects surrounding how news and information is produced, published and accessed on these platforms. Beyond being an economic and strategic regulatory response for online content providers to refer to themselves as 'platforms', Gillespie (2010) argues that platforms play a far more important role as the curators of public discourse. Helmond (2015: 1) suggests platforms are a prominent infrastructure, noting platformization 'entails the extension of social media platforms into the rest of the web and their drive to make external web data "platform ready"'. Bruns notes the shift away from news websites towards considering social media platforms as a prime space for accessing journalism, framing this shift as a problem for news organizations and the news process (2018: 6). He further observes that the news process flows from 'publication through dissemination to engagement – and (now) takes place immediately within the third-party spaces provided by the social media platforms themselves: the outlet's own Website now merely serves as the place where a story is published'. We note that an important exception to this general trend is access to news via publishers' mobile apps. Another important aspect of platform studies includes tracking influential online content producers who continue to dominate as their content is exposed to large audiences through strategic production processes. During a ten-year longitudinal research project on YouTube, Bärtl (2018) notes the top 85 per cent of all content consumed being created by a mere 3 per cent of YouTube content producers. With this production power rule as a backdrop, it can be seen that platforms and their operation are central to any contemporary analysis of the news and journalism process, especially in terms of news media pluralism.

In the Australian context, this situation of the market domination by platforms prompted the then Treasurer, Scott Morrison, to direct the Australian Competition and Consumer Commission (ACCC) to undertake a Digital Platforms Inquiry. A key probe of this inquiry was to highlight that

> there are important questions to be asked about the role the global digital platforms play in the supply of news and journalism in Australia, what responsibility they should hold as gateways to information and business, and the extent to which they should be accountable for their influence.
>
> (ACCC 2018: 1)

The preliminary report from the ACCC noted that although these digital platforms are increasingly performing similar roles as existing media businesses, there is little to no regulation. 'The regulation of media sectors supplying news and journalistic content varies by sector and different regulatory models and obligations apply for TV, radio, print and online publishers' (129). The ACCC, then, was very conscious of the pressures for regulation, or at least new forms of regulation. Responding to two of the Commission's preliminary recommendations, and from the specific perspective of online news and journalism, Flew and Dwyer (2019) argued:

> we support the recommendation (5) for the establishment of a regulatory authority to 'monitor, investigate and report on the ranking of news and journalistic content by digital platforms and the provision of referral services to news media businesses'. In addition, we support recommendation (6) to 'conduct a separate, independent review

[…] to ensure […] regulations are applied effectively and consistently', in relation to the production and delivery of news and journalistic content. (3)

The first of these recommendations was abandoned by the Commission in its final report (ACCC 2019) but the second was at least partly taken up in a government policy statement (Australian Government 2019). The push to make platforms more accountable through regulation extends far beyond the Australian inquiry alone. In the United Kingdom, The Cairncross (2019) Review was primarily concerned with shoring up 'high journalism' within the journalism environment we highlight above to solve the problem of 'broken journalism' (Barnett 2019). Most significantly, the Cairncross Report recommended the establishment of an Institute for Public Interest News to forge publisher/platform partnerships, distribute revenues accordingly and monitor the quality of journalism. This recommendation came at a time when Facebook itself was establishing its Oversight Board to monitor content governance, a response to increasing pressure from publics and Senate enquiries (Zuckerberg 2018). The vast array of platform attention, then, both externally and internally, and the pressure to more accurately regulate news access points has significantly increased in the last few years. The following Korean case studies demonstrate the role platforms, social media and portals have on the production and distribution of public and non-public affairs journalism.

Naver: A search engine plus

As the dominant source of news in Korea, the Naver portal is generally referred to as a 'search engine' in the sense referred to previously by Moller et al. (2019). But to place Naver into this category is only partly accurate. While it is certainly the case that a large search engine box sits across the top of the home page, it is not used in the way that Google or Yahoo search is used; although Google and Naver do share some common features. For example, both brands offer a news aggregation service that is algorithmically personalized, based on past user interactions. But the Naver homepage offers a wider range of functions including news stories, weather, shopping, blogs, cartoons, e-mail, a dictionary, stock market information, music and books. Therefore, it is easy to see why Naver can be considered as the 'Korean homepage for the Internet' (Marsden 2017). The Naver and Kakao portals actually prefer the 'Internet Service Provider' moniker, and shy away from any broadcast-like analogies, with their attendant regulatory assumptions (Kim 2019).

Yet, algorithmically, Naver and Google operationalize in quite different ways. Koreans use Naver as a destination to help them connect and explore in a more broadly culturally way; it's not perceived just as a means to hoover up page-ranked information on a specific topic or event (although it can do that as well). Koreans use the site as a hub and constantly morphing cultural palimpsest where they can see news on a range of their interests and receive suggestions and get ideas for things to search for. It acts as a cultural repository that users can browse, with a plenty of rich media content that may then lead users to search for more news on a topic of interest. This multi-dimensional functionality means that although users may go elsewhere for certain things such as e-commerce and travel sites, Naver operates the first port of call for most Koreans when they interface with the Internet, both on mobile and desktop and according to some, the portal has 'outsized control over what Koreans read and see' (Bogle 2017).

Naver provides search services in 'various collections such as a Web collection, a directory collection, an image collection, a news collection, an encyclopedia collection, a thesis and article collection, a knowledge collection, and so on' (Park et al. 2005: 206). Naver is the core source of information for many Koreans having a very strong relationship with the Korean publishers and news agencies. In 2017, Naver was reported to be negotiating fees for content agreements with 124 news outlets each year as Naver News In-Link partners (Bogle 2017). The In-Link system means that the partners' articles are published on the portal; and it's an effective way of keeping users bouncing around inside Naver's advertising world. Digital advertising revenue was reported as 2.97 trillion won (USD 2.7 billion) in 2017 making the In-Link partners total fees of USD 40 million look tiny in comparison (Bogle 2017). At the time of that assessment another 500 or so news outlets were unpaid 'search partners' and users would be sent to the originator's site, in a manner similar to *Google News* or Facebook's *Instant Articles*. These In-Link partners have entered into supply agreements with the portal, and consequently have become critical to the economics of the news industry in Korea. The main state-controlled news agency, Yonhap, (Kim 2019) has such a relationship and supplies around a quarter of all the news articles appearing on the Naver and Daum (Kakao) portals.

The news experience for a Naver user, like all news experiences, is ultimately a branded cultural experience that becomes a very familiar and accepted process of access and discovery. When Gillespie argues in *Custodians of the Internet*, 'Platforms are sociotechnical assemblages and complex institutions' he is therefore underscoring these cultural dimensions (2018: 18).

A common approach towards researching platforms and applications (apps) is to undertake a 'walk-through' method (Giddings 2006; Light et al. 2018). On performing a walkthrough on Naver, it becomes clear that the platform is designed to be a kind of 'one-stop-shop' for Koreans, as it provides a number of services beyond news articles. It also has a search function, an entertainment section, an e-mail client, a space for keeping notes organized, Web Toon, and a number of other functions. We therefore engaged the efforts of a native speaking Korean to translate the app and explain how it was used. Choi (2019: n.pag.) made these interesting observations:

> Korean people just wouldn't open up their phone and use Google to search the web. It's kind of our go to app for almost everything in that, say, I want to check the weather in Seoul, I will open up Naver to do this. I will probably then see what is happening in the K Pop world, and because I work in radio, I then start to check what news articles appear […] Because I use Naver [most of the time], I have subscribed to a number of news topics, so the news that is presented to me is usually what I am interested in. I understand the editorial process here, and am aware of the algorithmic process, but that's probably because I work in the media. I'm not sure that's the case for Koreans more broadly.

Choi also highlighted that the majority of news articles she sees come from Yonhap News and noted that unlike for the remainder of supplied content she rarely leaves the portal to go back to the native news site (Choi 2019). Indeed, the assemblage of technology and information that is presented on this app is Naver-branded and caters to a particular user experience. The editorial, both human and non-human, is designed to address a particular user and retain their time spent within this environment. The longer the user remains on the Naver app, the more 'normalized' the branded-experience becomes.

Kakao: A portal meets a killer messaging app

Kakao is a Korean internet company formed through the merger of Daum and Kakao in 2014 but was rebranded the following year and is now referred to as *Kakao*. Like Naver, Kakao has many applications associated with the core portal destination, *Daum*, including its super popular service, *KakaoTalk* ('Kakao'). 'Kakaotalk is a Korean mobile messaging application that allows users to set up a profile containing an avatar and a status message. Users can text each other or participate in a group chat with many friends' (Shim et al. 2012: 5).

By 2020 Kakao had over 220 million registered users and over 52 million active monthly users worldwide with more than 44 million based in Korea. It is available in 15 languages but used by more by 93 per cent of smartphone owners in Korea (Statistica 2020). For Korean users this represents an unassailable lead on rival messaging services such as Telegram, Facebook Messenger, Line, WeChat and Naver (also used for messaging). The closest messaging app in terms of popularity is the Line app, which may potentially gain some ground in Korea following a merger with the internet portal Yahoo Japan. Under the terms of the merger agreement a subsidiary of Softbank (another large Japanese corporation) and Line's parent company, Naver, each hold 50 per cent of the joint venture holding company (Mochizuki 2019). Merging the Japanese Line (the dominant chat app in Japan) and Yahoo databases, combined with the deep pockets of Softbank and Naver, may eventually be able to make some inroads into Kakao's near monopoly domination over chat messaging in Korea. Bearing in mind the global trend to increased usage of messaging for formerly social media network functions, this move may be one to watch. Interestingly, it was prescient that at the time of the merger the new company announced that they would aim to become 'one of the world's leading AI tech companies' (Mochizuki 2019).

One of the most popular aspects of Kakao is the Daum portal, which is the second largest in the country with 38 per cent share of the Korean news aggregation services (Newman et al. 2018). It operates in a similar fashion to a social network and chat app, and like Naver *pays* news organizations for access to their content. It's noteworthy that Daum has a storyfunding service 'by which users can donate money to citizen journalists, civic organisations, and investigative reporters' (Newman et al. 2018: 136). Our research interviewees agreed that with Naver's lead in market share, the Kakao-Daum portal is unlikely to catch up with them anytime soon. However, with a significant share of the market Kakao, is in a position to offer differentiated products and services (KakaoTalk and Kakaotaxi are just two of several service apps), and to also make it competitive, some suggest more conservative, news curation interventions (both human and algorithmic).

Algorithms and news in Korea

A critical area we wish to focus on in this chapter is problematizing the impact that algorithms are having on online news and media content diversity. Algorithms, recommender systems and personalization all shape exposure to new information in what Pariser (2011) refers to as a filter bubble – or an echo chamber of similar discussions amongst users who are all concerned with similar issues. Algorithms, 'understood as the coded instructions that a computer needs to follow to perform a given task, (they) are deployed to make decisions, to sort and make meaningfully visible the vast amount of data produced and available on the web' (Bucher 2018: 3), and they are key mechanisms on digital platforms that curate online news (Wilding et al. 2018). With news personalization, Pasquale (2015: 78) notes 'Google News might give pride of place to baseball, music, or left-wing politics according to the reputations we establish', suggesting the information we are exposed to is based on the historical access to news. Therefore, we can say that the combination of algorithms on digital platforms forms the basis for recommender systems which have 'the goal of enhancing the findability and exposure of their content, and to improve interactive services and personalisation' (Sørensen and Hutchinson 2018: 94). Online news discoverability through recommender systems is a useful tool for personalizing news to the user but one which also raises various algorithmic concerns, as well as significant data scandals which have been identified by a number of scholars and commentators (Moore 2018; Wylie 2019).

Noble (2018), for example, has argued algorithms can be inherently racist and exclusionary, are inherently political (Bucher, 2018; Forlano, 2018) and can impinge on civil rights through predictive policing (Civil Rights.org 2019). These concerns, then, are the basis for a number of inquiries and investigations from several global agencies, including the Data & Society Institute, AI Now Institute and the Leadership Conference on Civil and Human Rights for example, to ensure that plurality remains a significant public policy issue within digital intermediation (Moore and Tambini 2018; Napoli 2019).

Globally, there are an increasing number of calls for increased transparency, accountability and regulation for these digital platforms. According to the 2018 Reuters Digital News Report, social media users see misinformation, trust and transparency as a significant issue, where 60 per cent of Europeans have called for greater platform and content regulation, compared with 41 per cent in the United States. The *AI Now Report* (Whittaker et al. 2018) considered these same issues within the context of automation and artificial intelligence (AI), and constructed a series of key recommendations to address these concerns, along with labour issues, and the need for policy interventions around questions of race, gender and power. In this context the Silicon Valley rhetoric of 'move fast and break things' is now no longer an acceptable mantra given the potential harms it may cause to society, with journalism remaining a key vehicle for public issues on behalf of an informed citizenry.

Yet while many public interest groups are calling for greater transparency, this can be empty rhetoric for publics and users needing to interrogate what is, generally, a complex mathematical equation: an algorithm. Instead, the 2019 *Automating Society* report on automated decision making within the European Union region frames these concerns through arguably a more useful lens of 'understandability'. 'There are a number of ways we can enhance citizens' expertise to enable them to better assess the consequences of automated decision-making' (Algorithmic Watch: n.pag). In Finland for example, there are now free public courses available for citizens, in which 100,000 have enrolled, where 'some societal implications of AI are introduced, for example, algorithmic bias and de-anonymization, to underscore the need for policies and regulations that help society to adapt more easily to the use of AI' (Algorithmic Watch 2019: n.pag.).

If users are aware that their online news feed is manipulated by these sorts of mechanisms, they are better equipped to source diverse content in the absence of suitable regulation. Pasquale has undertaken a survey on the short history of 'algorithmic accountability' and observes that 'just as the "first wave" of algorithmic accountability research and activism has targeted existing systems, an emerging "second wave" has begun to address more structural concerns. Both waves will be essential to ensure a fairer, more emancipatory political economy of technology' (Pasquale 2019: n.pag.).

While this environment remains in transition as a regulatory grey area, the online news and journalism market in Korea is a significant case study for studying algorithms and news diversity not least for the massive national audiences their portals attract. In our view, the Korean news media ecology contains some important signposts in the debate for news media pluralism and its relation to questions of automation of editorial decision-making.

Key industry stakeholders in Korea's news market

The traditional Korean news industry is built on the recognizable foundations of most global media industries through its print, radio and television networks which have paved the way for the current networked media organizations, including the news portals. Many of these organizations are still in operation today, where many of them made significant landgrabs for telecom and internet service providers (ISPs) facilitated by key stakeholders including Korea Telecom (KT), SK Telecom (SK) and LG during the 1990s. Currently, KT, SK and LG are the largest providers of mobile and desktop internet access. In terms of broadcast news media, the main market players are KBS, MBS, JTBC, Yonhap TV, YTN, MBN and SBS. The main newspaper publishers are Chosunilbo, Joongangilbo, Dongailbo, Maeil Business, Kyunhyang and Hankyoreh.

In relation more specifically to the online news environment, there are a number of key players within the content publication and distribution landscape for the Korean market. A powerful player in the regulatory space is the Media Partnerships Evaluation Committee (MPEC) – a joint initiative by Naver and Kakao (then Daum) to establish a self-regulatory body to oversee the online news environment, and specifically the portals in 2015. Certainly, it appears to be partly a strategic response, often seen in the media sector, to ward off tougher black letter responses by government and regulatory authorities. Given their dominance in Korea it is not surprising that the portals have moved to a predominantly self-regulatory model in the 'Media Partnership Evaluation Committee'.

Officially, the MPEC's main purpose is to manage the fairness of news distribution on the portals. The portals had been criticized about their news partnerships and why particular articles surfaced more prominently on the platforms. This was, and continues to be, in a climate of strong criticism of the portals' manipulation of news articles, usually in favour of the incumbent political party. This was the case during the Park Geun Hye (2013–2017) led government, her subsequent impeachment, and then during the Moon Jae-In (2017–2022) government. It has been reported that the Committee serves two main functions: first, to evaluate which news outlets can supply news to the portals and second, to penalize news outlets that violate contract conditions, including publishing sponsored, violent content or clickbait articles (Bogle 2017).

The allegation has been aired that publishers will use trending topics to over produce clickbait articles, and thus there was a need to monitor and penalize, and in a few cases not renew partnership news supply agreements. To stop access to Naver's traffic firehose can potentially sound the death knell for publishers relying on the clicks and therefore advertizing dollars. This is a significant amount of power to be welded by an unelected body whose membership is made up of the portals themselves and media experts, major press outlets and broadcasters appointed by the portals; they are often criticized for the application of opaque assessment criteria in relation to news 'quality factors'. In effect, these judgement calls are defining the sorts of content that is appropriate for the Korean citizens, as well as which news sources are suitable to provide journalism to the news portals.

Interestingly, both news portals sponsor the Committee to remain in operation. Twice yearly, the Committee accepts applications from all news sources and agencies that would like to be included as providers to the news portals. The non-government affiliation, along with their connection to the news portals and their ability to enable or prohibit particular news agencies, positions them as significantly powerful players in shaping the news media within Korea. Naver itself also made changes to the portal's news curation in response to critics; in 2017, it announced that by 2018, it would be moving from a combination of human and machine curation to an entirely automated news selection model. Nonetheless, the company noted that humans would be creating the news selection algorithm and decisions regarding the partnership agreements with news outlets would be made entirely by humans (Bogle 2017).

The most significant online news outlets are the powerful Yonhap News Agency, News1.kr, Joins.com (JoongAng), Chosun.com, JTBC.Joins.com, Newsis.com, Donga.com, News.SBS.co.kr and Hankooki.com (*The Korea Times*), who are primarily responsible for Korean news agenda setting (Lim 2011). Of these major online outlets, one of the key news providers in the Korean context is the Yonhap News Agency. Yonhap News Agency is a wire service that 'delivers domestic and overseas news in real time' and covers 'all news topics from politics, business and social issues to culture and sports. The agency produces more than 3,000 news items daily, including articles, photos, graphics and video' (Yonhap 2019). According to Jin-Gyu Kim, an IT Manager at Yonhap, 'These items are provided to about 180 local news outlets, more than 120 Internet portals and new media platforms, some 210 government ministries and local authorities, and around 250 private businesses' (Lee and Joshi 2018: 226). Yonhap News Agency is one of the largest suppliers of news to the country and has approximately 25 per cent of the total amount of news on the two major news portals, Naver and Kakao. The media homogeneity compounds with a smartphone penetration rate of approximately 80 per cent (Statista 2018).

While the Korean news and journalism market appears to be relatively free and open on the surface, on closer inspection it can be seen to be significantly skewed to a small number of dominant news provider voices. The arrangement between the news organizations, the MPEC and the two dominating news portals significantly limits the diversity of sources for the Korean citizens. In the following section, we will explore this relationship using field data and policy documents.

Media contexts of disinformation

Park et al. (2010) have researched the broader context of Korean Internet regulation finding that 'Korea is a highly networked country, but Internet use has been strongly regulated'. In Korea, the majority of online platforms require a valid national ID number (and the real name) for verification when users first register. This system first gained traction in the wake of serious online social problems relating to defamatory language and rumour mongering, including the slander of celebrities and suicides linked with these communications.

The Korean Communication Commission (KCC) regulates the online industry, including Naver and Kakao. Content is closely monitored by the KCC, and our research confirms that news content on the portals is required under Korean law to be redistributed rather than originally produced (Kim 2019).

In previous years, there has been minimal traditional editorial intervention, amounting mainly to story selection, packaging and layout. Dae Woon Kim (2019), the Director Government relations & policy affairs team for Daum Kakao, noted 'Daum enhance the convenience of news consumption' (Kim 2019). Essentially the portals, as the major destinations for news seeking audiences, are *redistributing* news from traditional news organizations including Yonhap, Chosun or Joongang. Kim also highlighted that Kakao (Daum) has pre-determined categories from the main page and this is what they prioritize, hinting at a stronger focus toward automation over editorial.

Mixed with cultural edginess though are other unique political-economic traditions. Korea's new media is deeply influenced by the country's modern political and economic history. The press had been very tightly controlled under successive authoritarian governments until many restrictions were lifted when the Basic Press Law was repealed in 1987. Democratization and a more open outlook to global media led to an increase in the range of media sources (local and international) throughout the 1990s.

Yet the Korean press are still subject to direct and indirect pressure from the government, including through criminal defamation and national security laws, leading to international media watchdog Reporters Without Borders ranking Korea in 2019 at the 41st in its world press freedom index – an improvement on its 60th ranking in 2018 (Reporters Without Borders 2019). The press media outlets have generally shaped the mediasphere in terms of fostering party political alignments.

Newspapers in Korea have traditionally been divided along political lines – the leading, mainstream newspapers, *Chosun*, *JoongAng* and *Dong-A*, are generally conservative and broadly supportive of the major Korean business conglomerates, or Chaebol. In return, the Chaebol offered support (in the form of advertising revenue) for favourable (or limits on unfavourable) coverage.

Daniel Tudor, the former Korea correspondent for *The Economist*, has written that Korean media tends to contribute to an atmosphere of political division. He notes in relation to traditional media:

> There are five major national newspapers: *Chosun Ilbo, JoongAng Ilbo, Dong-A Ilbo, Hankyoreh, and Kyunghyang Shimun*. The first three are the most popular, with over two million daily copies sold each. They are also all editorially right-wing. Left-wing critics lump the three together as one, taking the first syllable of their names to make the pejorative composite word *Chojoongdong* though in reality the *JoongAng* has been perceived as more moderate than the *Chosun* or the *Dong-A*. The Hankyoreh and Kyunghyang Shimun are left-wing and less popular.

Tudor's general view of the news media in Korea is that there is only a limited free press and the majority of outlets 'lack balance and moderation. They present the same basic news but with different biases'. The power of the Chaebol within Korean society means 'harsh criticism of the likes of Samsung or Hyundai is rare in the mainstream media. If 20% of one's advertising revenue comes from one company, one is very unlikely to criticize that company'.

Online news sources have become more important since the turn of the century and the major internet portals are considered to be a threat to the business models of the legacy press. Tudor cites the 'citizen reporter' news site 'Ohmynews.com' as evidence of the existence of a left-wing media. In the intervening years, the site met with severe financial problems, with the English language site being shut down and archived.

Overall, the influence of online sources of news poses growing challenges to legacy media and the established institutions with which they are aligned. More than in some other industries (e.g., electronics, automobile manufacturing and heavy industry), these upstarts are demonstrating considerable resistance to the usually over-whelming power of the chaebol. Notably, the largest internet company, Naver, pointedly declined invitations from the Federation of Korean Industries (FKI) – composed of the major Korean chaebol – to join the key umbrella industry group. Naver instead remains a member of the Korea Medium Industries Association and publicly states its goal is to support the development of an 'Internet ecosystem' and the growth of small and medium businesses.

Most news content still originates from either a newspaper (or similar, i.e. a news magazine) or a news wire service, such as Yonhap. The news portals in Korea do not have newsrooms or any reporting (in fact, as noted above, their 'distributor' legal status prevents them under government regulation from doing so). Professional and personal blogs are still very popular sources of news and information in Korea. Blogs hosted on the portals are typically the most popular for the so-called 'angry 20–40 year old' demographic. These are widely read and shared on Twitter and via messaging apps such as Kakao and Line (Naver).

In their analysis of contemporary media pluralism policy in Korea, Youn and Lee note that 'the media law debates' of 2008–10 were basically an ideological conflict over deregulation between conservative and more progressive media and their party political parallels (Youn and Lee 2015). This battle was essentially over the power of corporations to shape public opinion in Korea; not surprisingly it continues and is inevitably framed by neo-liberal discourses of market deregulation. Government agencies formed in the wake of the 'media law debates', and the Committee on the Impact of Media Concentration and the Media Diversity Committee, are now grappling with evaluating the public policy and regulatory implications of this conflict (Youn and Lee 2015: 282).

Conclusion

This chapter has investigated an approach for researching media diversity policies and its relation to online news ecologies in China and Korea using both theoretical and empirical frameworks of analysis. Our argument has been that this requires taking steps to, in the first instance, de-westernize earlier approaches based on comparative frameworks which have been at best, overly universalistic and at worst, narrowly ethnocentric in their application. In our view, theorized understandings of diversification and pluralization offer valuable explanatory leverage in these online news media ecologies.

In addition to making inroads into and developing our understanding of media pluralities across divergent media systems, this research has applied computational techniques of data analysis. Our intention has been to extend existing media pluralism models in order that they might be applied to societies that are undergoing rapid changes to their media practices.

Our research into media pluralism and diversities has taken an approach that seeks to emphasize processes as well as systems and prompted reassessments of the dynamic interactions between structure, agency and pathways of policymaking. We have intentionally not made direct comparisons between Australian and these Asian media ecologies; rather, we have seen greater value in taking a first steps approach allowing researchers to identify similarities and differences using relevant theoretical framings and methodologies. There are overlaps with the EC's MPM which frames sufficient pluralism in terms of the risks present in nation state's media ecologies. Existing analysis in terms of diversification and pluralization recognize the unique characteristics of the media ecology in China, and we have built on this in theorising how diversity in online news media is manifested (Sukosd 2016). We have also argued that so-called 'platformization' needs to be a factor in any future reassessments of the way news articles surface on news platforms in China and Korea, as it does in any other national or regional internet location. Algorithmic visibility is structured through the role of commercial, personalized media delivery mechanisms; it is also a global factor in platform exposure to news articles from both individual and aggregate perspectives.

The data for online news articles in WeChat official accounts has provided a preliminary analysis of news distributed on this popular platform. We have argued that computational content analysis is highly complementary to the theoretical approach that we have taken; not only does it allow for nuanced assessments of important 'public affairs' content in platform intermediaries but it is also consistent with regulatory assessments that seek to monitor actual consumption in relation to meaningful and sufficient diversity.

Our research indicates that a common area of attention across the analysis of news articles in these nation-states concerns the role of automated curation of content relying on algorithmic manipulation of news stories. In a marketized and commercialized media ecosystem that is forced to spread their resources, news organizations in China are under increasing pressure to attract readers to their news brands. The WOA are an important part of the evolving suite of digital media audience marketing techniques that assemble their audiences by various means, including on Tencent's popular WeChat social media platform ecosystem.

In terms of media voice pluralism on the portals in Korea, our research indicates a very dynamic media market in Korea, and yet one still dominated by a relatively small set of players. In particular, the power of the portals over everyday news media consumption is very apparent since news is being selected from what is a mature, medium sized national news market, and this means that the pool of news providers inevitably results in a quite concentrated pool; this group are then filtered initially by the portals (and MPEC), and then further winnowed by both human and machine based curation processes.

It has been a turbulent few years in Korean politics, first with the 'candlelight revolution' and impeachment of former president, Park Guen Hye, and then disinformation and news manipulation scandals at Naver thought to have contributed to the election of the president, Moon Jae-In. This led to a major investigation into a key member of Moon's election team and hacker Kim Dongwon, subsequently found by an independent prosecutor to have manipulated public opinion on a massive scale at the Naver and Nate portals. These events have prompted changes in policies and practices at the portals. Clearly, this kind of hacking and manipulation of news is now a feature of our online news media ecologies, with significant consequences for democratic polities around the world.

REFERENCES

ACCC (2018), *Digital Platforms Inquiry: Preliminary Report*, Canberra, 10 December, https://www.accc.gov.au/focus-areas/inquiries/digital-platforms-inquiry/preliminary-report. Accessed 14 February 2022.

ACCC (2019), *Digital Platforms Inquiry. Final Report*, Canberra, 26 July, https://www.accc.gov.au/publications/digital-platforms-inquiry-final-report. Accessed 14 February 2022.

Algorithmic Watch (2019), 'Automating society: Taking stock of automated decision-making in the EU, Berlin', https://www.algorithmwatch.org/automating-society. Accessed 1 February 2023.

Australian Government (2019), *Regulating in the Digital Age: Government Response and Implementation Roadmap for the Digital Platforms Inquiry*, Canberra, 12 December, https://treasury.gov.au/publication/p2019-41708. Accessed 1 February 2023.

Barnett, S. (2019), 'Cairncross review: Two cheers and two fears for the future of UK journalism', *The Conversation*, 14 February, https://theconversation.com/cairncross-review-two-cheers-and-two-fears-for-the-future-of-uk-journalism-111658. Accessed 1 February 2023.

Bärtl, M. (2018), 'YouTube channels, uploads and views: A statistical analysis of the past 10 years', *Convergence: The International Journal of Research into New Media Technologies*, 24:1, pp. 16–32.

Bogle, A. (2017), 'Has the Google of South Korea found a way to save struggling news outlets?', *The Atlantic*, https://www.theatlantic.com/technology/archive/2017/12/naver-news-ad-revenue/547412/. Accessed 1 February 2023.

Bruns, A. (2018), *Gatewatching and News Curation: Journalism, Social Media, and the Public Sphere*, New York: Peter Lang.

Bucher, T. (2018), *If ... Then: Algorithmic Power and Politics*, New York: Oxford University Press.

Cairncross, F. (2019), *Cairncross Review: A Sustainable Future for Journalism*, Gov.UK, https://assets.publishing.service.gov.uk/government/uploads/system/uploads/attachment_data/file/779882/021919_DCMS_Cairncross_Review_.pdf. Accessed 4 September 2022.

Choi, K. (2019), personal interview, Seoul, 20 February.

Civil Rights.org (2019), 'Civil rights and tech advocates sound alarm on racial bias in predictive policing', https://civilrights.org/2016/08/31/civil-rights-and-tech-advocates-sound-alarm-on-racial-bias-in-predictive-policing/. Accessed 1 February 2023.

Council of the European Union (2020), *Council Conclusions on Safeguarding a Free and Pluralistic Media System (7 December 2020, 2020/C 422/08) paragraph 21*, https://eur-lex.europa.eu/legal-content/EN/TXT/PDF/?uri=uriserv:OJ.C_.2020.422.01.0008.01.ENG. Accesssed 8 February 2022.

Davis, M. and Xiao, J. (2021), 'De-westernizing platform studies: History and logics of Chinese and U.S. platforms', *International Journal of Communication*, 15:2021, pp. 103–22.

Deng, J. (2017), 'Telling little and beautiful China stories – The convergence international journalism of Sixth Tone', *International Communications (Duiwai Chuanbo)*, 5, pp. 63–65.

Deng, J. (2018), '*The Paper* Janus: How exceptionalism based on regaining influence and doing new media help a Chinese mobile news app negotiate censorship for better journalism', *Communication and the Public*, 3:2, pp. 113–33.

Dwyer, T. (2019), 'Media pluralism policies and the implications of social news sharing', in F. Martin and T. Dwyer (eds), *Sharing News Online. Commentary Cultures and Social Media News Ecologies*, Cham: Palgrave Macmillan, pp. 223–56.

Fenton, N., Freedman, D., Schlosberg, J. and Dencik, L. (2020), *The Media Manifesto*, Cambridge, Medford: Polity.

Flew, T. and Dwyer, T. (2019). *Response to ACCC Digital Platforms Inquiry Preliminary Report*, Canberra, https://www.accc.gov.au/system/files/Professor%20Terry%20Flew%20and%20Associate%20Professor%20Tim%20Dwyer%20%28February%202019%29.PDF. Accessed 24 February 2023.

Flew, T. and Wilding, D. (2020), 'The turn to regulation in digital communication: The ACCC's digital platforms inquiry and Australian media policy', *Media, Culture & Society*, 43:1, pp. 48–65, https://doi.org/10.1177/0163443720926044.

Forlano, L. (2018), 'Invisible algorithms, invisible politics', Public Books, http://www.publicbooks.org/invisible-algorithms-invisible-politics/. Accessed 1 February 2023.

Gibbons, T. (2015), 'What is "Sufficient" plurality?', in S. Barnett and J. Townend (eds), *Media Power and Plurality: From Hyperlocal to High-Level Policy*, London: Palgrave Macmillan, n.pag.

Giddings, S. (2006), 'Walkthrough: Videogames and technocultural form', Ph.D. dissertation, Bristol:University of the West of England.

Gillespie, T. (2010), 'The politics of platforms', *New Media and Society*, 12:3, pp. 347–64.

Gillespie, T. (2018), *Custodians of the Internet: Platforms, Content Moderation, and the Hidden Decisions that Shape Social Media*, New Haven, London: Yale University Press.

Gong, Q., Verboord, M. and Janssen, S. (2020), 'Cross-media usage repertoires and their political impacts: The case of China', *International Journal of Communication*, 14:2020, pp. 3799–818.

Hallin, D. and Mancini, P. (2012) (eds), *Comparing Media Systems Beyond the Western World*, New York: Cambridge University Press.

Hallin, D. and Mancini, P. (2004), *Comparing Media Systems: Three Models of Media and Politics*, Cambridge: Cambridge University Press.

He, Y. (2012), 'Let TV news reporting touch souls: An analysis of Zouzhuanggai's new space', *Journal of TV Research*, 10, pp. 17–20.

Helberger, N. (2018), 'Challenging media diversity – Social media platforms and a new conception of media diversity', in M. Moore and D. Tambini (eds), *Digital Dominance: The Power of Google, Amazon, Facebook and Apple*, New York: Oxford University Press, pp. 153–75.

Helberger, N. (2021), 'On the democratic role of news recommenders', in N. Thurman, S. C. Lewis and J. Kunert (eds), *Algorithms, Automation and News: New Directions in the Study of Computation and News*, London: Routledge, pp. 14–33.

Helmond, A. (2015), 'The platformization of the web: Making web data platform ready', *Social Media + Society*, 1:2, pp. 1–11.

Hong, Y. (2017), *Networking China: The Digital Transformation of the Chinese Economy*, Champaign: University of Illinois Press.

Hutchinson, J. and Sørensen, J. (2021), 'Can automated strategies work for PSM in a network society? Engaging digital intermediation for informed citizenry', in M. Túñez-López, F. Campos-Freire and M. Rodríguez-Castro (eds), *The Values of Public Service Media in the Internet Society*, New York: Palgrave Macmillan, pp. 59–75.

Jin, D. Y. (2021), 'Encounters with western media theory: Asian perspectives', *Media, Culture & Society*, 43:1, pp. 150–57.

Karppinen, K. (2006), 'Media diversity and the politics of criteria: Diversity assessment and technocratisation of European media policy', *Nordicom Review*, 27:2, pp. 53–68.

Kim, D. (2019), personal interview with the Director Government Relations & Policy Affairs, Kakao, Seoul, 19 February.

Kim, J.-H. (2019), personal interview, *Yonhap News Agency*, Seoul, 19 February.

Kwak, K. S. (2012), *Media and Democratic Transition in South Korea*, New York: Routledge.

Lee, K. and Joshi, K. (2018), 'IS supported global information exchanges in new media environments: An interview with Jin-Gyu Kim, manager of IT Operation of Yonhap News Agency, Seoul, Korea', *Journal of Global Information Technology Management*, 21:3, pp. 226–28.

Light, B., Burgess, J. and Duguay, S. (2017), 'The walkthrough method: An approach to the study of apps', *New Media & Society*, pp. 1–20.

Lim, J. (2011), 'First-level and second-level intermedia agenda-setting among major news websites', *Asian Journal of Communication*, 21:2, pp. 167–85.

Lingel, J. (2021), *The Gentrification of the Internet: How to Reclaim Our Digital Freedom*, Los Angeles: University of California Press.

Marsden, T. (2017), 'Google vs Naver. Google's Struggles – South Korea in Focus', 13 March, https://www.minttwist.com/blog/google-vs-naver-googles-struggles-south-korea-focus/. Accessed 1 February 2023.

Media Pluralism Monitor Report (2020), *European Commission, DG Connect. Centre for Media Pluralism and Freedom*, https://ec.europa.eu/digital-single-market/en/news/media-pluralism-monitor-report-2020. Accessed 24 February 2023.

Media Pluralism Project (2019), 'The role of a pluralistic media in Australia's democracy', Accessed 30 January 2023. https://mediapluralism.org.au/2019/05/the-role-of-a-pluralistic-media-in-australias-democracy/. Accessed 30 January 2023.

Media Pluralism Project Dashboard (2020), Computational tool available at https://mediapluralism.sydney.edu.au. Accessed 19 July 2023.

Media Reform Coalition (2019), *Who Owns the Media? Goldsmiths Leverhulme Media Research Centre, Department of Media, Communications and Cultural Studies*, London: Goldsmiths, University of London.

Mochizuki, T. (2019), 'Yahoo Japan and line link up', *The Australian* (from the WSJ), 19 November, n.pag.

Möller, J., Velde, R. N. v. d., Merten, L. and Puschmann, C. (2019), 'Explaining online news engagement based on browsing behavior: Creatures of habit?', *Social Science Computer Review*, pp. 1–17, https://doi.org/10.1177/0894439319828012.

Moore, M. (2018), *Democracy Hacked: Political Turmoil and Information Warfare in the Digital Age*, London: One World.

Moore, M. and Tambini, D. (eds) (2018), *Digital Dominance: The Power of Google, Amazon, Facebook, and Apple*, New York: Oxford University Press.

Morgan, R. (2018), 'Single source news data (top twenty online news sites)', http://www.roymorgan.com/findings/7595-top-20-news-websites-march-2018-201805240521. Accessed 30 January 2023.

Napoli, P. (2019), *Social Media and the Public Interest: Media Regulation in the Disinformation Age*, New York: Columbia University Press.

Nenadic, I. and Milosavljevic, M. (2019), 'Adapting the understanding of media market plurality to new digital realities', 5 February, https://cmpf.eui.eu/adapting-understanding-media-market-plurality-to-the-new-digital-realities/. Accessed 30 January 2023.

Newman, N., Fletcher, R., Kalogeropoulos, A., Levy, D. A. and Nielsen, R. K. (2018), *Reuters Institute Digital News Report 2018*, Oxford, https://reutersinstitute.politics.ox.ac.uk/sites/default/files/digital-news-report-2018.pdf. Accessed 30 January 2023.

Newman, N., Fletcher, R., Kalogeropoulos, A., Levy, D. A. and Nielsen, R. K. (2019), *Reuters Institute Digital News Report*, Oxford, http://www.digitalnewsreport.org. Accessed 30 January 2023.

Noble, S. U. (2018), *Algorithms of Oppression: How Search Engines Reinforce Racism*, New York: NYU Press.

Park, M. and Curran, J. (2005), *De-Westernising Media Studies*, London. Routledge.

Park, S., Lee, J. H. and Bae, H. J. (2005), 'End user searching: A web log analysis of NAVER, a Korean Web search engine', *Library and Information Science Research*, 27, pp. 203–21.

Pariser, E. (2011), *The Filter Bubble: What the Internet Is Hiding from You*, New York: Penguin Press.

Pasquale, F. (2015), *The Black Box Society: The Secret Algorithms That Control Money and Information*, Cambridge: MIT Press.

Pasquale, F. (2019), 'The second wave of algorithmic accountability', *Law and Political Economy*, 25 November, https://lpeblog.org/2019/11/25/the-second-wave-of-algorithmic-accountability/. Accessed 30 January 2023.

Reporters Without Borders (2019), *World Press Freedom Index Ranking*, https://rsf.org/en/ranking?#. Accessed 30 January 2023.

Shim, J. P., Dekleva, S., French, A. M. and Guo, C. (2012), 'Social networking and social media in the United States, South Korea, and China', *Communications of the Association for Information Systems*, 30, pp. 1–13.

Simons, M. (2012), 'Chinese activate "zouzhuanggai" media: Will it free the press?', Crikey.Com, 9 October, https://www.crikey.com.au/2012/10/09/chinese-activate-zoushuangai-media-will-it-free-the-press/. Accessed 19 July 2023.

Sørensen, J. and Hutchinson, J. (2018), 'Algorithms and public service media', in G. Lowe, H. V. d. Bulck and K. Donders (eds), *RIPE@2017: Public Service Media in the Networked Society*, Göteborg: Nordicom, pp. 75–91.

Sparks, C. (2017), 'Hegemonic shadows: USA, China and de-westernising media studies', *Westminster Papers in Communication and Culture*, 12:1, pp. 19–20, https://doi.org/https://doi.org/10.16997/wpcc.244.

Spry, D. and Dwyer, T. (2016), 'The representation of Australia in South Korean online news: October 2014–April 2015', *A Report for the Australia-Korea Foundation*, Canberra: Australian Government Department of Foreign Affairs and Trade, pp. 1–51.

Spry, D. and Dwyer, T. (2017), 'Representations of Australia in South Korean online news: A qualitative and quantitative approach utilizing Leximancer and Korean keywords in context', *Quality and Quantity*, 51:3, pp. 1045–64.

Statista (2018), 'Mobile phone internet user penetration in South Korea from 2015 to 2022', https://www.statista.com/statistics/284204/south-korea-mobile-phone-internet-user-penetration/. Accessed 24 February 2023.

Statista (2020), 'Kakaotalk', https://www.statista.com/statistics/278846/kakaotalk-monthly-active-users-mau/. Accessed 24 February 2023.

Sukosd, M. (2016), 'How to conceptualize media pluralization in China?', in P. Valcke, M. Sukosd and R. Picard (ed.), *Media Pluralism and Diversity: Concepts, Risks and Global Trends*, New York: Palgrave Macmillan, pp. 152–71.

Taffel, S. (2021), 'Google's lens: Computational photography and platform capitalism', *Media, Culture & Society*, 43:2, pp. 237–55, https://doi.org/10.1177/0163443720939449.

Transcript, (2020), interview with CPC Organ news site journalist, March.

Tudor, D. (2012), *Korea: The Impossible Country*, China: Tuttle Publishing.

Wilding, D., Fray, P., Molitorisz, S. and McKewon, E. (2018), *The Impact of Digital Platforms on News and Journalistic Content*, Sydney: University of Technology Sydney, https://www.accc.gov.au/system/files/ACCC%20commissioned%20report%20-%20The%20impact%20of%20digital%20platforms%20on%20news%20and%20journalistic%20content%2C%20Centre%20for%20Media%20Transition%20%282%29.pdf. Accessed 24 February 2023.

Whittaker, M., Crawford, K., Dobbe, R., Fried, G., Kaziunas, E., Mathur, V., Myers West, S., Richardson, R., Schultz, J. and Schwartz, O. (2018), *AI Now Report 2018*, New York: AI Now Institute, https://ainowinstitute.org/AI_Now_2018_Report.pdf. Accessed 24 February 2023.

Wylie, C. (2019), *Mindf*ck. Inside Cambridge Analytica's Plot to Break the World*, London: Profile Books.

Yonhap News (2019), 'About Yonhap News', https://en.yna.co.kr/aboutus/yonhapnews. Accessed 2 April 2019.

Youn, S. and Lee, H. (2015), 'The ongoing media pluralism debate in South Korea', in P. Valcke, M. Sukosd and R. Picard (eds), *Media Pluralism and Diversity: Concepts, Risks, and Global Trends*, Basingstoke, New York: Palgrave Macmillan, pp. 267–84.

Zhang, Z. (2020), 'Infrastructuralization of Tik Tok: Transformation, power relationships, and platformization of video entertainment in China', *Media, Culture & Society*, 43:2, pp. 1–18, https://doi.org/10.1177/0163443720939452.

Zhao, Y. (2008), *Communication in China: Political Economy, Power, and Conflict*, Lanham: Rowman & Littlefield.

Zhao, Y. (2012), 'Understanding China's media system in a world historical context', in D. Hallin and P. Mancini (eds), *Comparing Media Systems beyond the Western World*, New York: Cambridge University Press, pp. 143–74.

Zuckerberg, M. (2018), *A Blueprint for Content Governance and Enforcement*, https://www.facebook.com/notes/mark-zuckerberg/a-blueprint-for-content-governance-and-enforcement/10156443129621634/?hc_location=ufi. Accessed 30 January 2023.

7

Investigative Journalism and Media Pluralism: Voices from the Global South

Saba Bebawi

Introduction

Investigative journalism is a key component of media pluralism in terms of the production of truth-telling discourses in national and international polities. From this perspective, the availability of voices in the global south has emerged as critical for a political reportage that accounts for identity and structural inequality in nation states. In many parts of the global south, the media have been mainly state-controlled and the practice of investigative reporting, which aims to 'dig deeper' and uncover facts on various issues of concern, has been seen as a challenging form of journalism since reporting in these regions is controlled and opinion pieces are monitored. Nonetheless, investigative journalism in many countries of the global south is on the rise as a result of increased awareness towards the importance of such a form of journalism. The Panama Papers and the recent Pandora Papers, initiated by the International Consortium of Investigative Journalists, enabled reporters from the global south to have access to data they are more than often lacking. This was a successful exercise and an example of how investigative journalism can cut across the global north and south.

This chapter discusses the extent to which investigative journalism – as an essential component of media pluralism – is in fact developing in the global south. This chapter, therefore, focuses on how investigative journalism practice has been developing to provide in-depth news reporting in order to foster pluralism in transparent, deliberative contexts, which then are positioned to lead to sustainable and proactive political participation in countries of the global south. Investigative journalism is just one of the terms that have been used amongst others and which include 'muckraking', 'watchdog journalism' and 'accountability reporting'. Equally, there have been various definitions used to determine the parameters of this practice. In the *Story-Based Inquiry: A Manual for Investigative Journalists Used by Arab Training Journalists*, investigative reporting is defined as:

> exposing to the public matters that are concealed – either deliberately by someone in a position of power, or accidentally, behind a chaotic mass of facts and circumstances that obscure understanding. It requires using both secret and open sources and documents.
>
> (Hunter et al. 2011: 7)

This definition distinguishes investigative journalism from daily reporting through a methodological approach which includes continuous searching of these kinds of sources. Another methodological difference between daily reporting and investigative journalism, and which is also a defining factor between the two forms, is that of *in-depth* reporting, as noted in the definition provided by the Dutch-Flemish Association for Investigative Journalism (VVOJ), where investigative reporting is defined as 'critical and in depth journalism' (VVOJ 2011: n.pag.). Investigative reporting entails more vigorous research than conventional daily reporting, where '[i]nvestigative journalism does not just happen; it is not just a matter of journalists following their "natural instincts". Investigative journalism has to be organized, resourced and protected. It depends on trained journalists, supportive editors and a substantial budget' (Street 2011: 193). Yet of importance to this chapter on the role of investigative journalism as a *media pluralism tool*, this form of journalism actively seeks to uncover information and discourses that are not known or circulated with the aim of bringing to light issues that are of concern to the public. In essence, investigative journalism can be regarded as 'reporting, [primarily] through one's own work product and initiative, matters of importance which some persons or organizations wish to keep secret' (cited in Ullmann 1995: 2). Essentially, therefore, investigative journalism can be defined as a form of journalism that seeks to uncover a 'secret' which someone or some entity wishes to keep hidden from the public (Bebawi 2016).

In the 2021 Media for Democracy Monitor, economic crises – especially as a result of COVID-19 – have had a considerable impact on both investigative journalism teams and initiatives in parts of the world such as Chile, yet in countries such as Denmark the opposite is happening where there are substantial resources allocated to investigative journalism (Trappel and Tomaz 2021). The Media Democracy Monitor found that 'The indicator on journalists' self-perception as watchdogs is among the top-3 highest-scoring indicators of the entire monitor' (Trappel and Tomaz 2021: 428). It concludes that this indicates that journalists see that their mission is highly aligned with their role as investigative reporters, as a crucial democratic function. At the heart of its function, therefore, investigative reporting aims to deliver plurality in voices, discourses and perspectives; bringing these to the forefront thus expands the public debate and allows for more deliberative participation, ideally leading to social change, as will be discussed in the following section.

The deliberative role of investigative journalism

Considering the definitions outlined above, investigative journalism can become an active participant in the process towards democracy and pluralism through its deliberative role by informing the public, highlighting issues that are not known and, in turn, leading to change. By bringing to light various perspectives, voices and issues, investigative journalism becomes a key component of media pluralism. As John Street argues, '[t]he ability of journalists to investigate, rather than merely to report information given out at press conferences or in press releases, is often presented as a key defining feature of mass media in a democracy' (Street 2011: 193). He argues that '[t]he job of the journalist is to expose wrongdoing and deceit in public office, to act as a key mechanism of public accountability in a democracy' (Street 2011: 193).

James S. Ettema (2007) outlines the possible role of journalism in enhancing democracy, where he states that '[j]ournalism is considered […] as an instrument of institutional accountability, a means to hold the governors accountable to informed and powerful people and more fundamentally to the ideals and rules of the democratic polity itself' (Ettema 2007: 144). Ettema refers to Christopher Lasch, who argues that democracy requires debate, not information, and it is the duty of the press to enhance debate (Ettema 2007: 143). Yet, the duty of the press requires the need to uncover and provide information in order to enhance the debate. Michael Schudson argues that the media should not only align with people's beliefs but what they should do is shape moral values and value choices (Ettema 2007: 14). This relates to the role of investigative journalism, whereby investigative reporting taps into a standard set of collective moral standards where injustice is exposed and that this injustice is universally accepted as such. Yet, shaping people's values and choices is not an ideal task for the media; rather, what the press can do, as argued by Schudson, is at least to hold those in power accountable to the small number of the public who are informed and powerful (Ettema 2007: 144). Ettema states in relation to this:

> The concept of accountability within a system of morally sensitive language […] suggests standards of performance for journalism when it attempts to function not only as a resource for citizen education but also as a social institution

seeking the accountability of other institutions. At the same time, examining journalism as an exercise in institutional (or inter-elite) accountability can shed light on the possibilities for deliberative democracy within contemporary mass-mediated politics.

(Ettema 2007: 145)

Here, Ettema sees journalism acting as 'both a fair-minded moderator and a committed speaker', where journalism acts as 'a reasoning institution that aggressively pursues, rigorously tests, and compellingly renders reasons that satisfy the key criterion of deliberative democracy' (Ettema 2007: 145). Yet, according to Ettema (2007), there are a few 'procedural principles' that need to be taken into account when considering the role of journalism in processes of democracy. One of these is publicity, where although the media make known to the public what is happening and what the issues are, the public might not 'listen' or 'see' this knowledge. This, therefore, is seen to impede the process of democracy. Yet, there are two points to be considered here: the first is that the media need to assume that public information is gaining the attention of the public to some extent; and the other point is that even if the public is not concerned with what is being told by the media, at least bodies such as non-governmental institutions, interest groups and legislative committees are (Ettema 2007: 145–46). Here, I argue that investigative journalism, as a more in-depth form of journalism, has a role in enhancing and publicizing its findings to both the public and institutional bodies, by seeking to address issues that need to be exposed and which affect the public itself (Bebawi 2016).

Yet such practices, especially in the global south, become problematic if not impossible in the face of media control that is so entrenched in these parts of the globe. To better understand this, James Curran (2011: 15–16) refers to five different types of media control which I will briefly outline here. The first form of media control is achieved through repressive legislation from the state, where journalists are monitored, imprisoned or killed, and media publications and platforms are banned and closed down. The second form of control 'can be exerted through public ownership, licensing and regulation of the media' (Curran 2011: 15). In authoritarian states, public media follow the government's official line, and '[a]n effective way of muzzling commercial television has been to allocate licensed franchises to allies of the government and governing party or coalition' (Curran 2011: 15). This is common in many countries that want to be seen as pluralistic in their media landscape and not just operating through the main state broadcaster. The third form of control, according to Curran, is exercised through a second party that operates in collaboration with the government, especially owners of private media. Another type of control is 'intimidated through vigilantism' in countries where the law is weak and where 'crime is highly organised and has links to the state', in which case 'journalists are vulnerable to physical intimidation' (Curran 2011: 15). Finally, Curran points to other forms of media control, such as the 'indirect system of control [...] through the invisible threads of domination', where governments control the media using methods such as public relations (Curran 2011: 16). These various types of media domination showcase how media control is exercised in various ways and in different countries, whether they are authoritarian or non-authoritarian.

However, media domination is not the only challenge for the deliberative role of journalism. We assume that within a deliberative public sphere, the public is more often than not, responsive and interested in what the media have to say. Yet this is not always the case, especially in a fast-paced news environment where the rise of entertainment and the abundance of social media. Nevertheless, Curran argues that journalism has a deliberative role and obligation regardless of whether or not the public is responsive. He argues:

> It is sufficient for most people just to scan the news. But the news media have nonetheless certain responsibilities. They should provide a succinct, impartial news briefing, and be ready to sound an alarm if there is a crisis or acute problem that warrants the 'monitorial' citizen's urgent attention. In addition, there need to be quality media, inspired by a sense of professional mission providing intelligent, extensive news coverage and facilitating informed dialogue between elites.
>
> (Curran 2011: 81)

In this above statement, there are two points that relate to the responsibilities of investigative journalism as a key component of media pluralism. The first is that investigative journalism exposes and emphasizes issues that require the 'citizen's urgent attention'; and the second is that it facilitates informed dialogue (Bebawi 2016). Curran adds that 'through collective deliberation shaped by a sense of civic duty', the media have a role to play in informing the public, thus enabling the people to form opinions and judgements (Curran 2011: 81). In essence, investigative journalism has the potential to solicit pluralism by informing the public, promoting democratic participation and achieving change. This is echoed in the Media Pluralism Monitor (MPM), which is a tool that has been set up by the Centre for Media Pluralism and Media Freedom (CMPF) at the European University Institute. Since 2013/14, the MPM has assessed risks to media pluralism in a total of 32 countries based on twenty indicators across four main areas that define 'media pluralism'. According to the MPM2021, '[p]luralism of the media constitutes one of the essential pillars of democracy' (MPM 2021: 1).

Rise of investigative journalism in the global south

If we track the rise and development of investigative journalism in the global south, we notice that it has not been systematic or linear. In fact, its emergence can be better characterized as chaotic and dispersed, where its successes in achieving change and making an impact have been occasional. Hence, the evolution of investigative journalism does not translate into a continuous historical narrative in the global south; rather, it can be described as a cyclical evolution that is dependent on particular contextual factors such as media institution; the journalist; and the political, economic and social conditions at the time.

In relation to this, Mark Feldstein (2006) outlines a 'muckraking model' that classifies the historical evolvement of investigative reporting into four categories. These four categories illustrate how the evolution of investigative reporting has not been consistent, as its historical emergence can be better described as fluctuating in cycles not just in the global south but across the world. Looking through various accounts of historical cases of investigative reporting (Aucoin 2006; de Burgh 2008), it can be noted where contextual political, economic, social and journalistic factors have impacted the practice of investigative reporting. Based on demand and supply, Feldstein's (2006) muckraking model explains these periods and can be understood as follows: in category 1, there is both demand and supply for muckraking, and, as a result, this category includes prominent periods of investigative reporting, which occurred 'in the 1760s and 1770s, before and during the American Revolution; 1902 to 1912, during the heyday of the original muckrakers; and in the 1960s and 1970s during Vietnam and Watergate' (Feldstein 2006: 10). These periods were all characterized by political turmoil due to oppressive colonialism, and economic turmoil as a result of the Industrial Revolution, in addition to social turmoil caused by a war that was unpopular (referring here to the Vietnam war). These factors led to what Feldstein sees as a 'public demand for investigative reporting'; and new technologies that became prominent at the time, such as the printing press, national magazines and television, all of which contributed to an increase in the supply of investigative journalism (Feldstein 2006: 10). In category 2, however, slightly different from the first category, the demand is high for investigative reporting, yet the supply is low. Feldstein explains that '[t]his is what occurred during the Populist and New Deal eras, when economic dislocation and political foment was acute but mainstream media outlets, facing little journalistic competition, offered scant criticism of the status quo' (Feldstein 2006: 10). In contrast to this, in category 3, the supply of investigative journalism is high, but the demand is not, where 'new technologies of cable/satellite TV and Internet Web sites provide a kind of pseudo-muckraking, where titillation is more common than substantive public service journalism' (Feldstein 2006: 10).

Feldstein notes that this period corresponds with the 1830s, during which the 'Penny Press' emerged, focusing on sensationalist reporting of 'crime and high society' (Feldstein 2006: 10). Finally, category 4 has both low supply and low demand for investigative reporting during the middle of the nineteenth and twentieth centuries (Feldstein 2006: 10). This fourth category, labelled the 'Dark Ages' by Feldstein, is seen by many to be applicable to the state of investigative journalism today.

The current decline of investigative journalism has been noted by Street where he observes that '[m]ore recently, writers have argued that we are now witnessing the decline, and even the death of investigative journalism' (Street 2011: 193). He argues that 'the heyday of the 1960s and 1970s, when newspapers and television programmes exposed the Thalidomide and Watergate scandals, when miscarriages of justice were pursued and resulted in the release of the innocent, is now past' (Street 2011: 193–94). Others, however, perceive that investigative journalism has recently witnessed an awakening through the emergence of the internet and practices such as blogging. Websites such as Wikileaks are examples that have 'led some to ask whether a new era of investigative journalism is emerging' (Street 2011: 194). Of course, investigative journalism should not only consist of 'leaks' but should involve the actual compilation of an investigation by a reporter. In turn, modern-day leaks need to be developed into investigations, checking on sources and facts, in order for them to be considered investigative journalism. Yet this is not to say that technologies that override gatekeeping and facilitate easier research and sourcing have not made investigative reporting more possible. Nonetheless, in mainstream media, investigative units are being closed down due to limited resources and funding, and their operation in many parts of the world cannot be justified in an environment of fast, competing news production processes.

At a time when investigative journalism is facing a bleak future in most western countries, the global south has been experiencing a trend in the rise of investigative reporting in response to the dominance of state control. Although there are some commonalities in relation to the overall narrative of the limitations and challenges to investigative reporting around the world, there remain some variations that are dependent on contextual circumstances. Accordingly, investigative journalism is understood and practised differently and is therefore 'context specific' (Street 2011: 194). For example, in China, the practice of investigative journalism does not necessarily replicate the practice experienced in western countries. Haiyan Wang (2016) argues that investigative journalism in China was predominantly modelled on western practices, yet this approach was not sustainable in the long run due to the modes of governance in China. Instead, investigative reporters in China adopted a form of activist journalism which in turn allowed them to conduct investigations. Wang examines how activist journalism in China emerged and was practised with notable examples such as the Xiamen PX event, the Nansha petrochemical plant dispute, the Panyu GIP project and the death of Qian Yunhui which all occurred between 2007 and 2010, as the period seeing the emergence of waves of civic movement in China (Wang 2016: 102). These cases provide accurate illustrations of how civic engagement could be merged with journalism to enhance pluralism within the mediated public sphere.

There have been other attempts in Asia to develop investigative reporting. Of significance is the Philippine Center for Investigative Journalism (PCIJ) which was established in 1989 and is now regarded as a model for other investigative centres in the region, especially since it is one of the earliest training organizations. It receives nearly a third of its annual budget from the Ford Foundation and has published over a thousand investigative reports and over a thousand other stories in major Philippine newspapers and magazines, in addition to five full-length documentaries and a number of documentaries for television. In addition, the PCIJ organizes training courses for journalism trainers and for various news organizations in the Philippines and Southeast Asia. The organization has held over 120 training courses for journalists, journalism trainers and students in the Philippines, Indonesia, Thailand, Burma, Cambodia, Vietnam, Japan and Papua New Guinea, in addition to other countries in Southeast Asia, the Pacific Islands and the South African subcontinent. Another example of the development of investigative reporting in Asia is the Korea Center for Investigative Journalism, based in Seoul, which is the first non-profit online investigative reporting organization in South Korea. Launched by veteran broadcast journalists, the centre publishes its investigations through an online news website called Newstapa. The centre was established at the start of 2012 by a small group of journalists 'who felt the need for an independent news organization not subject to the kind of political pressure used against investigative journalism at the country's major media outlets' (Kaplan: n.pag.). Other examples in Asia include Transparency International Sri Lanka (TISL), which was established at the end of 2002 and is active in addressing corruption in Sri Lanka. Its mission is 'to contribute to increase understanding of corruption, strengthen anti-corruption structures and processes and to appreciate upholding of integrity' (TISL 2021: n.pag.). Although it is not solely focused on the development of investigative reporting, it is active in holding workshops to train journalists in investigative reporting skills. TISL has published its own investigative reporting training book called the IJ Toolkit. Other workshops are also held 'to equip officials of provincial government offices and community-based organizations with knowledge and skills to contribute to a more accountable public service, this includes Training of Trainers (TOT)' (TISL 2021: n.pag.).

In other locations in the global south, such as South America, the tradition of investigative reporting has historically been practised in 'marginal, nonmainstream publications during democratic periods, and to underground, clandestine outlets during dictatorial regimes' (Waisbord 2000: xiii). However, in recent times, investigative journalism has become more mainstream, 'making strides in media organizations that traditionally sacrificed the denunciation of power abuses for economic benefits and political tranquillity' (Waisbord 2000: xiii). Silvio Waisbord provides examples of this in dailies such as the influential Brazilian newspaper *Folha de São Paulo* and the Argentinian *Clarín*, in addition to the emergence of investigative units in newspapers such as the Columbian *El Tiempo* and the Peruvian *El Comercio* and *La República* (Waisbord 2000: xiii). Yet, there remain major hurdles in the face of investigative reporters, such as access to information, which are overcome when they 'combine personal efforts and information supplied by sources' (Waisbord 2000: xvi).

In Africa, there has been a tradition of investigative journalism since the 1950s. Particularly of importance is the establishment of the *Drum Magazine* in 1951, where investigative journalism was prominent through the investigations of Henry Nxumalo, who was nicknamed 'Mr Drum' and who exposed political and social injustices (South African History 2021). Investigative reporting has continued in Africa, where investigations are conducted on current issues such as arms deals, financial scams, corrupt politicians and hospital deaths (journalism.co.za 2021). The conditions for investigative reporters in Africa are extremely difficult, whereby '[i]nvestigative journalists in Africa often operate in environments which seem by default designed to shut them down' (Konrad Adenauer Foundation 2021: n.pag.). The challenges investigative reporters face in African countries include '[r]epressive media laws, lack of resources and a widespread culture of secrecy' (Windeck 2016: n.pag.). Nonetheless, there have been factors, such as internet technologies and the support of global non-governmental organizations, that have made the work of investigative reporters in Africa slightly easier.

From these examples stemming from the global south, it is necessary to highlight that investigative journalism develops differently from one country to another; even among regions of the global south where conditions such as corruption, media control and economic restraints on investigative journalism remain common obstacles. In turn, due to these common challenges facing the development of investigative reporting in the global south, there is a need to develop some form of dialogue and cooperation between these parts of the world. During an international workshop, *Investigative Journalism: A South-South Dialogue*, held on 22 November 2010 in São Paulo, organized by the International Policy Centre for Inclusive Growth (IPC-IG) of the United Nations Development Programme (UNDP), a group of journalists, researchers and experts from South Africa, Brazil, India, Mexico, Switzerland and Qatar, in addition to UN representatives and civil society activists, met to discuss the development of investigative reporting in the global south. The discussion highlighted the role that investigative journalism could play in '[a]dressing issues such as money laundering, international paedophilia, drug and people trafficking, poverty, climate change, and slavery [which] requires collaboration among different actors in different countries' (International Policy Centre for Inclusive Growth 2010: 25). At the workshop, Maurício Hashizume, director of the Repórter Brasil Organisation at the time, argues that through strategic international partnerships, reporting on all the above issues becomes easier. He argued that: 'We have a heavy flow of business and (a) flow of little experiences of civil society and media. We must keep up those relationships' (International Policy Centre for Inclusive Growth 2010: 25). Collaboration between various parts of the global south that face similar obstacles and challenges could assist in improving the practice of investigative reporting in these areas, and in turn increase representation of their voices within the global public sphere.

Investigative journalism in the Arab region

As discussed in the previous section, to understand the emergence of journalism in the global south, it is necessary to take into account the political, social and economic factors that have played a role in shaping it. When going through the historical development of Arab journalism as an example of a region within the global south, two key observations emerge in relation to widening its pluralistic role within the region. The first observation is that the tradition of journalism that historically developed was a result of individual journalists playing an active role in transforming the field, with the aim of pursuing pluralism in views and perspectives. Investigative journalists are now once again finding themselves needing to transform the field and become independent drivers of change, especially after the 'Arab Spring' protests. The second observation that emerges is that although Arab journalism evolved based on western traditions of journalism by borrowing many of its values, it eventually transformed to become a form of journalism that was specific to the region as affected by unique political, social, economic and cultural influences. Today, Arab investigative journalism is being shaped in a similar way: by becoming a form of investigative reporting that is adopting western teachings and techniques of investigative reporting, while accommodating cultural practices specific to the Arab culture of journalism (Bebawi 2016). This is important to note, as talking about pluralism in western media takes on different shapes and variations in non-western contexts in the global south. With these two observations in mind, I will provide a historical account of how Arab journalism evolved in general, and investigative journalism specifically, in the region.

In his book, *The Press in the Arab Middle East: A History*, Ami Ayalon provides a comprehensive and detailed account of the rise of journalism in the Arab world, which I will rely on here as a background to understanding the development of investigative journalism in the region. Generally speaking, journalism in Arab countries operated in an environment of state governance and hegemony. Ayalon explains:

> The ruler was expected to govern effectively, and it was desirable that he be just; the ruled were required to obey him, regardless of the quality of his justice. The basic principle underlying this concept was that effective government was essential for the stability and proper functioning of the community, and obedience was vital in assuring such effectiveness.
>
> (Ayalon 1995: 109)

The media were, therefore, regarded as playing a focal role in assuring the obedience of the people. Arab journalism broadly acted as the mouthpiece of the state, thus avoiding political, religious and cultural questioning. The earliest legislation to affect the Arab press came under the Ottoman Law of Printing and Publications in January 1857. This law stipulated the need to gain permission from the Council of Education and the Ministry of Police in order to establish a press. Yet what was particularly vital to the notion of a free press in this case was that this law obliged anybody who had a press licence to submit all texts that were intended for publication for council approval. A year later, a penal code imposed punishments, which included closures and fines, on those who did not submit material for prepublication approval (Ayalon 1995: 111). As Ayalon notes, '[l]icensing, prepublication censorship, and prescribed punishments – a set of preventative measures – would become the cornerstone of government control of printed self-expression by individual subjects' (Ayalon 1995: 112). This, unavoidably, led to journalists' self-censorship of what to report on and what to avoid in their publications. They were fully aware of political, religious and social red lines they were not allowed to cross. Having said this, '[t]he rules for what was permissible or prohibited were seldom consistent, and interpretation depended largely on the understanding, or ignorance, of the censors. This resulted in endless ridiculous situations' (Ayalon 1995: 114). These situations included, for example, the monitoring of words that could have double meanings or words that could be negatively associated with the monarchy or the ruler. Hence, throughout the nineteenth and twentieth centuries, the region's leaders 'were irritated not only by the conduct of the press but by its very existence as well. Freedom of expression, a novel concept and a newly coined phrase in Arabic, was part of an alien system' (Ayalon 1995: 117).

Nonetheless, there were Arab free thinkers and intellectuals, such as Rifa'a Rafi' Al-Tahtawi, who rose to promote enlightenment thought in Egyptian society in the 1830s and beyond. There were those who 'were drawn to the press under the inspiration of a foreign example [and] pursued journalism successfully in the 1860s and 1870s' (Ayalon 1995: 216). They

> showed that it was possible to publish opinions on public affairs and have an impact without antagonizing the government beyond an acceptable point, produce a saleable commodity, and even make a living out of it – in other words, to turn writing on current affairs into a career.
>
> (Ayalon 1995: 216)

The development of the profession itself, therefore, began with the introduction of western concepts and teachings of journalism into Arab journalism. Such concepts included notions of objectivity and fairness. However, within such a tightly monitored Arab media environment, such concepts were not always easy to apply. This meant that Arab journalism was forced to develop a different method of reporting from that of western journalism, as the political, social and cultural factors affecting Arab journalism were different. Accordingly, Arab 'journalism developed as a variation distinct from the European prototype in the social and political roles it filled' (Ayalon 1995: 215). Prominent journalists who became influential included Mustafa Kamil, Ahmad Lutfi Al-Sayyid, Muhammad Al-Tabi'i, Amin Al-Rafi'i, Mohammad Hassanain Heikal, Abbas Mahmuod Al-Akkad, Sa'd and Fathi Zaghlul, Abdul Qadir Hamza and Mahmuod Azmi from Egypt; Jibran and Ghassan Tuwayni, and Muhi Al-Din Al-Nusuli, from Lebanon; the Rayyis cousins, Muhammad Kurd Ali, and Yusuf Al-Isa and Nassuh Babil from Syria; Tawfiq Al-Sam'ani and Rafa'il Batti from Iraq; and Isa Al-Isa from Palestine (Ayalon 1995: 217). The number of newspapers established by the end of 1929 rose to 3000 Arabic periodicals (Ayalon 1995: 217). At the time, there were minimum requirements for setting up a non-governmental private newspaper, whereby licence conditions included a minimum age of 20–25 years, no criminal record and a financial guarantee (Ayalon 1995: 217). In some cases, 'a writer would establish a paper, and slowly, as other like-minded people were attracted to it, they formed a party that became active on the political scene' (Rugh 2004: 148), especially during French and British rule. Later in the century, however, there were numerous restrictions which meant that only the state had access to the media. Currently, the media space is opening up within the Arab world with the advent of the internet; however, independent news websites are continuously being closed down, as witnessed in the aftermath of the Arab Spring uprisings.

One interesting aspect of Arab journalism is the culture of journalism at the time, which focused on the 'desire to satisfy literary cravings', where writers regarded newspapers as an outlet to produce literary work (Ayalon 1995: 219). Such examples include the work of the Amin brothers in the 1930s and 1940s in Egypt. The Amin brothers, Mustafa Amin and Ali Amin, who were twin brothers, were 'advocates of Western-style democracy', western liberalism, free enterprise and a free press, which would, in turn, assist in liberalizing Egypt (Jehl 1997). Prior to the nationalization of Egypt's press in 1960 by President Gamal Abdul Nasser, the Amin brothers were publishers of five publications, which included *Al-Akhbar* and the weekly *Akhbar Al Youm*. Their journalism critiqued those in power, which led to continuous imprisonment. Mustafa Amin was imprisoned in 1939 for criticizing King Farouk and in the early 1950s during Nasser's rule (Jehl 1997). Ihsan Abdul Quddoos was also prominent in writing investigative stories for the publication *Rose Al Yusif*, which was founded by his mother Fatima al Youssef. He syndicated columns for government newspapers and magazines. His column, entitled *At a Café on Politics Street*, addressed current issues circulating in cafes in Egypt at the time, thus extending discourses from the physical public sphere to the mediated public sphere. In the 1960s and 1970s, he was also editor of Akhbar Al Yawm and Al Ahram newspapers (*New York Times*, 16 January 1990). Mohammad Hassanain Heikal was another Egyptian journalist who was influential in his investigative reporting. He was the editor-in-chief of the Cairo-based newspaper *Al Ahram* and was keen on developing a tradition and practice of investigative reporting at the paper, and therefore would train graduates in investigative journalism and employ them. Unlike the Amin brothers, Heikal had strong ties with President Nasser and therefore gained access to information. Accordingly, he had consent from the authorities to publish his work, which included his investigations. However, during the rule of Anwar Sadat following Nasser, Heikal continued to report, however 'when he spoke out too obviously in opposition to government policy he simply lost his platform' (Rugh 2004: 153).

Recent individual attempts at investigative reporting have also existed. An example of this is the work of Rana Al-Husseini in Jordan, who set out to uncover honour killings and bring them to the attention of the mediated public sphere. This was significant, given this was a taboo topic to be addressed and critiqued in public. Working for the *Jordan Times*, Husseini would visit various police stations and inquire about, follow up and uncover various cases of honour crimes and investigate why they were done and how they were dealt with. Through a series of investigative stories that created social awareness of the issue, she exposed the legal deficiencies in dealing with this social practice, thus calling for a legislation reform. As a result, a National Jordanian Committee was formed to eliminate crimes of honour, which managed to collect 15,000 signatures in the form of a petition demanding stronger punishment for honour crimes (Biography of Rana Husseini). Between 1999 and 2003, amendments to the law were presented to the Jordanian parliament but have been rejected a number of times. Despite not achieving a concrete change in this case, Husseini's work brought the magnitude of the problem to both local and global attention.

It should be noted that all the historical and recent individual cases of investigative reporting were isolated and not sustainable since there were no institutionalized units for investigative reporters. Nonetheless, media organizations in the Arab world now understand the importance of investigative journalism and are giving it some attention. The reason behind this is because they can see the effects of investigative reporting and understand its power (Al-Omari 2013). In recent times, there has been a renewal of investigative reporting through media institutions such as *Al Jazeera*. Yosri Fouda, who was *Al Jazeera*'s chief investigative correspondent, conducted investigative stories through the programme *Sirri lil-Ghaya*, translated as 'Top Secret'. Fouda tells how the programme began:

> After the launch of *Al Jazeera* in 1996, I summoned my courage and put an 'outlandish' idea across to its management: to be allowed to disappear for two months every other year in return for a bi-monthly, 45-minute investigative piece. Sarcastically, the norm in Arab TV then was that you were only allowed to disappear for 45 minutes if you promised to come back with two months' worth of rushes.
>
> (Fouda 2009: n.pag.)

Despite this rough start, the programme began its broadcasts in 1998 and ran for ten years. In June 2010, *Al Jazeera* announced the establishment of its investigative unit. The director general at the time, Wadah Khanfar, said

> this was a ground-breaking initiative, at a time major news networks [were] retreating from investigative journalism the new unit represents an important step forward for the Network, not only to expand the breadth of our reporting, but also to drive further into stories for deeper narratives.
>
> (Press release 2010: n.pag.)

The unit consisted of three investigative teams, whose aim was to conduct their own investigations and also commission stories from external sources for output across all *Al Jazeera* channels, platforms and languages (Press release, 29 June 2010). Another *Al Jazeera* investigative unit was established in April 2013 as part of *Al Jazeera America*, and in January 2011, the network launched the *Al Jazeera Transparency Unit*, which aims to mobilize its audience – both in the Arab world and further afield – to submit all forms of content (documents, photos, audio & video clips, as well as 'story tips') for editorial review and, if merited, online broadcast and transmission on our English and Arabic-language broadcasts.

(*Al Jazeera Investigates*: n.pag.)

Al Jazeera's investigative unit deals with regional and global issues, and it is necessary to note that, accordingly, the investigations it conducts are therefore done at a regional and global level.

With the assistance of Arab Reporters for Investigative Journalism (ARIJ), various investigative units have been set up in the region to be part of the institutional make-up of media organizations in different Arab countries. In 2010, ARIJ set up a joint programme with the Washington-based International Center for Journalism, setting up five investigative journalism units in Jordan, Palestine and Egypt. Since then more units have been developed in all countries where ARIJ operates, with the aim 'to ensure sustained professional media development' (ARIJ: n.pag.). Rana Sabbagh, who was its founding executive director of ARIJ, explains the idea behind establishing investigative units:

We decided on working on parallel levels, working with journalists individually and working with newspapers where we have trained most journalists, [we] structure [the investigative units] – we continue funding them and then pull out hoping that over time they create brands and a reputation, and they become self-sustained units. Of course a lot depends on the chief editor, but if you look at it so far 'it is a miracle'.

(Sabbagh 2013: n.pag.)

The 'miracle' Sabbagh is referring to here concerns the teething difficulties that are faced when setting up an investigative unit. For example, *Al Ghad* newspaper introduced an investigative unit with the assistance of ARIJ but since the newspaper only employed one journalist to work in the unit, this was not sustainable and eventually it closed down. Sabbagh notes that some investigative units were set up and then had to shut down, such as *Al Nahar* TV in Egypt, *AlMaghrib* newspaper and *Radio Shams* FM in Tunisia, *Al Shorouq* newspaper and *Al Nahar* TV in Egypt, *Al Ghad* newspaper and *Ro'ya* TV in Jordan (Sabbagh 2014).

Generally speaking, through the case of Arab investigative journalism, it can be noted that investigative reporting was used as a tool for democratizing the Arab-mediated public sphere. It tried to adopt fact-based, evidence-based journalism as opposed to 'emotive journalism' (Bebawi 2019) based on literary expressions. More importantly, and in relation to this volume, it allowed for pluralism in perspectives, issues and discourses to emerge not only within the Arab region through local investigative units but also at a global level through investigative units such as that from *Al Jazeera*. It is important to recognize, however, that each region of the global south has its own narrative in this struggle to promote investigative journalism as a form of democracy building that is similar to that of the Arab world.

Conclusion

Uncovering information, holding those in power accountable and enhancing debate are what have been traditionally expected from investigative reporting. From the definitions outlined in the introduction section of this chapter, investigative journalism was defined as a form of in-depth reporting that aims to uncover a 'secret' that is of interest and concern to the public, based on existing standards of morality. Here it is necessary, as I argue, to note that the role of investigative journalism is to allow for a plurality of voices, discourses and representation from the global south. This democratic function, as outlined at the start of this chapter and as discussed through the cases from the global south and specifically the Arab world, is not easy and is often not always achieved. Although this places a heavy responsibility on investigative reporters, the notion of pursuing a diversity of voices in relation to issues that are under investigation serves to enhance the depth and strength of a deliberative public sphere.

As outlined in this chapter, investigative reporting sets its own agenda by identifying issues that relate to the public's interest and well-being and, in turn, their right to be informed. It is then conducted through a rigorous and in-depth process of investigating and uncovering facts that are unknown to the public, rather than merely quoting both sides. This then leads to the publication of the findings, which is often a challenge in itself. Many investigative reporters stop here; however, there is a need for investigative journalism to take this further and aim for pluralistic representation.

Examples in this chapter have showcased that investigative reporters in the global south are not only keen on getting their stories published but are themselves acting as agents of social change and they are adamant to create awareness of various voices for reform. This has been further possible through the use of new technologies, automation and social media. The rising popularity of these platforms in the Arab region was showcased during the 'Arab Spring' uprisings and continues to develop today through investigative journalism in the region with the rise of various projects – especially with a focus on data journalism. New media platforms in the region are, therefore, becoming increasingly influential and used as sources for 'news' and information.

REFERENCES

Al Jazeera Investigates, 'About the transparency unit', http://transparency.aljazeera.net/en/aboutus/. Accessed 24 February 2023.

Al-Omari, Jawad (2013), in-person interview with author, Amman, Jordan, 27 June.

ARIJ (2021), 'About us', http://arij.net/en/about-us. Accessed 19 July 2023.

Aucoin, J. (2006), *The Evolution of American Investigative Journalism*, Columbia: University of Missouri Press.

Ayalon, Ami (1995), *The Press in the Arab Middle East: A History*, New York: Oxford University Press.

Bebawi, Saba (2016), *Investigative Journalism in the Arab World: Issues and Challenges*, London: Palgrave.

Bebawi, Saba (2019), 'Data journalism and investigative reporting in the Arab World: From emotive to evidence-based journalism', in B. Mutsvairo, S. Bebawi and E. Borges-Rey (eds), *Data Journalism in the Global South, Palgrave Studies in Journalism in the Global South*, London: Palgrave, pp. 193–204.

Biography of Rana Husseini (2016), http://www.ranahusseini.com/Biography2.html. Accessed 19 July 2023.

Curran, James (2011), *Media and Democracy*, Oxon: Routledge.

de Burgh, H. (2008), *Investigative Journalism*, New York: Routledge.

Ettema, J. S. (2007), 'Journalism as reason-giving: Deliberative democracy, institutional accountability, and the news media's mission', *Political Communication*, 24, pp. 143–60.

Feldstein, Mark (2006), 'A muckraking model investigative reporting cycles in American history', *The International Journal of Press/Politics*, 11:2, April, pp. 105–20.

Fouda, Yosri (2009), 'Arab investigative journalism', *Ammon*, 20 November, http://en.ammonnews.net/article.aspx?articleNO=4833#.VK8KSyjB5UQ. Accessed 19 July 2023.

Hunter, Mark Lee, Hanson, Nils, Sabbagh, Rana, Sengers, Luuk, Sullivan, Drew and Thordsen, Pia (2011), *Story-based Inquiry: A Manual for Investigative Journalists*, Paris: UNESCO.

International Policy Centre for Inclusive Growth (2010), *Investigative Journalism: Issues for a South-South Debate*, New York: UNDP.

Jehl, Douglas (1997), 'Mustafa amin, liberal editor jailed by Nasser, dies at 83', *The New York Times*, 16 April, http://www.nytimes.com/1997/04/16/world/mustafa-amin-liberal-editor-jailed-by-nasser-dies-at-83.html. Accessed 24 February 2023.

Journalism.co.za (2021), 'Investigative journalism', http://www.journalism.co.za/investigative-journalism-homepage/. Accessed 24 February 2023.

Kaplan, David E. (2014), 'GIJN welcomes new members from Argentina, Korea, S. Africa', in *Global Investigative Journalism Network*, http://gijn.org/2014/04/09/gijn-welcomes-new-members-from-argentina-france-korea-s-africa/. Accessed 24 February 2023.

Konrad Adenauer Foundation (2021), *Investigative Journalism Manual*, http://www.investigative-journalism-africa.info/. Accessed 24 February 2023.

Media Pluralism Monitor (MPM) (2021), *Monitoring Media Pluralism in the Digital Era*, in K. Bleyer-Simon, E. Brogi, R. Carlini, I. Nenadic, M. Palmer, P. L. Parcu, S. Verza, V. de Azevedo Cunha and M. Žuffová (eds), Florence: Centre for Media Pluralism and Media Freedom, European University Institute.

New York Times (1990), 'Ihsan Abdel Kuddous, an Egyptian writer', 71, 16 January, http://www.nytimes.com/1990/01/16/obituaries/ihsan-abdelkuddous-an-egyptian-writer-71.html. Accessed 19 July 2023.

Press Release (2010), 'Al Jazeera Network launches a new unit for investigative journalism', 29 June, https://www.facebook.com/notes/al-jazeera-english/al-jazeera-network-launches-a-new-unit-for-investigativejournalism/402479163262. Accessed 24 February 2023.

Rugh, William A. (2004), *Arab Mass Media: Newspapers, Radio, and Television in Arab Politics*, Westport: Praeger.

Sabbagh, Rana (2013), Executive Director of Arab Reporters for Investigative Journalism, interview with Author, Amman, Jordan, 16 June 2013.

Sabbagh, Rana (2014), 'Closing speech at ARIJ Annual Conference', Amman, Jordan, 7 December.

South African History Online (2021), 'Henry "Mr Drum" Nxumalo', http://www.sahistory.org.za/people/henry-mr-drum-nxumalo. Accessed 24 February 2023.

Street, John (2011), *Mass Media, Politics & Democracy*, 2nd ed., London: Palgrave Macmillan.

TISL (2021), 'Our organisation', http://www.tisrilanka.org/?page_id=2. Accessed 19 July 2023.

Trappel, Josef and Tomaz, Tales (eds) (2021), *The Media for Democracy Monitor: How Leading News Media Survive Digital Transformation*, vol. 2, Gothenberg: Nordicom.

Ullmann, John (1995), *Investigative Reporting; Advanced Methods and Techniques*, New York: St Martin's Press.

VVOJ (2011), 'Objectives', Vereniging van Onderzoeksjournalisten, http://www.vvoj.nl/cms/vvoj-english/objectives/. Accessed 19 July 2023.

Waisbord, Silvio (2000), *Watchdog Journalism in South America: News, Accountability and Democracy*, New York: Columbia University Press.

Wang, Haiyan (2016), *The Transformation of Investigative Journalism in China: From Journalists to Activists*, London: Lexington Books.

Windeck, Frank, (2016) 'Preface', *Investigative Journalism Manual*, http://www.investigative-journalism-africa.info/?page_id=194. Accessed 19 July 2023.

8

Conclusion

Tim Dwyer and Derek Wilding

In the Introduction, we referred to instances where the unmitigated power of platforms to control the delivery of news content has been apparent for all to witness. We argued that these events are clear evidence of the consequences for society of decisions made by platforms. Underpinning our assessment was a view that algorithmic changes lack transparency and manipulate news content visibility for the audiences who have become accustomed to a daily 'drip feed' by way of a variety of devices and platform locations. Analyzing the broader social and cultural implications of these hidden changes, as well as the more direct consequences of automated curation of news in mediatized online ecosystems for pluralism, has been an underlying theme in the book. We have argued that automated processes of online news curation rely on the shifting priorities of algorithmic mechanisms, that in turn have capabilities to shape content diversity and plurality in our mediatized infospheres (Floridi 2014: 42).

By identifying 'automated curation' as a key concern in the book, we wished to emphasize the machinic, non-human agencies that accompany platform distribution of news. Public debate about these agencies is attracting a growing level of academic analysis and critique. The author of one recent study of editorial judgment in online news invokes a 'sociomateriality framework to disentangle the interplay of the human and the algorithmic' (Reidl 2022: 374). His exploration of 'critical realist agency and agential realism' approaches is relevant to our concluding comments in this chapter. The former 'acknowledges both human and non-human agency but treats them as separate'; the latter argues for the social and the material being 'mutually constitutive and discursively constructed', thereby defusing the binary understanding inherent in a critical realist agency view. The author further argues that social media platforms such as Facebook, Twitter and LinkedIn now 'fulfill functions previously thought to belong to media outlets, such as news distribution, advertising and editorial choices' (Reidl 2022: 375).

This kind of sociomaterial approach supplements existing literature in the sociotechnical space of platforms and news, to view aspects of automated curation as akin to the editorial judgement that takes place in more traditional media organizations (Napoli and Caplan 2017: n.pag.). These frameworks are also capable of assisting us in conceiving of algorithmic curation as inevitably normative, and therefore, constitutive of encoded biases and ethical decision-making that will have consequences for online news readers (Eubanks 2017; Bucher 2018; Kearns and Roth 2020). Machine learning and automation in online news distribution too easily lead to a 'bad equilibrium', as computer scientists term the process, whereby readers are encouraged 'to become less informed about, and less tolerant of, opposing perspectives' (Kearns and Roth 2020: 124). But is it possible that outcomes do not always mean polarization for society if news recommender design (Helberger et al. 2018, 2021) is optimized for an informed and deliberative public primed for a diet of diverse viewpoints, including oppositional ones?

Platformization, disinformation and 'quality' news

As we have indicated throughout the book, the global platform context for media pluralism is unavoidably embedded in the power dynamics of these intermediary infrastructures (Nielsen and Ganter 2022). In that sense, Terry Flew argues that platformization and platform power have themselves become integrally connected in the evolution of the latest internet phase (Flew 2021). On the point in relation to the untrammelled power of platforms, Flew writes:

> When, in February 2021, Facebook withdrew the access of Australian news media sites to its global news feed, as part of a bargaining strategy designed to influence the federal government's proposed News Media and Digital Platforms Bargaining Code, it made explicit forms of power that had long been tacit in the media environment.
> (Flew 2021: 13)

Similarly, these giant intermediaries of the platform media world are implicated in shaping how the public sphere itself is now informed. In *Digital Democracy, Social Media and Disinformation*, Iosifidis and Nicoli (2021) have developed an important set of arguments that connect the three major themes in the title of their book. They argue that disinformation is inevitably bound up with the dynamics of social media platforms and a populist politics that is damagingly polarized and that this has generated significant consequences for the fabric of nations and societies. Further, these communicative developments rely on networked ecologies and 'emotion-laden' communication (2). This networked ecosystem that underpins automated curation, a clickbait economy and disinformation, is the core explanation offered in their book for the overwhelming evidence of the damage being wrought on democracies. The authors have used case studies on the US 2016 presidential elections and Russian and Ukrainian disinformation campaigns to show how these processes have worked in practice.

Iosifidis and Nicoli's Habermasian inspired theoretical framework of a corrupted and irrational public sphere is exemplified using the European Commission's (2018) *Tackling Online Disinformation* report, to make the argument that the media information industries are incentivized to amplify populist narratives and thus political emotions. As we have suggested in the book, media pluralism in terms of diverse sources of information, must now contend with how platform infrastructures are integral to the provision of information. The authors of the European Commission's report make a related point, arguing that 'some platforms have taken on functions traditionally associated with media outlets, entering the news business as content aggregators and distributors without necessarily taking on the editorial frameworks and capabilities of such outlets' (EC 2018: 4).

The report approaches online news and information, in terms of freely available diverse quality information, as a constitutive factor in participatory and inclusive democratic processes. Key to 'pluralistic public debate', such provision is particularly important in election contexts. The report notes that sources of disinformation can destabilize public opinion and lead to poor policy outcomes for society. However, it is the explicit connections drawn between disinformation, intermediary platforms and the need for journalism that produces quality information that make this a significant contribution:

> Quality news media – including public media – and journalism play an important role in providing citizens high quality and diverse information. By ensuring a pluralistic and diverse media environment, they can uncover, counterbalance, and dilute disinformation. In an evolving digital environment, there is a need to invest in high quality journalism, reinforce trust in the key societal and democratic role of quality journalism both offline and online, and encourage quality news media to explore innovative forms of journalism.
>
> (EC 2018: 14)

Giotis, Molitorisz and Wilding (2023) observe that in the Australian industry code that adapted the original 2018 EU Code of Practice on Disinformation, the concept of quality was largely absent, and that a single provision dealing with quality in the News Media Bargaining Code has had no impact as a result of the code provision remaining inactive in the face of side deals between news media and each of Google and Meta. The authors argue that while assisting to build capacity among local news businesses, the scheme, as a result of the decision to use competition law in place of media regulation, could in fact incentive the creation of poor quality content.

There are of course other variables for pluralistic outcomes at play, and the EC report singles out citizen media literacy campaigns, the need for journalists to embrace digital skills made available by data analytics for fact-finding and verification, as well as support for public service media and public interest initiatives (EC 2018: 12–16). To this we would add support for the evolving role of investigative journalism, such as that in the global south, described in Chapter 7. In a more recent development, the proposed European Media Freedom Act (EMFA) includes safeguards for the independence of public service media providers (Article 5, 2022/0277) as well as a requirement for very large online platforms to take measures to advise media service providers in advance on any actions that might restrict or suspend the supply of its service and to 'engage in a meaningful and effective dialogue' to find a solution as well as to report annually on any such actions (Article 17). While the proposed EMFA has been welcomed by some (Tambini 2022), an EU Parliamentary committee hearing in early 2023 showed that some of its provisions, including those mentioned here, have been subject to vigorous critique (European Parliament 2023). In a slide presentation to the Committee and in separately published comments, Professor Matthias Cornils, Director of the Mainz Media Institute, described the Act as 'an almost "revolutionary" expansion of Union competences in the field of media regulation' (Mainzer Medieninstitut 2023: n.pag.).

Many of the issues of concern are recognized in Ofcom's (2021) recent report to the Secretary of State. Its statutorily mandated review of ownership rules in the United Kingdom involved consultation with industry (news publishers, platforms, representative bodies), civil society, audience/consumer and academics stakeholders, and drew the conclusion that there was potential risk to media plurality arising from several factors. First, Ofcom noted that online intermediaries and their algorithms control the prominence they give to different news sources and stories. Second, the basis on which online intermediaries serve news via their algorithms is not sufficiently transparent. And third, consumers do not always critically engage with the accuracy and partiality of online news. As a result of its consultations Ofcom considered that some changes to the existing framework were required.

A significant reform in terms of our research, as discussed in Chapter 2, was the Ofcom recommendation to the Secretary of State that the scope of the Media Public Interest Test (PIT) be broadened to include a wider range of 'news creators', to encompass forms of online news in relevant merger situations (Ofcom, 2021: 2, 26–30, para. 4.55). Ofcom proposed subsequent amendments to the PIT in Section 58 of the Enterprise Act 2002 whereby 'news creators' would be included within an assessment of 'a sufficient plurality of views' (s.58 (2B)) and 'a sufficient plurality of persons with control' (s.58 (2C)(a)) dealing with respectively, 'internal' and 'external' plurality.

Ofcom's rationale is that these amendments would then 'enable the Secretary of State to refer mergers on plurality grounds relating to online news provision' (para. 4.590).

Ofcom defines the new category of 'news creators' as covering 'entities who have editorial control over the creation and publishing of news material by journalists, irrespective of platform' (para. 4.37, 36). The general intention is that the category would capture stand-alone online only news providers such as Vice, and other online news providers 'involved in the creation of news'. Although Ofcom does not directly address our category of 'social media *news* influencers' (distinguishing them from brand-based social influencers) or other news-focussed weblog or vlog providers discussed in Chapter 5, the breadth of 'news creators' should mean that the PIT would address the risk to plurality that arises where a highly popular YouTube vlogger was 'bought' by a major news publisher. It seems to us that shifts in news media consumption are occurring across many different forms of intermediary platforms and 'public affairs' news genres, and regulatory frameworks need to pivot to take account of these developments.

In its report, Ofcom notes that the growth of online news challenges its ability to consider news plurality:

> the introduction of online intermediaries, and the lack of transparency as to the algorithms they use to serve news, has made this role much harder by challenging our ability to measure accurately what news people are consuming, and to understand the significance and influence of different news sources (48. A1.21) [...]. Not only has the shift online made it more difficult to measure and to assess plurality, but it has also potentially created new plurality concerns, or exacerbated existing ones – which makes it even more important to address our reduced ability to assess plurality accurately.
>
> (49. A1.24)

A number of stakeholders expressed detailed concerns in relation to the role and impact of algorithms on media plurality, arguing that regulatory reform for greater modernization was long overdue. For example, the Guardian Media Group, the Media Reform Coalition, Dr Crawfurd Smith and the National Union of Journalists (NUJ) agreed that Ofcom needed new powers to obtain data from platforms to better understand consumer behaviour and engagement with news content (13). The NUJ argued that Ofcom should be able to 'monitor, assess and publicly report on the methodologies, and impact of news algorithms (on) media consumption and plurality' (3.26, 13).

The submissions received from these news organizations provide valuable insights into the competitive online news environment in the United Kingdom. The Guardian Media Group notes for example:

> The online intermediaries are now so large that it is impossible to argue that their dominance does not raise worrying concerns about media plurality. There is a wide and growing range of other media organisations, civil society activists and academics who believe that media pluralism is under threat due to new sources of power, concentration and dominance that are not adequately captured in existing competition rules or tests.
>
> (GMG, quoted in Ofcom 2021: n.pag.)

There was a considerable support for the case of bringing online intermediaries within scope of the current UK regulatory framework to deal with media plurality. The National Union of Journalists noted

> the current framework is insufficient to address the increasingly concentrated news and media landscape. The Council of Europe have recommended that countries 'limit the influence which a single person, company or group may have in one or more media sector'. We would argue this should apply across all types of media as well as to print, broadcast and online media specifically.
>
> (NUJ, quoted in Ofcom 2021: n.pag.)

These stakeholders to the Ofcom pluralism review made a compelling case for monitoring and intervention that went beyond the scheduled three-year plurality reviews, or action triggered by merger situations under the Enterprise Act 2002. Their argument was that the existing framework is unable to respond to expansions of influence that arise from market power, from companies leaving a market, and consolidation achieved through network effects (3.30, 15).

Despite this support for the proposition of bringing online intermediaries within the regulatory framework for media plurality, Ofcom's recommendations to the Secretary of State were limited. Ofcom said that any proposal by an online intermediary to acquire a large newspaper publisher or significant broadcasting service – or a 'news creator', should its recommendations on that aspect be accepted – would likely fall within scope of the existing PIT as a 'relevant merger' (Ofcom 2021: 27). Further consideration of the role of intermediaries was deferred to its discussion document issued the following year, 'Media Plurality and Online News' (Ofcom 2022a). As we note in Chapter 3, this paper raised a mix of regulatory and other approaches that could provide greater oversight of online intermediaries, even if, in the first instance, this only extends to giving Ofcom information-gathering powers. While giving ACMA information gathering powers is among the measures announced by the Australian Government in early 2023 in relation to mis- and disinformation (Rowland 2023), on media plurality Australia is only at the stage of considering how to design a measurement framework, with no policy process to address other aspects of regulation. As we argue in Chapters 2 and 3, the need to address decades of neglect in media policy calls for a holistic approach to media pluralism comprising a measurement framework, a public interest test for media mergers, and mechanisms for taking account of automated curation and other conduct of digital platforms.

Networks, automated curation and news sources

Axel Bruns in his polemically framed book *Are Filter Bubbles Real?* debates an issue which many will regard as core business to any analysis of the contemporary dynamics of media pluralism and online news. This debate has tended to be caricatured by both the affirmative and negative sides; for Bruns, this means prosecution of the 'against' side where he seeks to dispel the 'myth of the echo chamber and filter bubble' (93).

Bruns brings empirical nuance to the debate by advancing a range of evidence: he explains the *modus operandi* of platforms in assembling networked communities or interest-issue and topic clusters, from the 'mildly homophilous' to the strongly 'hyperpartisan'. He suggests that rather than focusing on the ill-defined concepts of 'echo chambers' and 'filter bubbles' researchers would be better advised to spend time investigating the 'human causes of polarisation and their very real and alarming impacts on society and democracy' (107). It is a point well made – although it needs to be said that it may be at the cost of any sustained interrogation of the automated bias and even harms that frequently accompany the algorithmic processes inherent in search and social media platformization (Bucher 2018; Vaidhyanathan 2018). Bruns does, nonetheless, give that aspect of the debate a limited hearing, by noting that:

> Importantly, their comparative innocence on this count does not absolve *Google*, *Facebook*, *Twitter*, and other providers of their responsibility in other critical contexts though; while their affordances and algorithms do not cause echo chambers and filter bubbles, they do materially affect user experience in other ways that are just as crucial [...] these platforms play an ever more critical role as key brokers of information flows in contemporary society.
>
> (116)

His underlying argument is that the terms 'echo chamber' and 'filter bubble' are much abused, and typically ill-defined. To address this issue, Bruns brings his own clarity to the situation by developing definitions for each (29). Interestingly, he is at pains to insist that both phenomena emerge when the group participants either 'preferentially connect' in the case of echo chambers, or 'preferentially communicate' in the case of filter bubbles. In other words, his contention is that this is primarily a process involving *choice* by the individuals involved. We would not disagree that for many in such networks active decisions will be made to perpetuate the existence of the group or indeed create a group on Facebook. This also works when participants police the borders of their group in terms of how the membership is maintained through linking with the like-minded in an @mention, comment, like, share or retweet in the case of Twitter.

Interestingly, a study undertaken as part of Ofcom's own 'Media Plurality and Online News' investigation in 2022, which relied on rich Twitter API data, was significantly more qualified regarding the evidence of user homophily, and plurality of viewpoints in general. The study found that there were 'some users whose networks exhibit relatively high levels of homophily according to our metric and these tend to follow/like the content of only a few news outlets' (Ofcom 2022b: 5). It's worth noting that in its Discussion Paper, Ofcom combines these computational metrics with more traditional approaches to assess diversity:

> we consider our homophily metrics jointly with simple measures of diversity: the number of news outlets followed or the number of outlets whose content a consumer liked. The match of the underlying measure between the homophily and diversity metrics – i.e., following or liking – is useful, because it allows for a more fundamental link between homophily and diversity [...] Homophily combined with a diverse news outlet followership/liking profile means that a given user and their friends are exposed to a relatively wide range of news sources. Homophily combined with following fewer or linking behaviour focused on fewer news outlets, by contrast, is evidence suggestive of an echo chamber that involves access to few news sources. The latter scenario is more of a concern from a media plurality standpoint.
>
> (Ofcom, 2022b: 27. par. 5.9)

Yet Bruns' position complements those researchers who similarly assert a reluctance to embrace these widely circulating common-sense discourses regarding the state of our infospheres. Following their extensive survey of predominantly political science-oriented literature researching the dynamics of echo chambers and filter bubbles, the Reuters Institute team at Oxford University identify three summative messages regarding the existence, causality and impact of such 'bounded media spaces' and information structures generally (Arguedas et al. 2022). These authors note that

> a growing amount of research rejecting the filter bubble hypothesis should not be confused with a Panglossian belief that we live in the best of all possible worlds, or

that our increasingly digital, mobile, and platform-dominated media environment does not come with any serious societal challenges. There are many, including the frequently overlooked fact of pronounced inequality in news and information use.
(Arguedas et al. 2022: 30)

To this list of challenges they add misinformation, as we too have discussed previously, together with online harassment and abuse, invasive data collection and 'serious disruption of the established business of news and market concentration'. The final challenge listed here is curious, given that we regard this as actually being one of the most critical factors in the debate. Yet the authors raise this in only an indirect fashion. They argue that the news and information that is visible to people is a result of the interplay of media supply, media distribution and media demand. For them, this is only partly a 'supply' issue – and while we agree with that proposition, we would emphasize the continuing relevance of media concentration (or voices) in a media market. In Australia, for example, three companies, News Corporation, Nine Entertainment and Seven West Media control over 90 per cent of the news market (Dwyer et al. 2021: 60). In the United Kingdom, by 2015 'three companies controlled 71% of national newspaper readership; by the end of 2018, the same three companies – Rupert Murdoch's News UK, DMG Media (publisher of the Mail titles) and Reach (publisher of the Mirror titles) accounted for 83%' (Schlosberg and Freedman 2021: 13). As we have tried to show in this volume, 'supply' of news has differing dimensions in national or regional media markets and policy environments. In the Philippines, for example, authorities have actively sought to impede the pursuit of investigative journalism, while in Australia, inadequate media ownership rules and a lackadaisical approach to the suitability of competition law have resulted in the loss of local news content for sizeable regional populations. In the second of these examples, problems with 'media supply' manifest most clearly in the form of a lack of localism but this is inextricably linked to market consolidation and the vulnerability of local communities to a news organization that can exercise near monopolistic control.

This fundamental media ownership reality shapes 'media supply', including the dominance of those companies in the available online news sites (this is discussed further below). In the Australian example discussed above, the 'end of print' and the redirection of news consumers to the paywalled online news sites of one supplier has resulted in a distinct loss of diversity. This over-riding media ownership and concentration situation renders problematic the Reuters' report contention that:

Most people have diverse media diets, those who rely on only one source typically converge on large sources with politically diverse audiences such as commercial or public service broadcasters, and only small minorities, often only a few percent, exclusively get news from partisan sources.

(Arguedas et al. 2022: 16)

The assertion, therefore, of a media diet being 'diverse' in this context of concentrated news media market would require various caveats around the amount of public service media consumed, genre, different markets and cross-media exposure. The access pathway (automated or algorithmic selection via social media, search, apps) does little to change this basic reality in national media contexts. Of course, for the minority who consistently seek out and engage with diverse news media diets, automated personalization will deliver it to them (Thorson 2020). Importantly, Arguedas et al. (2022: 18) make the point that 'automated serendipity' (when, for example, an unlikely result is returned on a search) and 'incidental exposure' (where readers bump into a news story they would not ordinarily see) work in the commercial self-interests of platforms in terms of the engagement experience and time spent on a platform; these experiences are not driven by some higher-minded pluralistic objective.

The second concluding point in the Reuters Institute research notes that risks of polarization and 'attitude-consistent information' are smaller than many think. However, in saying this the researchers recognize that minority cohorts can be very influential on others' belief frameworks, and in 'driving public and policy debate'. They also recognize that offline social communities can result in cohorts holding 'very strong views' despite their media consumption habits. Their third concluding point is important because it notes that much of the existing research has occurred in the United States and it has therefore neglected 'several important established platforms and many newer and smaller platforms' (30).

It is interesting to observe that Twitter itself has tinkered with some alternatives to the platform's default position of an algorithmically provided tendency to polarization. The previous CEO of Twitter, Parag Agrawal, admitted in an interview in 2020 that the company needed to do some work on the recommender algorithms so that, 'how we direct people's attention is leading to a healthy public conversation' (Kelly 2021: n.pag.). Relatedly, the idea of 'building your own social network' or in other words, agentially picking and choosing one's accounts to follow, is core to these kinds of proposals. Public Service Media recommender systems (as discussed in Chapter 5) would make these pluralized content recommendations (Helberger, et al. 2020). The idea was that algorithms are coded to suggest a range of viewpoints in the feed of social media and other news-oriented platforms. These would not be just the polarized viewpoints but also more nuanced positional arguments that inform audiences on important issues. With Twitter, the observation is also made that it is possible to deselect the default setting so that tweets then appear in a reverse-chronological fashion, thereby avoiding what the algorithms push in the feed. Twitter has experimented with this kind of 'challenger mode' in the past (Kelly 2021). In those experiments, a group of participants were automatically shown tweets with opposing points of view to those they would typically consume. It is reported that the new feature was loathed by those Twitter users involved in the experiment. This makes sense – it seems that polarization via retweets, likes and a bump in followers is actually what tends to attract most Twitter users. A former VP for Europe, the Middle East and Africa, Bruce Daisley, was reported to note:

> If you retweeted Owen Jones or a *Guardian* journalist it would say 'here's what Andrew Neil is saying on this in the *Spectator*', and people were furious about it [...] What you generally discover is people believe that plurality of opinion is something everyone else should see, but they don't want to see it themselves.
>
> (Kelly 2021: n.pag.)

This sort of third-party effect is also a factor in policy debates about investment in media literacy programs. And the related question of user 'technacy' (or media tech-competency) needs to be included in the conversation as well. In this context, Elvestad and Phillips prefer the idea of 'user-customized recommender systems', in relation to the capabilities of people to freely build their own 'Daily Me' online news diet (Dwyer and Martin 2019; Elvestad and Phillips 2018). In *Sharing News Online*, Dwyer and Martin wanted to highlight the 'myth of user agency' (295) to make the point that the liberal choice paradigm discursively plays into a kind of neutral and platform-friendly understanding of 'algorithmic nudging'; this contrasts with how people actually negotiate participation in their technologically dependent lives, cultures and societies.

Such free choice decisions are probably more pertinent in the case of Twitter, which is generally speaking, a social media platform used by the news and information cognoscenti (and only used, according to the *Digital News Report* 2021, by 18 per cent of Australians). The argument made in Martin and Dwyer's *Sharing News Online* was that the automated shaping of news and information appearing in Meta newsfeeds was a consequence of algorithmic decisions based on the platforms' aggregated signals and ranking data, which led people to click on items which surfaced at the top the feed. This argument can be counterposed to that of liberal media theorists, who as Elvestad and Phillips (2018: 6) note:

> see choice-making as inherently empowering and audiences as: 'rational and purposeful agents who work, individually and collectively, to choose among available options to best meet their perceived personal and social needs' (Meyrowitz 2008: 649)[...] [for them]

the Internet appears to be an excellent means of enabling rational choice and thereby increasing plurality via demand [...] [It] was hailed as a networked public sphere (Benkler 2006) in which everyone would be able to edit their own news (Negroponte 1995: 153).

The recent parliamentary inquiry into Media Diversity in Australia recorded contemporary expressions of this liberal media theory on the part of technology companies – Meta claimed that 'Technology has democratised the sharing of ideas and information. Australians are no longer dependent on a small number of gate-keepers [...]' – and on the part of news organizations that sought to justify the repeal of media ownership laws (Australian Senate 2021: 11–12).

As we discussed in the Introduction, one of the key aspects of people knowing more and having access to reliable, truthful information is the ability to actually locate this in a sea of misinformation. This goes to the discussion of media literacies and key competences for discovering trustworthy news sources. The liberal media theory approach also demonstrates a misunderstanding of the way media power works to proliferate amenable forms of news content across platforms and in that process, influence political agendas.

We have noted the reasons why diverse media sources remains an important goal for Australia in this volume and in the *Media for Democracy Monitor 2021*:

> the Internet potentially offers a wide array of news sources, but this has not abated continuous declines in regional and local reporting [...] (and) as a result of deregulation, Australia's media is dominated by two large commercial media corporations (Nine Entertainment Co Ltd and News Corp) and there are no longer any larger scale independent media voices.
>
> (Dwyer et al. 2021: 71)

The rhetorical argument that is often made is that, as the newspaper sector is in historic structural decline, with fewer people reading newspapers and especially younger cohorts being less interested in these legacy mastheads, surely it no longer matters?

There are several reasons why this is not the situation on the ground. The first is that the brands that dominate legacy media in Australia also dominate online news media. News Corp Australia and Nine Entertainment own many of the most visited online sites (Morgan 2018b). The exceptions (such as the *Guardian* and *Daily Mail*) only reinforce the point, as they are often established legacy media from other countries.

Second, with the removal of cross-media laws, which prevented co-ownership of TV, radio and newspapers, this dominance will only continue and intensify. The convergence of digital media has resulted in news media being re-used across platforms (Dwyer 2010). The search engines and aggregators online and on mobile phones only exacerbate this dominance in their algorithms that give preference to established media (Athey et al. 2017).

And third, these major brands tend to set the news agenda for the rest of the media because they control the bulk of the journalistic resources. Do social media improve news voice diversity? Social media platforms, in large measure, distribute and amplify existing news stories amongst like-minded networked groups. As is widely known, these platforms are often responsible for amplifying the worst kinds of speech (Sunstein 2018) and providing a means for algorithmic news manipulation as witnessed in the Cambridge Analytica and other incidents by extremist groups. So, while audiences are increasingly discovering their news on social media platforms, the contribution of those sources to news diversity is a more nuanced story (Newman et al. 2020).

The Media Pluralism Dashboard tool discussed in Chapter 3 highlighted the role and significance of 'public affairs' news content for media pluralism policies. Our research indicates that automated news distribution brings a heightened risk that publics will get their news in ways that are shaped by the platformized distribution logics. This means that news agendas will no longer be driven entirely by human editors and that algorithmic decisions are standard fare.

The automated curation of news cultures in 'news feeds' on intermediary platforms is a central component in our networked connectivity and infosphere interactions. At a deeper philosophical level, the consequences for society of this shift in news provision are a feature of the information infrastructure of our everyday lives.

The meanings of these changes are manifold and are inevitably tethered to the socio-cultural and political economic foundations of contemporary societies. In their book *Risk and Hyperconnectivity: Media and Memories of Neoliberalism*, Hoskins and Tulloch argue that large-scale informational and news risk events (including, we suggest, media concentration and waning voice plurality) take on meanings that inform emerging epistemic formations. An important inflection point in their arguments is that the twenty-first century risks to the participatory public sphere ushered in by hyperconnectivity entail elements of both 'overhearing' and 'spectacle' (290). The contribution of emergent media in this process and the concept they term 'hyperconnectivity' 'includes the competitive reconfiguration of the discourses of neoliberalism'. 'New memories' are 'shaped and understood through the metaphors, media and technologies of the day [...] through hyperconnectivity' (297).

Future directions for media pluralism and online news research

Recognition of the impact of the broader context of ongoing structural transformations in digitalized public spheres (Habermas, 2022) underpins the preamble to a set of recommendations on principles for media and communication governance by the Council of Europe Committee of Ministers. Recommendation CM/Rec(2022)11 of the Committee of Ministers is intended to act as a guide for member States to modernise principles for governance of media and platforms. There are fifteen principles that range from 'transparency and accountability', 'openness and inclusiveness', 'independence and impartiality' through to 'promoting media pluralism and safeguarding the sustainability of journalism', and perhaps most significantly for this book, 'mitigating the risks posed by algorithmic curation, selection and prioritization'.

Various aspects of governance and democratic ideals are identified as ripe for renewal. Recommendations are put forward for regularly reviewing and evaluating member state frameworks and policies that are designed to protect freedom of expression and journalism, media pluralism and threats from ownership concentration. The Ministers highlight that these developments usher in many opportunites for access to information in novel platform contexts; however, they also note that

> platforms are not neutral but have assumed an active curatorial or editorial role, including through the use of algorithmic systems, in the dissemination of content produced by media and others, and thus have a huge impact on the way people perceive the world, and are exposed to other information and ideas.
>
> (CoE 2022: 1)

In a similar spirit of renewal, in Chapter 3, we reviewed the best currently available options for media pluralism interventions. Starting with the ground-breaking measurement framework first introduced by Ofcom in 2015, we noted the reservations expressed by some researchers regarding the design and effectiveness of the framework. The multifactorial approach, taking into account availability, consumption, impact and contextual factors, is arguably the most sophisticated attempt to date by a media regulator to assess the public interest implications of a merger on the available range of news sources in terms of on media pluralism, in any given media market. That it was applied at retail and wholesale levels is also an indication of its practical sophistication.

Yet it is not without shortcomings. As we discussed, Ofcom itself is now in the process of considering how the framework can better account for online news. A legitimate critique of the existing model is that it relies on a discretionary ministerial trigger to bring it to life in any given *merger* situation, and it offers no leverage in other circumstances. Furthermore, there is also a critique in relation to the inability of the measurement framework to provide insight into 'real world' agenda-setting power, which limits its overall value. Despite these problems, we see it as a clear advancement in the application of media pluralism policy in multi-platform media environments. Another noteworthy and innovative element is the 'consumption' metric, moving the tool into the terrain of 'exposure diversity' for the first time in media plurality assessments. Deployed with the notion of a 'share of references', incorporating frequency of usage, the tool has become a proxy for measuring media influence. Ofcom has made some attempts to include digital intermediaries (including Meta, Twitter and Google), but the oversized impact of the BBC in the 'share of references' metric remains an Achilles heel: we noted the 2013 example where the BBC had a 44 per cent share of references, while the News Corp newspapers had just 4 per cent. There is also the problem of double counting noted by Scholsberg and Freedman (2020) since the methodology disguises the actual sources of news content, and BBC content on Meta could also be counted, leading to the perception of more plurality than legitimately consumed.

Leveraging off the successes of Ofcom's measurement framework we noted that the ACMA's policy development work would arguably offer greater sophistication, given the inclusion of a 'localism' dimension for media diversity assessment. However, as we explained, ACMA has a general monitoring remit for media diversity but not an active capability to intervene enshrined in its operational legislation; this is a significant shortcoming, and therefore a public policy problem that requires remedial action by government.

We see that this limitation calls for revitalized thinking for a media policy agenda to deal with the trends to platform power and concentrated media power that pose ongoing risks to public interest journalism in Australia, and globally. We won't repeat all the categories and their detailed components that the ACMA's measurement metric includes (outlined in Chapter 3 for its 'Indicators of Diversity and Localism' matrix), however, it is clearly a refinement over the Ofcom model. It calls out for application in Australia, and could perhaps be adapted for other similar jurisdictions.

We have recommended that the media regulator be rebuilt with powers and responsibilities that enable it to effectively monitor the whole of the legacy and digital media landscape; the introduction of a baseline assessment of media plurality; and a public interest test to assess the state of media diversity. We have suggested that in the contemporary media environment characterized by the presence of international media brands and the operation of digital platforms' news recommenders, the public interest in a vibrant and sustainable news media sector means that merger decisions that assess whether there is a 'reduction in diversity' should have a more expansive policy focus than in the past. This would include consideration of:

- the sustainability of local businesses
- the encouragement of original and local news content

- quality of content, in terms of the promotion of news standards
- modes of delivery and consumption, including the 'automated curation' of digital platforms.

We have proposed that these functions be allocated to the media regulator for two reasons. First, we think it desirable to build on the existing competency of an agency that has long had responsibility for aspects of licensing and content regulation. Second, despite the seemingly unshakeable faith of neoliberal governments in the benefits of competition, we have witnessed the abject failure of competition law to protect media diversity in the absence of sector-specific media ownership controls and/or content obligations. This is despite acknowledgment from competition regulators themselves, as well as economists and lawyers, that the tests and tools of competition law are not suited to the social policy outcomes associated with media diversity. On this aspect of regulatory design, we have strongly supported the warnings offered by UK researchers who have argued for the avoidance of ministerial discretion over decisions that are likely to be subject to intense lobbying and inducements of one kind or another (Humphreys 2015; Schlosberg and Freedman 2020; Craufurd Smith 2021). Interestingly, in the proposed European Media Freedom Act, the European Commission clearly separates the anticipated assessment of transactions that result in media concentration and their impact on media pluralism from competition law assessments under merger control rules (see Article 21 of 2022/0277).

As we discussed in the introduction and in Chapters 3 and 5, although in Australia the idea of an 'algorithm regulator' has been explicitly rejected by the ACCC and government, we believe that it should be introduced as an element of ACMA's media pluralism and diversity monitoring role. Its main purpose would be to consider the ways in which algorithmic delivery of news via recommender systems, and any actions users can take to influence these systems, affects the content that is seen by audiences (i.e., an aspect of exposure diversity), but it could also monitor the ways in which local news providers engage with the practices of digital platforms and news aggregators. In performing this second function, the media regulator could conduct the oversight of algorithmic changes and the impact of news media. While embedded in the News Media Bargaining Code, this aspect has had no application in the absence of any government decision to hit the trigger for the formal implementation of the scheme.

An alternative to relying solely on a 'reduction in diversity' test as part of a decision on media mergers (and a precursor to such a test) would be the inclusion of indicative thresholds in the baseline and subsequent assessments of media plurality. We agree with arguments made by Schlosberg and Freedman (2020) that indicative thresholds would bring greater clarity and certainty to debates regarding 'sufficient' plurality and the ability of regulators to assess plurality outside of specific merger situations. More specifically, they argue that 'effective plurality reform must start with new legislation that sets out indicative thresholds and detailed guidance on the meaning of plurality sufficiency' (1).

This goes some way to addressing the concerns discussed above with Ofcom's existing Measurement Framework for Media Plurality. The setting of indicative thresholds will necessarily differ at the national level across jurisdictions. One important differentiating factor we have identified here is the presence and strength of public service media in any market. But even within the one country, thresholds will vary among metropolitan and regional markets and those that may contain even smaller markets, even though they cover vast remote areas. As an indication of this difference, the geographic area of the Rockhampton radio licence area, one of the regional Queensland areas mentioned in Chapter 2, is about one-fifth greater than that of the nation of Wales in the United Kingdom, even though the population of Wales is about 16 times that of the Rockhampton region. Despite these difficulties, it is possible to benchmark areas against realistic targets – for example, a regional town with a population of a certain size that does not have at least a weekly print or online news source with a certain quantity of local content would be likely regarded as falling below the indicative threshold, regardless of whether it was also in a large, aggregated television market that supplied some content of relevance to the community.

As in the United Kingdom,

> we urgently need new legislative guidance on assessing existing levels of media plurality amidst all the complexities of a converged media environment, which identifies the material risks to plurality posed by *combinations of control* in respect of different platforms, markets and metrics ... and we need for a baseline plurality review outside of merger activity.
>
> (Schlosberg & Freedman 2020: 127–28)

And we need a baseline plurality review outside of merger activity.

The computational tool developed in the Media Pluralism Project discussed in Chapter 3 (Media Pluralism Project 2019) demonstrated some aspects of the application of future thinking and data-driven approaches to assessing media pluralism. While other researchers have followed a related big data approach for analyzing emerging questions of diversity of content in the context of the algorithmically mediated distribution of news media (Makhortykh et al. 2021), few have attempted this kind of methodology to connect normative media policy research with large-scale taxonomy of corpora of news articles. The empirical methods, underpinning such content studies, have tended to look for consumption patterns between and within digital brands, rather than linking the content to research questions attempting to explain a changing dynamic of the digital news media distribution landscape, and the broader implications and consequences of these transformations for society. In our project, we have wanted to evaluate these bigger picture, aggregate, automated and structural developments and trends, and their impact on media pluralism, rather than focus on how online news consumption has changed at the level of individual routines and repertoires. Wider research questions in relation to morphing digital news content consumption are inextricably connected with those issues by way of research into the algorithmic design, for example, of personal recommender systems.

One of the more interesting findings of research by Makhortykh et al. (2021) is that insights that may arise from how online news content is consumed by audiences are, ultimately, adding little to the foundational knowledge of the structural availability or access in terms of plurality or diversity. The authors note:

> Our analyses emphasise the essential role of content supply that aligns with earlier arguments about the importance of availability factors for the composition of individual news repertoires (Taneja et al. 2012). Independently of how different users consume news, their information diets seem to generally align with the distribution of the supplied content.
>
> (2795)

However, probably of more importance to us from the perspective of rejuvenating media pluralism policies is the observation the authors make in relation to the implications for the impact of this sort of research about time and content-based habits of news consumption. In particular, they comment that their research raises 'a number of questions concerning the possible impact of algorithmic news recommenders on the user reading habits'. They note, for example, that there may be a gap between 'the goal to increase users' engagement and the rate of return to news websites via personalised content suggestions' and the actual usage patterns as indicated in clickstream data (and other kinds of studies). So, it is suggested that the question could be posed, 'how significant will the impact of news recommenders be on the existing reader habits?' and how universal will their application be to remain helpful for the users of particular media brands/outlets? (2795).

Alternative policy paradigms

As we have noted elsewhere, journalism in Australia has been in a crisis for some years, echoing the 'news deserts' around the globe, and this can be seen in the number of closures that are a matter of public record:

> The advocacy group Public Interest Journalism Initiative has documented 200 news 'contractions' in the sector (meaning title, masthead, or newsroom closures, the end

of a print edition, a move to digital-only, or a merger) since January 2019 (Public Interest Journalism Initiative 2020) [...]. In May 2020, News Corp announced it would cease printing 112 community and regional newspapers, transitioning 76 titles to digital-only and closing 36 of their titles completely (Mason 2020). A number of commentators noted that COVID-19 had accelerated a plan initiated by News Corp in 2018 to transition its print publishing operations to digital-only. The company announced it would retain 375 jobs in its regional and community sector – a sector that was previously employing some 1,200–1,300 jobs.

(MDM 2021: 64)

Most of the interventions discussed in this book, and particularly in Chapter 3, concerned mechanisms to monitor media pluralism and diversity, and where necessary prevent further reductions of media voices from occurring. Alternative, or perhaps, 'positive' structural regulatory approaches are also possible. This can occur in the form of financial assistance to whole sectors (e.g., the Public Interest News Gathering, or PING fund, or the Regional and Small Publishers Innovation Fund that currently exist in Australia), as tax relief, or as more targeted financial interventions including philanthropic support for investigative reporting in countries where governments and markets are unlikely to recognize its crucial contribution to media freedom and pluralism. In Nordic countries, subsidies have been the main mechanism for achieving goals of media diversity and pluralism for decades.

We agree with those arguing that it is time for the Australian government to seriously consider the Nordic 'welfarist' approach that provides long-term funding for threatened forms of public interest journalism, 'providing certain accountability measures are in place' (Bennett and Rae 2021: 211–15), and as part of a suite of measures that would continue to include some financial contribution by digital platforms to the local news environment. As the ACCC's Digital Platform Inquiry concluded, the power imbalance between digital intermediaries and traditional news media organizations is not going to get any better. Therefore, a long-term strategy to address this situation is required to remedy a situation that amplifies Australia's already dire concentrated media market (ACCC 2019).

The policy rationale of providing direct subsidies to newspaper outlets is that such an intervention supports the survival of specific media market voices, and in that way supports diversity for democratic ends. They take the form of financial assistance for production and distribution, as well as relief from paying taxes. An example of the former would be in Norway, where the second-largest newspaper (by circulation) in each city is provided with direct financial support. The main purpose of the mechanism is to prevent monopolies from occurring in news and current affairs publishing. As Bennett and Rae note, 'the main argument for direct support to the less dominant newspapers was to uphold political diversity and geographical diversity among newspapers' (Bennett and Rae 2021: 215). Public broadcast media are funded through licence fees, and this is also intended to support and boost voice plurality. Denmark and Sweden also use subsidy mechanisms to support publishers who are not the market leaders. Supporting public interest journalism has been accepted as a public good in these Nordic countries.

The new law that requires Meta and Google to make payments to news publishers in Australia has arisen as a result of the recognition that, left to their own dynamics, the platforms may sound the death knell for existing news media organizations. However, there is a view that once the largesse of the payments flowing from the platforms under the News Media Bargaining Code runs out, the situation for news will not be so rosy (Meese 2021). Arguably, if there was a system-wide approach it could be a sustainable solution for regional newsrooms as well. There is a great risk, though, that in the absence of ongoing subsidy mechanisms, many existing news publishers will not survive. In the past, media inquiries have concluded that permanent mechanisms for government funding of news media would not be acceptable (Finkelstein 2012).

The more recent review conducted as part of the Senate Inquiry into Media Diversity found that the media regulatory framework in Australia was 'not fit for purpose' (Senate: x). Although the inquiry advanced debate regarding the possible forms of regulation for progressive media outcomes, its recommendations – particulary the call for a judicial inquiry with the powers of a royal commission into media diversity – are unlikely to be adopted, even by the new Labor Govermnent. In his dissenting report, Sen. Bragg, Deputy Chair of the Environment and Communications References Committee and a member of the conservative Liberal Party, found no problem with the state of news provision in Australia. Sen. Bragg observes 'Australian news consumers have never been exposed to a more diverse media environment' (para. 1.57, 141). In support of this thesis, he cherry picks a number of sources used by minority cohorts for news, such as younger Australians' use of TikTok and Reddit. He notes that Australians can read *The Guardian*, the *ABC online* and *news.com.au* for free and can use their phones to access news. He observes that 'While it is true that there are two major newspaper outlets, this is not a proxy for media diversity' (para. 1.8, 136). It appears, from Sen Bragg's analysis, that we should just carry on basking in the abundance of news sources provided by the internet.

Having heard this kind of explanation for several decades, many in the community now recognize such fare as the standard neoliberalist ideology of 'choice' that often results in fewer, rather than more, voices to critique the actions and decisions of those in power. Our hope is that this approach will be challenged through parliamentary and other inquiries, innovative regulation, research that connects the experience of those across the globe, and a growing community awareness of the need for enhanced recognition of media pluralism in the online, platformized era.

REFERENCES

ACCC (Australian Competition and Consumer Commission) (2019), *Digital Platforms Inquiry: Final Report*, https://www.accc.gov.au/publications/digital-platforms-inquiry-final-report. Accessed 26 July 2019.

Arguedas, Amy Ross, Robertson, Craig T., Fletcher, Richard and Nielsen, Rasmus Klein (2022), *Echo Chambers, Filter Bubbles, and Polarisation: A Literature Review, Reuters Institute for Journalism*, Oxford: University of Oxford. https://reutersinstitute.politics.ox.ac.uk/echo-chambers-filter-bubbles-and-polarisation-literature-review. Accessed 20 January 2022.

Athey, Susan, Mobius, Markus and Pal, Jeno (2017), *The Impact of Aggregators on Internet News Consumption*, Stanford University Graduate School of Business Research Paper Nos. 17-8, https://ssrn.com/abstract=2897960. Accessed 24 February 2023.

Australian Senate (2021), *Media Diversity in Australia. Senate Environment and Communications References Committee*, Canberra: Commonwealth of Australia, https://parlinfo.aph.gov.au/parlInfo/download/committees/reportsen/024602/toc_pdf/MediadiversityinAustralia.pdf;fileType=application%2Fpdf. Accessed 9 February 2022.

Bennett, Ebony and Rae, Maria (2021), 'Towards a more diverse media and stronger public broadcasting', in A. Scott and R. Campbell (eds), *The Nordic Edge: Policy Possibilities for Australia*, Melbourne: Melbourne University Press, pp. 195–215.

Bruns, Axel (2019), *Are Filter Bubbles Real?* Cambridge: Polity.

Bucher, Taina (2018), *If … Then: Algorithmic Power and Politics*, New York: Oxford University Press.

Council of Europe (2022), *Recommendation CM/Rec (2022) 11 of the Committee of Ministers to Member States on Principles for Media and Communication Governance*, https://search.coe.int/cm/Pages/result_details.aspx?ObjectID=0900001680a61712. Accessed 18 May 2022.

Craufurd Smith, Rachael (2021), *Submission to Ofcom: The Future of Media Plurality in the UK Including Ofcom's Consultation on the Media Ownership Rules*, https://www.ofcom.org.uk/consultations-and-statements/category-2/future-media-plurality-uk. Accessed 20 November 2021.

Dwyer, Tim (2010), *Media Convergence*, Maidenhead: Open University Press.

Dwyer, Tim and Martin, Fiona (2019), 'The future of journalism in a sharing ecology', in F. Martin and T. Dwyer (eds), *Sharing News Online: Commendary Cultures and Social Media News Ecologies*, Cham: Palgrave Macmillan, pp. 285–304.

Dwyer, Tim, Wilding, Derek and Koskie, Tim (2021), 'Australia: Media concentration and deteriorating conditions for investigative journalism', in J. Trappel and T. Tomaz (eds), *The Media for Democracy Monitor 2021*, Gothenburg: Nordicom, pp. 59–94.

Elvestad, Eiri and Phillips, Angela (2018), *Misunderstanding News Audiences: Seven Myths of the Social Media Era*, London and New York: Routledge.

Eubanks, Virginia (2017), *Automating Inequality: How High-Tech Tools Profile, Police and Punish the Poor*, New York: St. Martin's Press.

European Commission (2018), *Tackling Online Disinformation: A European Approach*, (Report No. 52018DC0236), https://eur-lex.europa.eu/legal-content/EN/TXT/?uri=CELEX%3A52018DC0236. Accessed 11 February 2022.

European Parliament (2023), 'Committee on education and culture, hearing on 6 February 2023', https://multimedia.europarl.europa.eu/en/webstreaming/cult-committee-meeting_20230206-1500-COMMITTEE-CULT. Accessed 8 February 2023.

Finkelstein, Ray (2012), *Report of the Independent Inquiry into the Media and Media Regulation* ('The Finkelstein Inquiry'), https://apo.org.au/node/28522. Accesssed 28 February 2022.

Flew, Terry (2021), *Platform Regulation*, London: Polity.

Floridi, Luciano (2014), *The 4th Revolution: How the Infosphere Is Reshaping Human Reality*, Oxford: Oxford University Press.

Giotis, Chrisanthi, Molitorisz, Sacha and Wilding, Derek (2023), 'How Australia's competition regulator is supporting news, but not quality', in P. M. Napoli and R. Lawrence (eds), *News Quality in the Digital Age*, New York: Routledge, pp. 169–86.

Habermas, Jurgen (2022), 'Reflections and hypotheses on a further structural transformation of the political public sphere', *Theory, Culture & Society*, 39:4, pp. 145–71, https://doi.org/10.1177/02632764221112341.

Helberger, Natalie (2021), 'On the democratic role of news recommenders', in N. Thurman, S. C. Lewis and J. Kunert (eds), *Algorithms, Automation and News: New Directions in the Study of Computation and News*, London: Routledge, pp. 993–1012.

Helberger, Natalie, Karppinen, Kari and D'Acunto, Lucia (2018), 'Exposure diversity as a design principle for recommender systems', *Information, Communication & Society*, 21:2, pp. 191–207, https://doi.org/10.1080/1369118X.2016.1271900.

Helberger, Natalie, Moeller, Judith and Vrijenhoek, Sanne (2020), *Diversity by Design – Diversity of Content in the Digital Age*, Canada: Canadian Department of Canadian Heritage and the Canadian Commission for UNESCO. https://www.canada.ca/en/canadian-heritage/services/diversity-content-digital-age/diversity-design.html. Accesssed 18 February 2022.

Hoskins, Andrew and Tulloch, John (2016), *Risk and Hyperconnectivity: Media and Memories of Neoliberalism*, Oxford and New York: Oxford University Press.

Humphreys, Peter (2015), 'Transferable media pluralism policies from Europe', in S. Barnett and J. Townend (eds), *Media Pluralism and Plurality: From Hyperlocal to High-Level Policy*, London: Palgrave MacMillan, pp. 151–69.

Iosifidis, Petros and Nicoli, Nicholas (2021), *Digital Democracy, Social Media and Disinformation*, New York: Routledge.

Kearns, Michael and Roth, Aaron (2020), *The Ethical Algorithm: The Science of Socially Aware Algorithm Design*, New York: Oxford University Press.

Kelly, Jemima (2021), 'Twitter's new team should institute a "challenger mode"', *Australian Financial Review*, 10 December.

Makhortykh, Mykola, de Vreese, Clais, Helberger, Natali, Harambam, Jaron and Bountouridis, Dimitrios (2021), 'We are what we click: Understanding time and content-based habits of Online News Readers', *New Media & Society*, 23:9, pp. 2773–800.

Mainzer Medieninstitut (2023), 'Prof. Cornils on the European Media Freedom Act – statement in the CULT', https://www-mainzer--medieninstitut-de.translate.goog/prof-cornils-zum-european-media-freedom-act-stellungnahme-im-cult/?_x_tr_sl=de&_x_tr_tl=en&_x_tr_hl=en&_x_tr_pto=sc. Accessed 8 February 2023.

Mason, Max (2020a), 'News Corp print closures leave regional media on life support', *Australian Financial Review*, 28 May, https://www.afr.com/companies/media-and-marketing/news-corp-print-closures-leave-regional-media-on-life-support-20200528-p54x7m. Accessed 30 January 2023.

Media Pluralism Project Dashboard (2020), Computational tool available at https://mediapluralism.sydney.edu.au. Accessed 19 July 2023.

Media Pluralism Project website (2019), 'The role of a pluralistic media in Australia's democracy', Media Pluralism Project, https://mediapluralism.org.au/2019/05/the-role-of-a-pluralistic-media-in-australias-democracy/. Accessed 30 January 2023.

Meese, James (2021), 'Why Google is now funnelling millions into media outlets, as Facebook pulls news for Australia', *The Conversation*, 18 February, https://theconversation.com/why-google-is-now-funnelling-millions-into-media-outlets-as-facebook-pulls-news-for-australia-155468. Accessed 30 January 2023.

Napoli, Philip and Caplan, Robyn (2017), 'Why media companies insist they're not media companies, why they're wrong, and why it matters', *First Monday*, 22:5, https://journals.uic.edu/ojs/index.php/fm/article/view/7051. Accessed 24 February 2023.

Newman, Nic, Fletcher, Richard, Schulz, Anne, Andi, Simge and Nielsen, Rasmus Kleis (2020), *Reuters Institute Digital News Report 2020. Reuters Institute for the Study of Journalism*, Oxford: University of Oxford, http:// www.digitalnewsreport.org/. Accessed 15 September, 2021.

Nielsen, Rasmus Kleis and Ganter, Sarah Anne (2022), *The Power of Platforms: Shaping Media and Society*, New York: Oxford University Press.

Ofcom (2021), *Statement: The Future of Media Plurality in the UK*, 17 November, https://www.ofcom.org.uk/__data/assets/pdf_file/0019/228124/statement-future-of-media-plurality.pdf. Accessed 24 February 2023.

Ofcom (2022a), 'Media Plurality and Online News', 16 November, https://www.ofcom.org.uk/research-and-data/multi-sector-research/media-plurality. Accessed 30 January 2023.

Ofcom (2022b), 'News Consumption and Media Plurality on Twitter in the UK', 16 November, https://www.ofcom.org.uk/research-and-data/economics-discussion-papers/news-consumption-and-media-plurality-on-twitter. Accessed 30 January 2023.

Park, Sora, Fisher, Caroline, McGuinness, Kieran, Lee, Jee Young and McCallum, Kerry (2021), *Digital News Report: Australia 2021*, 23 June, Canberra: News & Media Research Centre, University of Canberra, https://apo.org.au/node/312650. Accessed 30 January 2023.

Public Interest Journalism Initiative (2020), 'Number of public interest news contractions in Australia tops 200', Media Release, 28 May, https://piji.com.au/piji_media_releases/number-of-public-interest-news-contractions-in-australia-tops-200/. Accessed 30 January 2023.

Reidl, Martin J. (2022), 'Negotiating sociomateriality and commensurability: Human and algorithmic editorial judgment at social media platforms', *Journalism Studies*, 23:3, pp. 374–91.

Rowland MP, The Hon Michelle (2023), 'New ACMA powers to combat harmful online misinformation and disinformation', *Media Release*, 20 January, https://minister.infrastructure.gov.au/rowland/media-release/new-acma-powers-combat-harmful-online-misinformation-and-disinformation. Accessed 30 January 2023.

Roy Morgan (2018b), 'It's official: Most Australians now visit news or newspaper websites', 24 May, http://www.roymorgan.com/findings/7595-top-20-news-websites-march-2018-201805240521. Accessed 30 January 2023.

Schlosberg, Justin and Freedman, Des (2020), 'Opening the gates: Plurality regulation and the public interest', *Journal of Digital Media and Policy*, 11:2, pp. 115–32.

Sunstein, Cass R. (2018), *#Republic: Divided Democracy in the Age of Social Media*, Princeton: Princeton University Press, https://doi.org/10.2307/j.ctv8xnhtd.

Tambini, Damian (2022), 'The democratic fightback has begun: The Europena Commission's new European Media Freedom Act', *LSE*, 16 September, https://blogs.lse.ac.uk/europpblog/2022/09/16/the-democratic-fightback-has-begun-the-european-commissions-new-european-media-freedom-act/. Accessed 30 January 2023.

Taneja, Harsh, Webster, James G., Malthouse, Edward C. and Ksiazek, Thomas B. (2012), 'Media consumption across platforms: Identifying user-defined repertoires', *New Media & Society*, 14:6, pp. 951–68.

Thorson, Kjerstin (2020), 'Attracting the news: Algorithms, platforms, and reframing incidental exposure', *Journalism*, 21:8, pp. 1067–82, https://doi.org/10.1177/1464884920915352.

Vaidhyanathan, Siva (2018), *Anti-Social Media: How Facebook Disconnects Us and Undermines Democracy*, New York: Oxford University Press.

Contributors

SABA BEBAWI, professor, is the head of discipline for journalism and writing in the School of Communication at UTS. She has published on media power and the role of media in democracy-building, in addition to investigative journalism in conflict and post-conflict regions. She is author of *Media Power and Global Television News: The role of Al Jazeera English* (2016); *Investigative Journalism in the Arab World: Issues and Challenges* (2016); and co-author of *The Future Foreign Correspondent* (2019); in addition to co-editor of *Social Media and the Politics of Reportage: The Arab Spring* (2014) and *Data Journalism in the Global South* (2020).

* * * * *

TIM DWYER, associate professor, is the degree director of the master of media practice at the University of Sydney and a visiting foreign professor at the College of Media and International Culture, Zhejiang University. His research focuses on the critical evaluation of media and communications industries, regulation, media ethics, law and policy in an era of convergent media, algorithmic mediatization and the use of personal data. His current Australian Research Council funded research is investigating the links between the preparedness of individuals to pay for news, the value of news brands and organizational cultures of news publishers, and the social value of news in promoting a democratic public sphere. He is the author of several books including *Sharing News Online* (2019) (with Fiona Martin) and *Convergent Media and Privacy* (2016).

* * * * *

JONATHON HUTCHINSON is a senior lecturer in online communication and media at the University of Sydney, Chair of Discipline, and a chief investigator on the Australian Research Council Discovery Project, Media Pluralism and Online News. His research explores public service media, cultural intermediation, everyday social media, automated media and algorithms in media. He is the editor of the *Policy & Internet* journal and the president for the Australian and New Zealand Communication Association (ANZCA). He is the author of *Cultural Intermediaries: Audience Participation in Media Organisations* (2017) and *Digital Intermediaries* (2023).

* * * * *

KARI KARPPINEN's research interests include media and communication policy, media freedom and pluralism, theories of democracy and the public sphere, and questions about digital rights and internet governance. He is the author of *Rethinking Media Pluralism* (Fordham University Press, 2013), and his work has also appeared in journals such as the *European Journal of Communication, Information, Communication & Society, Journalism Studies, The Information Society, Journal of Information Policy* and *First Monday*. He has been a visiting research fellow at the University of Sydney, Westminster University and Fordham University.

* * * * *

DEREK WILDING, professor, is the co-director of the Centre for Media Transition (CMT) at the University of Technology Sydney. Prior to this he worked as executive director of the Australian Press Council and for the Australian Communications and Media Authority (ACMA) where he managed the implementation of the federal government's media ownership reform package. His research focusses on media and digital platform regulation. He is the author of numerous policy submissions to government inquiries and research reports, including research commissioned by the Australian Competition and Consumer Commission (ACCC) and the ACMA. He has published in journals such as *Federal Law Review*, *Media Culture Society*, and *Media International Australia*.

Index

Arabic personal names ignore the definite article (you will find Muhammad Al-Tabi'i under T for example) but titles of organizations and publications are indexed under 'A' (Al-Jazeera, *Al Maghrib*).

5/4 minimum voices rule 42, 55
21st Century Fox 46, 49
75 per cent reach rule 42

A
ABA (Australian Broadcasting Authority) 58
ABC (Australian Broadcasting Corporation) 15, 124, 137
ABC Online 216
Abidin, C. 128–29
ACCC (Australian Competition and Consumer Commission) 5, 38, 50–52, 57 *see also* Digital Platforms Inquiry (DPI)
accountability 107–11
    and algorithms 166–67
    and investigative journalism 181–82
    of platforms 162
    see also transparency
accountability reporting 179 *see also* investigative journalism
ACMA (Australian Communications and Media Authority) 6, 40, 48, 202–03, 211, 212–13
    and automated curation 87–88
    and digital platforms 87–88
    and dis/misinformation 78
    and localism 78–81
    and media diversity 28, 77–79, 83, 87, 91–92, 211
    and media pluralism 74, 87–88
    and PIT 57
    power of 87–88
    and regulation 59
    see also News Measurement Framework
Action Plan Against Disinformation (EU) 103 *see also* dis/misinformation
advertising revenue 163
Africa, investigative journalism 187
aggregators 8, 68, 89, 199, 212
Agrawal, Parag 206
AI (Artificial Intelligence) 125, 166
AI Now Institute 125, 166
AI Now Report (Whittaker et. al.) 166
Akhbar Al Youm 191
Al Ahram 191
Al-Akhbar 191
Al-Akkad, Abbas Mahmuod 190
Al Ghad 193
Al Jazeera 192–93
Al Maghrib 193
Al Nahar 193
Al Shorouq 193
algorithm imaginary 118
algorithm regulator 212

Algorithm Watch 34, 166
algorithmic culture 124
algorithmic suitability 118
algorithmic visibility 120 *see also* visibility
algorithms 2, 17–18, 107–13
    accountability 166–67
    auditing 35–39, 87
    China 18
    and civil rights 166
    definitions of 165
    and digital platforms 32
    DRCF reports 17–18
    Korea 165–67
    and media pluralism 166, 201
    and news delivery 32, 86, 212
    ontological politics of 34
    Philip DeFranco Show 131–32
    and platformization 146
    and PSM 123–26
    and racism 166
Ali, Muhammad Kurd 190
Alphabet (Google) 18
America, and media pluralism 101 *see also* United States
Amin, Mustafa and Ali 191
Apple 18
Apple News 8
Arab region, investigative journalism and press freedom 188–94
Arab Reporters for Investigative Journalism (ARIJ) 193
Arab Spring 188, 190, 194
Are Filter Bubbles Real? (Bruns) 203
Argentina, journalism 187
Arguedas, Amy Ross 206
ARIJ (Arab Reporters for Investigative Journalism) 193
Arnott, Craig 84
Arriagada, A 121
Asia, investigative journalism 186

ASMR (Autonomous Sensory Meridian Response) 122
At a Café on Politics Street (Quddoos) 191
AT&T 41
attention, shares of 72, 83–84, 87
audiences 3–4, 8, 125 *see also* public; users of digital platforms
auditing 13, 35–39, 87, 110 *see also* automated curation; regulation; transparency
Australia
    codes of practice 15, 40, 43–44
    Facebook shut down 6–8, 10–11, 13, 35, 198
    financial support 215–16
    and Google 6, 199
    human rights 35
    licensing 40–41
    media concentration 45, 205
    media control 41–44
    media diversity 28, 41, 43–44, 54–56, 91–92, 208, 216–17
    media markets 50–52
    media ownership 41–45, 208–09
    and media pluralism 28, 40–45, 58, 87–88, 202–03, 213
    and mergers 40, 50–52
    news consumption 72–74
    newspapers 44–45, 52
    policy and regulation 4, 40–45, 59, 92, 211–13, 215–16
    and quality news 199
    radio 44–45, 213
    TV 40, 41, 42, 43, 45
    Twitter usage 207
    see also ACCC; ACMA; News Media Bargaining Code
The Australian 45, 89
Australian Broadcasting Authority (ABA) 58
Australian Broadcasting Corporation (ABC) 15, 124, 137

Australian Communications and Media Authority (ACMA) *see* ACMA
Australian Communications and Media Authority Act 2005 48, 58, 77, 78
Australian Competition and Consumer Commission (ACCC) *see* ACCC
The Australian Financial Review 45, 89
automated curation 22, 84, 197–98, 203–09
    and ACMA 87–88
    assessment of 85–88
    China 172
    and citizenship 16–19
    digital platforms 84, 87
    and ethics 33–35
    and Ofcom 85–88
    see also auditing
automated platformization 158 *see also* platformization
automated serendipity 206
Automating Society (Algorithm Watch) 166
Autonomous Sensory Meridian Response (ASMR) 122
availability (Ofcom measure) 68–70
Ayalon, Ami 189
Azmi, Mahmuod 190

B

Babil, Nassuh 190
Baidu 18, 148
Baidu Tieba 146
Baker, C. Edwin 101, 112
bargaining code *see* News Media Bargaining Code
Barnett, Stephen 83
Barrett, Bridget 107, 109
Bärtl, M 161
Batti, Rafa'il 190
BBC (UK) 71–72, 76, 83, 85, 211
Bebawi, Saba 221

Belgium, mergers 52
Bennett, Ebony 215–16
Bernays, Edward L. 144
Berry, Mark 51
Bishop, Sophie 4, 130
BJs (Broadcast Jockeys) 129
black box 35, 110
blogs, Korea 171
Bodó, Balázo 2
Bolivia, and Facebook 8
bounded media spaces 204 *see also* echo chambers; filter bubbles
Bourdieu, P. 9, 127
Brand, Russell 131, 133–35, 138
Brazil
    journalism 187–88
    news sources 6, 159
bright-line regulation 53, 91
Broad Tones *see Sixth Tone*
broadband access 146 *see also* internet
Broadcast Jockeys (BJs) 129
Broadcasting Act 1990 (UK) 46
Broadcasting Code (UK) 76
Broadcasting Legislation Amendment (News Media Diversity) Bill 2013 (Australia) 53
Broadcasting Services Act 1992 (Australia) 40, 41–42, 55, 57–58, 77
Brogi, Elda 58–59, 106, 111
Brüggeman, Michael 106
Bruns, Axel 109, 161, 203
Bucher, Tania 33–34, 124, 125
Van den Bulck, Hilde 52, 126
Van der Burg, Miriam 52
Burma, journalism 186
Burri, M. 126
Bytedance 18

C

Cairncross Review (UK) 31, 162

Cambodia
    and Facebook 8
    journalism 186
Canada
    media diversity 44
    regulation 58
CCTV 152
censorship, Arab region 189–90 *see also* press freedom
CDEI (Centre for Data Ethics and Innovation) 38
Chaebol 170, 171
Chartbeat 7–8
Charter of Fundamental Rights of the European Union 100 *see also* human rights
chatbots 124
Chile, investigative journalism 180
China 18, 147–58, 169
    automated curation 172
    investigative journalism 185–86
Choi, K. 164
Choojoondong 170
Chosun.com 168
Chosunilbo 167
Chosun Ilbo 170
citizenship, and automated curation 16–19
civic journalism 79–80 *see also* journalism
Civil and Human Rights, Leadership Conference on 166
Civil Liberties, European Parliament Committee on 29
civil rights 29, 166 *see also* human rights
Clarín 187
clickbait 157, 158, 168, 198–99
CMA (Competition and Market Authority) 17, 38, 46, 58, 86
codes of practice
    Australia 15, 40, 43–44
    Europe 199
    see also ACMA

Columbia, journalism 187
commercialization, China 148
Communications Act 2003 (UK) 45–46, 48
Communications, UK House of Lords Select Committee 49, 52
Communist Party of China (CPC), Propaganda Department 147
competition 50, 51 *see also* mergers
Competition and Consumer Act 2010 (Australia) 33, 40, 50, 55
Competition and Market Authority (CMA) 17, 38, 46, 58, 86
connection (aspect of localism) 80
connectivity 1–2 *see also* hyperconnectivity
constructivist recommenders 3, 150 *see also* recommenders
consumption 79, 205–06
    Australia 72–74
    and Facebook/Google 85–86
    and media pluralism 70–74
    Ofcom survey 75(fig)
    and social media platforms 10, 74, 119, 159, 209
    YouTube 161
content 1–2, 87
    analysis 89–90, 172
    and ethics 136
    and media pluralism 75–77
    and regulation 33, 136
    and social media 15, 37, 130, 146, 207
    see also content diversity
content creation 3–4, 121–23, 129–30, 138, 146
    YouTube 132, 134–35
    see also Brand; DeFranco; friendlyjordies
content diversity 30–31, 79–80, 81, 84, 122, 165, 197 *see also* media diversity
content providers, concentration of 146
    see also media concentration

contextual factors 75–77, 84–85
Convergence Review (Australia) 41, 53–56
Cook, Tim 13
core news 11, 56 *see also* news
Cornils, Matthias 200
Council of Europe *see* Europe
The Courier Mail 52
couriermail.com.au 89
covered news 6, 11, 56 *see also* news
COVID-19 13–14
Craufurd Smith, Rachael 58, 83, 91, 201
crisis narrative 106–07
cross-media rule (Australia) 42
cross-media rule (UK) 45–46
cross-media usage, China 146
cultural diversity 4, 43, 150 *see also* media diversity
cultural intermediaries 127–29 *see also* intermediation
cultural production, platformization of 120–23, 138
Culture, Media and Sport, Department of (UK) 49
curation *see* automated curation; news curation
Curran, James 144, 182–83

D

Daily Mail and General Trust (DMGT) 54
Daily Mail Group 17
Daisley, Bruce 207
Dark Ages 185
Data Ethics and Innovation, Centre for (CDEI) 38
Data & Society Institute 166
data surveillance flows 1–2, 149–50
datacasting services 42, 77
Daum (Kakao) 159, 164–65, 169
Davis, M. 145
Deep Tones *see Sixth Tone*

DeFranco, Philip 131–33, 138
deliberative recommenders 3, 150 *see also* recommenders
democracy 107–09
Democracy Action Plan (EU) 99, 103, 105
Democratic Corporatist or North/Central European model of media 144
Deng, J. 152
Denmark
    investigative journalism 180
    newspapers 216
de-platforming 125 *see also* platformization
deregulation, Australia 41, 42 *see also* regulation
de-westernization 143–47, 171
De-Westernizing Platform Studies: History and Logics of Chinese and U.S. Platforms (Davis and Xiao) 145
Digital Competition, Unlocking. Report of the Digital Competition Expert Panel (Furman Report) 16, 38–39
Digital Democracy, Social Media and Disinformation (Iosifidis and Nicoli) 198–99
digital intermediation 120–21, 124–25 *see also* intermediation
digital journalism, China 152 *see also* journalism
digital literacy 146, 208 *see also* education; media literacy
Digital Markets Act (EU) 32
Digital Markets Unit (UK) 38
Digital News Report (University of Canberra) 5–6, 73, 207
digital platforms 84–88
    and algorithms 32
    and journalism 105–07
    and legacy media 105–07
    and media pluralism 32–33, 87
    and personalization 2–3
    and policy 39

digital platforms (*Contd*)
    power of 8–16, 18, 20, 111, 198
    problem definition 98–100, 105–07
    regulation 6, 32–33, 103, 161
    and transparency 110
    and users 111, 119, 207
    see also platforms
Digital Platforms Inquiry (ACCC) 37–38, 51–52, 106
    recommendations 6, 16, 37–38, 86, 161–62, 215
    see also ACCC
Digital Regulation Cooperation Forum (DRCF) 17–18, 39
Digital Services Act (EU) 32, 36, 99, 103, 108, 110, 111–12
Digital Strategy (EU) 103, 105
Digital, Culture, Sport and Media Committee, UK House of Commons 128
Van Dijck, J. 113
discoverability 4, 87, 150, 166 *see also* findability
disinformation 13–16, 78, 109, 198–203 *see also* news manipulation
Disinformation, Action Plan Against (EU) 103
Disinformation, Code of Practice on (EU) 199
Disinformation and Misinformation, Australian Code of Practice on 15
Disinformation, Tackling Online (EC) 199
distribution 1–2, 146, 199
    China 149–50
diversity *see* media diversity
Diversity Index (US) 20
DMG Media Limited 49, 70, 72, 205
DMGT (Daily Mail General Trust) 54
documentaries 148, 186
Dong-A 170
Donga.com 168
Dongailbo 167

Douban.com 146
Douyin (TikTok) 18
Doyle, Gillian 30
Drum Magazine 187
DRCF (Digital Regulation Cooperation Forum) 17–18, 39
Dutch-Flemish Association for Investigative Journalism (VVOJ) 180
Dwyer, Tim 10, 42, 121, 161–62, 207, 221

E
EC *see* Europe
echo chambers 109, 203–05 *see also* filter bubbles
Economic Legislation Committee, Senate, Australia 10–11
The Economist 170
education 166–67, 186, 200, 207 *see also* digital literacy
Egypt, journalism and press freedom 190–91, 193
El Comercio 187
El Tiempo 187
electoral processes 9, 143, 146
Elvestad, Eiri 207–08
empowerment (Ofcom measure) 87
Enterprise Act 2002 (UK) 46, 49, 53, 200–01, 202
ethics 33–35, 136
Ethics and algorithmic processes for decision making and decision support (Algorithm Watch) 34
Ettema, James S. 181–82
Europe
    action plans 99, 103, 105
    civil and human rights 29, 100
    and disinformation 103, 199
    intermediation 104
    and media pluralism 100–04, 150, 172, 199–200, 212

policy and regulation 4, 58–59, 99, 150, 166, 210
  see also Digital Markets Act; Digital Services Act; Media Freedom Act
European University Institute 102, 183
The Evening Standard 47, 49
Explore Feed, Facebook 8
exposure diversity 30, 43, 44, 70, 85, 108, 211 *see also* incidental exposure; media diversity

F
Facebook
  Australia shutdown 6–8, 10–11, 13, 35, 198
  content 15, 37, 130, 207
  and COVID-19 14
  defence of platform 208
  and dis/misinformation 15–16
  and news consumption 85–86
  and News Media Bargaining Code 7, 10–11, 13, 35, 216
  news platforms 159
  and news publishers 216
  Oversight Board 162
  power of 10
  and regulation 13
Facebook News 5
Facebook News Feed 37
Fairfax Media 51
Fairfax New Zealand 51
false balance 44
FCA (Financial Conduct Authority) 17
Federation of Korean Industries (FKI) 171
Feldstein, Mark 184
Fenton, Natalie 9, 39, 146
filter bubbles 97, 108–09, 165, 203–05
Financial Conduct Authority (FCA) 17
financial support
  Australia 215–16
  investigative journalism 180–81
  Korea 165
findability 4, 9, 150, 166 *see also* discoverability
Finkelstein Inquiry (Australia) 53
Finland, AI education 166
Finn, E. 35
First Draft News 15
fit and proper person test (UK) 46
FKI (Federation of Korean Industries) 171
Flew, Terry 106, 161–62, 198
Flipboard 8
Folha de São Paolo 187
Ford Foundation 186
Ford, H. 124
Foster, Robin 59
Fouda, Yosri 192
Foxtel 40, 45
France, and digital platforms 103
Freedman, Des 12, 58, 84, 85–86, 211, 212–13
freedom of expression 146 *see also* Media Freedom Act; press freedom
Freelon, Deen 108
friendlyjordies 131, 135(fig), 136–37
  see also Shanks, Jordan
Frydenberg, Josh 10
Furman Report (*Unlocking Digital Competition*) (UK) 16, 38–39

G
Germany
  and digital platforms 103
  news sources 5–6
Gibbons, Thomas 10, 84, 146
Gillespie, T. 160, 163
Giotis, Chrisanthi 199
Given, Jock 42
Glover, Richard 7

Google
   in Australia 6, 199
   and dis/misinformation 15–16
   litigation 137
   and Naver 162
   and news consumption 85–86
   and News Media Bargaining Code 10, 13, 216
   and news publishers 216
   power of 10
Google Chrome Suggestions 8
Google News 8
governance testing 87 *see also* regulation
The Guardian 208, 216
Guardian Media Group 201–02
Guatemala, and Facebook 8
Guokr.com 146

H
Hallin, D. 144
Hamza, Abdul Qadir 190
Hankooki.com (*The Korea Times*) 168
Hankyoreh 167, 170
hard news 31 *see also* news
Hashizume, Mauricio 188
headline baiting 156 *see also* clickbait
Heikal, Mohammad Hassanain 190, 191
Helberger, Natalie 3–4, 9, 29, 32, 44, 85, 87, 112, 150
Helmond, A. 160
Hitchens, Lesley 40, 48, 53, 58
homophily 204
Hongxing News 152
honour crimes 191–92
Hootsuite 132
Hoskins, Andrew 209
Huawei 18
human/machine relations 33–35, 150
human rights 35, 100, 108, 125, 166 *see also* civil rights

Human Rights, European Court of, and media pluralism 100
Human Rights, Leadership Conference on Civil and 166
Human Rights and Technology Final Report 2021 (Australian Human Rights Commission) 35
Humphreys, Peter 57, 58
Al-Husseini, Rana 191–92
Hutchinson, Jonathon 124, 127, 221–22
hyperconnectivity 209 *see also* connectivity

I
i (UK national newspaper) 49, 54, 70, 72
Ibáñez, F. 121
ICO (Information Commissioner's Office) 17
IJ Toolkit 186
image counts, WOA 157–58
impartiality 74, 76, 77
incidental exposure 206 *see also* exposure diversity
The Independent 47, 49
Independent Media Inquiry (Finkelstein Inquiry) 53
India, journalism 187–88
Indonesia, journalism 186
Industrial Revolution 184
influence 59, 77
influencers 56, 127–29, 138 *see also* recommenders
Information Commissioner's Office (ICO) 17
information pluralism 103–04 *see also* media pluralism
informed users 111 *see also* users
In-Link partners 163 *see also* Naver
Instagram 120, 130, 159
Institute for Public Interest News 162
intermediation 104, 120–21, 124–25, 130–37 *see also* cultural intermediaries

INDEX

International Policy Centre for Inclusive Growth (IPC-IG) 187–88
International Center for Journalism 193
International Consortium of Investigative Journalists 179
internet
    access 146
    Korea 167–68, 169–71
    and newspapers 72
investigative journalism 179–82, 184–94, 200 *see also* journalism
Investigative Journalism, International Consortium of 179
Investigative Journalism, Korea Center for 186
Investigative Journalism: A South-South Dialogue (IPC-IG workshop) 187–88
Iosifidis, Petros 198–99
IPC-IG (International Policy Centre for Inclusive Growth) 187–88
Iraq, journalism 190
Al-Isa, Isa 190
Al-Isa, Yusuf 190
ITV (UK), share of references 71

J

Jankowski, Nicholas W. 169
Japan 165
journalism 186
Jaume-Palasi, Lorena 34
Jin, D. Y. 145
JIPI (Public Interest Journalism Initiative) 45, 88
Johnston, Boris 133–34
Joins.com 168
Jolly, Sanjay 45, 78
Joongang 169
Joongangilbo 167

JoongAng 170
Jordan, journalism 191–92, 193
Jordan Times 191
journalism 105–06, 186–88, 190–93, 205
    civic 79–80
    digital 152
    China 152
    decline of 214–15
    DeFranco 132–33
    financial support 215
    and news influencers 138
    and platformization 5
    public interest 29–32
    and quality news 199
    regulation 161–62
    UK 162
    see also investigative journalism
Journalism, International Center for 193
journalists
    in China 147–48
    safety of 146
    see also journalism
JPI Media Publications Limited 49, 70
JTBC 167
JTBC.Joins.com 168

K

Kakao 162, 164–65, 167, 169, 171
Kamil, Mustafa 190
Karppinen, Kari 30, 149, 222
KBS 167
KCC (Korean Communication Commission) 169
keystone media 56
Khanfar, Wadah 192
Kim, Dae Woon 169
Kim, Dongwon 173
Kim, Jin-Gyu 169

Korea 159, 162–71
    cultural intermediaries 129
    investigative journalism 186
    and media pluralism 173
    news supply and politics 168, 169, 170, 173
    platformization 21
Korea Center for Investigative Journalism 186
Korea Medium Industries Association 171
Korea Telecom (KT) 167
Korean Communication Commission (KCC) 169
Koreanclick.com 159
KT (Korea Telecom) 167
Kyunhyang 167
Kyunhyang Shimun 170

L

La República 187
Lasch, Christopher 181
Lasswell, Harold 144
Law of Printing and Publications (Ottoman) 189
Lebanon, journalism 190
Lee, H. 171
Lee, K. 4
legacy media 105–07, 113
liberal recommenders 3, 150 *see also* recommenders
licensing 40–41 *see also* regulation
Line 164, 165, 171
Lippmann, Walter 144
literature, and newspapers 191
localism 67–68, 78–81, 82(fig), 205

M

machine-determined automation, and human-driven curation 150 *see also* human/machine relations
Maeil Business 167
Mainz Media Institute 200
Makhortykh, Mykola 214
Malaysia, news platforms 159
Mancini, P. 144
Mandatory News Media Bargaining Code *see* News Media Bargaining Code
market plurality (MPM measure) 29, 145 *see also* media pluralism
markets 29, 50–52, 68, 145 *see also* audiences
Martin, Fiona 121, 207
Marwick, A. 128
MBN 167
MBS 167
meaningful plurality 10, 146 *see also* media pluralism
Media and Audiovisual Action Plan (EU) 99, 103, 105
media concentration 45, 205–06 *see also* mergers
Media Concentration, Committee on the Impact of (Korea) 171
media control 41–44, 182–3 *see also* regulation
media diversity 29–30, 57–58, 119, 143, 172
    and ACMA 28, 77–79, 83, 87, 91–92, 211
    Australia 28, 41, 43–44, 54–56, 91–92, 208, 216–17
    Canada 44
    China 147–58
    and citizenship 16
    and competition 50–51
    in consumption 79–80, 156
    false balance 44
    and financial support 215–16
    Korea 158–73
    and localism 78, 80(fig), 82(fig), 83
    measurement 28–29, 41, 57, 59, 67, 79–81, 204, 212–13

and mergers 35, 50–52
and ownership 32, 41–42, 43, 54
and policy 29, 126
protection of 44–45, 53
and public service media 123–24, 138–39
reduced 84, 205, 211–13
and social media platforms 21–22
and technology 125
UK 91
and visibility 129–30
see also content diversity; cultural diversity; exposure diversity; news diversity; media pluralism; source diversity; viewpoint diversity
Media Diversity in Australia. Senate Environment and Communications References Committee 44, 171, 208
Media Diversity Bill (Australia) 54–55, 56
Media Diversity Committee (Korea) 171
Media Diversity, Senate Inquiry Into (Australia) 44, 51–52, 91, 216–17
Media for Democracy Monitor 180
Media Freedom Act, European 55, 86, 200, 212
Media Freedom and Pluralism, High Level Group on (EC) 108
media literacy 111, 200, 207, 208 *see also* digital literacy
Media Merger Guidelines (ACCC) 50
Media Partnerships Evaluation Committee (MPEC) 167–68
Media PIT *see* public interest test
media pluralism 9–10, 20, 29–33, 105, 143, 172, 209–14
and ACMA 74, 87–88
and algorithms 166, 201
America 101
Australia 28, 40–45, 58, 87–88, 202–03, 213

and availability 68–70
China 149
and consumption 70–74
and content 75–77
discursive shift 107
economic concerns 101
Europe 100–04, 150, 172, 199–200, 212
and investigative journalism 181
Korea 173
of markets 29, 145
non-Western contexts 188
and Ofcom 46–49, 68–77, 85–86, 87
and public interest 101
risks to 183
and social media platforms 21, 103
sufficient 10, 47–48, 84, 146
UK 46–47, 58, 160, 200–02
US 101
see also media diversity
Media Pluralism and Online News project 1, 30, 88–90, 213–14
aims of 31–32
Media Pluralism Dashboard 209
and policy 149
and terminology 56
WeChat analysis 152–56
Media Pluralism and Media Freedom, Centre for 58–59, 102, 183
Media Pluralism Monitor (MPM) 20, 29–30, 67, 68, 98, 99, 183
aims of 102–03, 104, 106, 110, 145–46
and automated curation 85–88
and China 146–47, 149
and digital platforms 85–88
and Europe 172
Media Plurality (UK House of Lords Select Committee on Communications) 52
Media Plurality Framework (Ofcom) 67, 69(fig), 83–85, 91, 210–11

Media Plurality and Online News (Ofcom) 19, 202, 204
Media Plurality in the UK, Statement: The Future of (Ofcom) 200
media policy studies, de-westernizing 143–47
Media Reform Coalition (MRC) 160, 201
media systems, and political systems 144
Media Watch (Australia) 137
Mediterranean or Polarized Pluralist model of media 144
Melbourne, news sources 89
mergers 32, 40, 46–48, 50–52 *see also* media concentration; monopolies; ownership
Meta (Facebook) 18, 199
metro papers 148
Mexico, journalism 187–88
microcelebrity 128
Milner, Simon 10–11
Milosavljević, Marko 100, 103
minimum voices rule (5/4 rule) 42, 55
misinformation 13–16, 78 *see also* disinformation
Misinformation in the COVID-19 Infodemic (UK) 13–14
Moe, H 126
Molitorisz, S. 4, 199
Möller, J. 160, 162
monetization 120, 136
monopolies, and power 12 *see also* mergers
Moon, Jae-In 173
Morrison, Scott 161
MPEC (Media Partnerships Evaluation Committee) 167–68
MPM *see* Media Pluralism Monitor
MRC (Media Reform Coalition) 160, 201
muckraking 179, 184–85 *see also* investigative journalism
Mukbang 129
Murdock, Graham 16
must show rules 150
My video went viral. Here's why (Veritasium) 122

N

Nansha 186
Napoli, Philip M. 30, 41, 79
Nasser, Gamal Abdul 191
Nate 173
National Union of Journalists (NUJ) 201, 202
Naver 159, 162–64, 165, 167, 171, 173
    news curation 168
    news supply 169
Nenadic, Iva 103, 104
Netherlands, mergers 52
network effect 12, 17, 111, 202
networks 126, 127–29, 159, 198, 203–09
    Korea 167, 169
    radio 44
    TV 42, 44–45
neutrality 104, 133, 146
New Deal Era 184
new public square/post public sphere 35
New Zealand, media diversity 51
New Zealand Commerce Commission 51
news
    accessing 160
    core 11, 56
    covered 6, 11, 56
    decline of 214–15
    definitions of 11
    hard 31
    platforms 159, 172
    quality 43, 198–203
    see also journalism; online news
News Consumption in the UK (Ofcom) 71
News Corp Australia 44–45, 52, 208
News Corporation 17, 40, 83, 89–90, 205, 211, 215

news creators 47–48, 56, 119, 129, 200–01, 202 *see also* Brand; content creation; DeFranco; friendlyjordies
news curation 14–15, 19, 150, 168, 169
news delivery, and algorithms 32, 86, 212
news diversity 21, 88, 106–07, 118, 157–58, 167, 209 *see also* media diversity
news engagement 70, 74, 81
news environment 119–23, 167, 201–02
news infrastructure 69, 81, 84
news manipulation 209 *see also* disinformation
News Measurement Framework (ACMA) 54, 56, 57, 67–68
News Media Bargaining Code (Australia) 6–7, 10–11, 33, 56, 57
    and algorithms 86, 212
    and content 87
    and Facebook 7, 10–11, 13, 35, 216
    and Google 10, 13, 216
    and quality news 199
News Messenger Service (ABC) 124
news output *see* content
news sources 5–6, 80, 89, 203–09 *see also* source diversity
news supply, Korea 168, 169, 170, 173
News UK 205
News, Algorithms and Automation (Bodó) 2
news.com.au 89, 216
News.SBS.co.kr 168
News1.kr 168
Newsis.com 168
newspapers 72, 191, 215–16
    Arab region 190
    Australia 44–45, 52
    China 148
    Korea 167–68, 170
    UK 47, 68, 71(fig), 205
Newstapa 186
Nicoli, Nicholas 198–99

Nieborg, D. B. 121
Nielsen, Rasmus Kleis 56
Nine Entertainment 45, 51, 89–90, 205, 208
Noble, Safiya Umoja 125, 166
non-public affairs reporting 31 *see also* PA/NPA classification; public affairs; reporting
North Atlantic or Liberal model of media 144
Northern and Shell Media Group 49
Norway, newspapers 215
Nothman, Joel 11
NUJ (National Union of Journalists) 201, 202
Al-Nusuli, Muhi Al-Din 190
Nxumal, Henry (Mr Drum) 187
NZME 51

O
OECD 5
Ofcom 17, 19, 46, 59
    and automated curation 85–88
    consumption survey 75(fig)
    and digital platforms 85–88
    and media diversity 204
    and media pluralism 46–49, 68–77, 85–86, 87
    news measurement framework 67, 69(fig), 83–85, 91, 210–11
    and PIT 54, 56
    scope of reviews 202
    and Twitter 204
Ohmynews.com 170
Online Harms and Disinformation, UK House of Commons Sub-committee 13–14
online news 88–90, 146, 161–62, 209–14
    China 151–52
    Korea 168
    see also news
Online Safety Act 2021 (Australia) 32
Online Safety Bill (UK) 32

originality (aspect of localism) 80
ownership 110, 205
    Australia 41–45, 208–09
    and media diversity 32
    UK 45–46
    see also mergers

P

PA/NPA classification 88–89, 90(fig), 153–54(fig), 155(fig) *see also* public affairs
Palestine, journalism 190, 193
Panama Papers 179
Pandora Papers 179
Paper, The (*Pengpai*) 151–52
Panyu GIP project 186
Papua New Guinea, journalism 186
Pariser, E. 165
Park, Guen Hye 168, 173
Park, Han Woo 169
Park, M. 144
participatory recommenders 3, 150
    see also recommenders
Pasquale, Frank 165, 167
pay TV 40, 42, 45
PCIJ (Philippine Center for Investigative Journalism) 186
Pengpai (*The Paper*) 151–52
Penny Press 185
persona studies 127–28
personal importance (Ofcom measure) 74
personalization 2–3, 37, 126, 165–66
Perth, news sources 89
Peru, journalism 187
The Philip DeFranco Show 131–33
Philippine Center for Investigative Journalism (PCIJ) 186
Philippines, journalism 186, 205
Phillips, Angela 207–08
Picard, Robert 57, 100

Pickard, Victor 45, 78
PING (Public Interest News Gathering) fund 215
PIT (public interest test) 46, 47–48, 53–59, 200–01
platform studies 145, 160–61
platformization 1–2, 157–58, 160–61, 172, 198–203
    and algorithms 146
    China 18, 21, 149–50
    of cultural production 120–23, 138
    de-platforming 125
    and journalism 5
    Korea 21
platforms *see* digital platforms; social media platforms
pluralism *see* media pluralism
Pluralism, High Level Group on Media Freedom and (EC) 108
plurality *see* media pluralism
Poell, T. 121
polarization 109, 206
policy 9–10, 112, 145
    Australia 4, 40–45, 59, 92, 211–13, 215–16
    and digital platforms 39
    Europe 4, 58–59, 99, 150, 166, 210
    and power concentration 112
    and problem definition 98–100, 113
    UK 28–29, 58, 59
    see also regulation
political independence (MPM measure) 145
political systems, and media systems 144
politics, and news supply, Korea 168, 169, 170, 173
Populist Era 184
portals, Korea 143, 158–73 *see also* Kakao; Naver

post-Mao economic reform, China 147
post public sphere 35, 39
power
    of ACMA 87–88
    concentration of 111–12, 113
    of digital platforms 8–16, 18, 20, 111, 198
    and monopolies 12
    and policy 112
press freedom
    Arab region 189–90
    Egypt 190–91, 193
    Korea 170–71
    see also Media Freedom Act
The Press in the Arab Middle East: A History (Ayalon) 189
Printing and Publications, Ottoman law of 189
problem definition
    accountability 109–11
    algorithms 107–09
    digital platforms 98–100, 105–07
    and policy 98–100, 113
    power concentration 111–12, 113
    transparency 109–11
Productivity Commission (Australia) 50, 53, 84–85
PSM (public service media) 3–4, 123–26, 138–39, 206
public 183 see also audiences; users of digital platforms
public affairs 1, 29–31, 56 see also PA/NPA classification
public interest 46, 53–54, 101
public interest journalism 29–32 see also journalism
Public Interest Journalism Initiative (JIPI) 45, 88
Public Interest News Gathering (PING) fund 215

public interest test (PIT) 46, 47–48, 53–59, 200–01
public service media (PSM) 3–4, 123–26, 138–39, 206
publishers 216

Q
Qatar, journalism 187–88
Qian, Yunhui 186
Qiupai News 152
quality news 43, 198–203 see also news
Quddoos, Ihsan Abdul 191
Qzone 146

R
race, and technology 125, 166
radio
    Australia 44–45, 213
    UK 47
Radio Shams FM 193
Rae, Maria 215–16
Al-Rafi'i, Amin 190
Rayyis cousins 190
Reach 49, 205
Recommendation CM/Rec(2022) 11 (EC) 210
recommenders 3–4, 85, 150, 165–66, 206–07, 214 see also influencers
reduction in diversity test 84, 212 see also media diversity
references, shares of 70–72, 73(fig), 83, 211
referral traffic 4, 6, 9, 33, 36, 86
Regional and Small Publishers Innovation Fund 215 see also financial support
Register of Controlled Media Groups 57

regulation 19, 91
  Australia 4, 40–45, 59, 92, 211–13, 215–16
  Canada 58
  China 18, 147
  and content 33, 136
  digital platforms 6, 32–33, 103, 161
  Europe 4, 58–59, 99, 150, 166, 210
  and Facebook 13
  governance testing 87
  impact of 44–45
  and journalism 161–62
  Korea 169–71
  online news 161–62
  and social media platforms 16, 36, 103
  structural 33
  UK 28–29, 58, 59
  US 166, 210
  see also ACCC; ACMA; auditing; Ofcom; media control
reliability (Ofcom measure) 74
Reporter Brasil Organisation 188
Reporters Without Borders 170 see also press freedom
reporting 31, 171 see also investigative journalism; journalism
Reset Australia 35–37
Reuters Digital News Report (2018) 166
Reuters Institute for the Study of Journalism 5, 204–06
revenue and reach test 55–56
Risk and Hyperconnectivity: Media and Memories of Neoliberalism (Hoskins and Tulloch) 209
Rockhampton, radio licences 213
Rodriguez, Pablo 58
Rose Al Yusif 191
Roy Morgan Single Source News data 72–73, 88
Ro'ya TV 193

Rudd, Kevin 92
Russell Brand YouTube Channel 131, 133–35, 138

S

Sabbagh, Rana 193
Sadat, Anwar 191
Al-Sam'ani, Tawfiq 190
Santow, Ed 35
São Paolo, workshop 187
Al-Sayyid, Ahmad Lutfi 190
SBS 167
Schifferes, S. 126
Schlesinger, P. 9
Schlosberg, Justin 58, 84, 85–86, 212
Schmidt, J. 125
Schudson, Michael 181
search engines 68 see also Google; Naver
Senft, T. M 128
Seoul, Korea Center for Investigative Journalism 186
Serbia, and Facebook 8
Seven West Media 45, 89, 205
Shanghai Daily 152
Shanghai United Media Group 151–52
Shangyou News 152
Shanks, Jordan 136–37, 138 see also friendlyjordies
share of attention 72, 83–84, 87
share of references 70–72, 73(fig), 83, 211
Sharing News Online (Martin and Dwyer) 207
Shine 157–58
SIH (Sydney Informatics Hub) 88–89
Simons, M. 148
Sims, Rod 6, 50, 52, 57
Sina-Weibo 146
Sirri lil-Ghaya (Top Secret) 192
Sixth Tone 151–52, 157
SK Telecom 167

INDEX

Sky Plc 46, 49
Sky/21C Fox 49, 51, 55, 68, 74, 77, 86
Slovakia, and Facebook 8
smartphones, Korea 164, 169
smh.com.au 89
Snapchat 127, 159
social inclusiveness (MPM measure) 145
social media platforms 68, 118, 160–61, 197, 203
    China 146, 148–49
    and content 15, 37, 130, 146, 207
    content creation 122–23, 129–30, 138, 146
    and dis/misinformation 13–14, 16, 18, 198
    and influencers 56
    media diversity 21–22
    and media pluralism 21, 103
    news consumption 10, 74, 119, 159, 209
    news curation 14–15, 19
    and news diversity 209
    and news distribution 199
    regulation 16, 36, 103
    and virality 121
    and visibility 120, 123, 124–25, 156
    see also Facebook; Instagram; platforms; TikTok; Twitter; WeChat; YouTube
soft news 31 *see also* news
Softbank 165
Sohu 152
Sørensen, J. 124, 125
source diversity 32, 44, 53–54, 79–80, 108, 169 *see also* media diversity; news sources
South Africa
    journalism 187–88
    news platforms 159
South America, investigative journalism 186–87

Spain, news platforms 159
Sparks, Colin 143–44
Spielkamp, Matthias 34
Spittle, George 51
Sri Lanka, and Facebook 8
Srnicek N. 12
Stan 45
status, and visibility 128
Stratton, Allegra 134
Street, John 181
Striphas, Ted 124
structural regulation 33 *see also* regulation
substantial lessening of competition test 51
sufficient plurality 10, 47–48, 84, 146
    see also media pluralism
suitable licensee test 43
Sukosd, M. 149
Super Followers, Twitter 120
Sweden, newspapers 216
Switzerland, journalism 187–88
Sydney, news sources 89
Sydney Informatics Hub (SIH) 88–89
Syria, journalism 190

T
Al-Tabi'i, Muhammad 190
Tackling Online Disinformation (EC) 199
Al-Tahtawi, Rifa'a Rafi' 190
targeting 3–4
technacy (media tech competency) 207
    see also media literacy
technology, and race 125
Tencent Holdings Ltd 18, 152
Thailand, journalism 186
Thalidomide 185
Thurman, N. 126
Tianya Club 146
TikTok 15–16, 130
Time Warner 41

TISL (Transparency International Sri Lanka) 186
topic distribution 90(fig) *see also* media diversity
transparency 5, 58–59, 87, 113, 166
    and digital platforms 110
    problem definition 109–11
    and personalization 126
    see also accountability; auditing
Transparency International Sri Lanka (TISL) 186
Treasury Laws Amendment (News Media and Digital Platforms Mandatory Bargaining Code) Act 2021 (Australia) 10–11
Trinity Mirror PLC 49, 68, 72, 74, 76
Trump, Donald 125
trust (Ofcom measure) 74
Tudor, Daniel 170
Tulloch, John 209
Tunisia, journalism 193
Tuwayni, Jibran and Ghassan 190
TV
    Arab region 193
    Australia 40, 41, 42, 43, 45
    China 146, 148
    UK 47, 71
Twitter 15–16, 120, 125, 171, 204, 206–07
two-out-of-three cross-media rule 42

U
UK
    and journalism 162
    media concentration 205
    media diversity 91
    media pluralism 46–47, 58, 160, 200–02
    mergers 46–48
    news platforms 159
    newspapers 47, 68, 71(fig), 205
    ownership 45–46
    policy and regulation 28–29, 58, 59
    radio and TV 47, 71
    see also Ofcom
understandability 166
United Nations 187
United States
    Capitol attacks 13
    media pluralism 101
    news platforms 159
news sources 6
regulation 166, 210
    users of digital platforms 111, 119, 207
    see also audiences

V
Vaidhyanathan, S. 14
Valcke, P. 10, 30
verification 36 *see also* auditing
Veritasium 122–23
Vice 56, 201
video-on-demand, Australia 41
Vietnam, journalism 186
Vietnam War 184
viewpoint diversity 32, 43–44, 59, 69–70, 81
    see also media diversity
virality 2, 15, 121, 122
visibility 127–30
    and monetization 136
    and social media platforms 120, 123, 124–25, 156
    and virality 121
Vivid Tones *see Sixth Tone*
VVOJ (Dutch-Flemish Association for Investigative Journalism) 180

W
Waisbord, Silvio 187
Wang, Haiyan 185–86

watchdog journalism 179 *see also* investigative journalism
Watergate 184, 185
Web Toon 163
WeChat 18, 146, 148, 172
WeChat Official Accounts (WOA) 152–58, 172
Weibo 18, 148
Wells, Chris 108
WhatsApp 159
Wikileaks 185
Wilding, Derek 2, 42, 106, 199, 222
Winseck, Dwayne 12, 13
WOA (WeChat Official Accounts) 152–58, 172

X
Xiamen PX event 186
Xiao, J. 145
Xiaomi 18
Xinhua 152

Y
Yahoo Japan 165
YLE, Finnish PSM 3, 150
Yonhap 163, 164, 169
Yonhap News Agency 168–69
Yonhap TV 167
Youn, S. 171
al Youssef, Fatima 191
YouTube
    consumption study 161
    content 130
    creator advice 132, 134–35
    Korea 159
    monetization 120
    and news 123
    and visibility 120, 122–23
    see also Brand; DeFranco; friendlyjordies
YTN 167

Z
Zaghlul, Sa'd and Faith 190
Zhao, Y. 147, 148
Zhihu.com 146
Zouzhuanggai policy 147–51